A FAULKNER GLOSSARY

A Faulkner Glossary

HARRY RUNYAN

The Citadel Press

NEW YORK

TO
Mother Gassèr

CONTENTS

PREFACE

THIS BOOK is a reference book, and as such it has been arranged to facilitate finding specific information. The Glossary is an alphabetical arrangement of all titles, characters, and places in the published writings of Faulkner. Actual places—such as Mississippi, New Orleans, Memphis, and the like—and actual people, with two and possibly three[1] exceptions, are not included. Cross-reference is used every time it seemed there might be confusion among titles or characters. With the latter, family names, when known, are used for the alphabetical entry. One exception to this is the family of Roskus and Dilsey, their family name—Gibson—being mentioned only once, and not generally known.

The Appendices are, for the most part, self-explanatory. Numbers II, III, and IV are essentially bibliographies, and although they repeat titles listed in the Glossary, here they are listed chronologically so that the reader can find all the writings in any given category without hunting. The "histories" of the various families of Yoknapatawpha County gather together all information about them from the several stories and novels in which members of the families appear, and the sources at the end of each give the titles of those pieces. The "documents" are, of course, the stories and novels themselves, and they are examined in terms of the over-all history. I have tried to avoid plot summaries, for by no means is this book intended to be a substitute for Faulkner's own writing.

For the pieces readily available, I have not listed any of the various reprintings. With the novels only the first publication

[1] See "Faulkner," "Forrest," and "Stone" in the Glossary.

is listed unless there has been something different or unusual about a later edition. With the short stories I have listed only their first publication and their "final disposition," that is, their inclusion in novels or collections of Faulkner's writings. For the pieces not readily available—a few short stories and much of the poetry and nonfiction prose—I have tried to list all the reprintings known to me, for the obvious reason that their first publication in many instances is extremely difficult of access. Except for two Japanese publications of Faulkner material no foreign editions are listed. The bibliographies are not definitive and they are not to be taken as such.

The listings are as complete and correct as one man has been able to make them, but such an undertaking can easily leave margin for error. There are likely to be errors of omission, and perhaps some of commission as well. I should be grateful to anyone sending me the information on what I may have overlooked.

I wish to acknowledge help from Elizabeth Findly of the University of Oregon Library, John H. Driscoll of Batten, Barton, Durstine & Osborn, James B. Meriwether, Carl Petersen, James B. Stronks, and especially Dorothy Oldham of the University of Mississippi Library. All have helped to make this book more complete and correct than it would otherwise have been.

HARRY RUNYAN

University of Illinois
Navy Pier, Chicago

A FAULKNER GLOSSARY

A FAULKNER GLOSSARY

A

Absalom, Absalom!   A novel published by Random House, New York, 1936. Chapter I was preprinted in *The American Mercury,* August 1936. Chapter II was reprinted in *The Portable Faulkner* under the title "Wedding in the Rain." Contains a map of Yoknapatawpha County. About the Sutpen family, told largely by Quentin Compson to his roommate at Harvard, Shrevlin (Shreve) McCannon. The time of the novel is 1807-1910, with most of it focusing around 1833-1869. The title is from 2 Samuel 18, and refers to the fact that Sutpen, like David, lost his sons through fratricide.

Academy, The.   A kind of junior college in Jefferson, or at least an institution that seemed to be something more than a high school and less than a college. It was founded by the grandfather of Doctor Wyott, himself a former head there. Apparently at one time it was for girls only, for it was popularly known as the "Female Academy." Charles Mallison, Jr. attended the Academy, however, as did Linda Snopes for awhile. Miss Melissa Hogganbeck taught history there. It seems also that it was known to some as the "Seminary," for that was what V. K. Ratliff called it. It is mentioned in "Knight's Gambit," *The Town,* and *The Mansion.*

Acey.   A friend of Rider's who attended Mannie's funeral and tried to pursuade Rider not to return alone ("Pantaloon in Black" in *Go Down, Moses*).

✶ **Acheron.**   A racing horse belonging to Colonel Linscomb. It was known variously as Akron and Akrum by the Negroes *(The Reivers).*

A Clymène.   A poem in *The Mississippian,* IX (Apr. 14,

1920), 3. Subtitled "From Paul Verlaine." Reprinted in *William Faulkner: Early Prose and Poetry*, ed. Carvel Collins, p. 61.

Adams, Mr. The mayor of Jefferson immediately preceding Manfred de Spain. He was beaten for re-election in 1904 by de Spain *(The Town)*.

Adams, Theron. The youngest son of Mayor Adams *(The Town)*.

Ad Astra. A short story in *Collected Stories*. First published in *The American Caravan*, IV (1931). Reprinted in *These 13*. It is included in *The Portable Faulkner*. About American and British soldiers still in France right after World War I. Bayard Sartoris appears in it. The title means "To the stars," and is from the motto of the Royal Air Force: "Per ardua ad astra." The story was adapted for television and presented on CBS *"Camera Three,"* September 7, 1958, with George Voskavek.

Addresses by Faulkner:

Address upon the award of the Nobel Prize for Literature. Delivered in Stockholm, Sweden, Dec. 10, 1950. Reprinted in *The Faulkner Reader* and *Faulkner at Nagano*. Read by Faulkner on Caedmon long playing record number TC-1035.

Address to the graduating class of University High School, Oxford, Mississippi. Delivered May 28, 1951. In the Oxford *Eagle*, May 31, 1951, p. 1. Reprinted in *The Harvard Advocate*, CXXXV (Nov. 1951), 7, under the title "Never Be Afraid."

Address upon being made an officer of the Legion of Honor. Delivered in New Orleans, Louisiana, Oct. 26, 1951. The manuscript (in French) is reproduced in facsimile in *The Princeton University Library Chronicle*, XVIII (Spring 1957), Plate 1.

Address to the annual meeting of the Delta Council. Delivered in Cleveland, Mississippi, May 15, 1952. In the Greenville *Delta Democrat-Times*, May 18, 1952, p. 9. Published as a pamphlet under the title *An Address Delivered by William Faulkner* by the Delta Council, 1952. Reprinted in *Vital Speeches of the Day*, XVIII (Sept. 15, 1952), 728-730, under the title "Man's Responsibility to Fellow Man."

Address to the graduating class of Pine Manor Junior College,

Wellesley, Massachusetts. Delivered June 8, 1953. Printed in *The Atlantic Monthy,* CXCII (Aug. 1953), 53-55, under the title "Faith or Fear."

Address upon receiving the National Book Award for Fiction. Delivered in New York, Jan. 25, 1955. Printed in *The New York Times Book Review,* Feb. 6, 1955, pp. 2 and 4.

Address at the University of Oregon. Delivered April 13, 1955. Printed in *Harper's Magazine,* CCXI (July 1955), 33-38, under the title "On Privacy. The American Dream: What Happened to It." [Faulkner had planned to include this as a chapter in a book of essays to be called *The American Dream.*]

Address to the annual meeting of the Southern Historical Association. Delivered in Memphis, Tennessee, Nov. 10, 1955. Printed in the Memphis *Commercial-Appeal,* Nov. 11, 1955, p. 8. Reprinted in *The Christian Century,* LXXII (Nov. 30, 1955), 1395-1396, under the title "To Claim Freedom Is Not Enough." Also in *Three Views of the Segregation Decisions,* Atlanta: The Southern Regional Council, 1956, under the title "American Segregation and the World Crisis."

Address upon receiving the Silver Medal of the Athens Academy, 1957. Delivered in Athens, Greece, Mar. 28, 1957. Printed in James B. Meriwether, *The Literary Career of William Faulkner,* Princeton University Library, 1961, p. 51.

Address to the Raven, Jefferson, and ODK Societies. Delivered in Charlottesville, Virginia, Feb. 20, 1958. Printed in *The University of Virginia Magazine,* II (Spring 1958), 11-14, under the title "A Word to Virginians." Reprinted in *Faulkner in the University.*

Address to the English Club of the University of Virginia. Delivered April 24, 1958. Printed in *Faulkner in the University* under the title "A Word to Young Writers."

Address to the seventh national conference of the U.S. National Commission for UNESCO. Delivered in Denver, Colorado, Oct. 2, 1959. Printed in *Saturday Review,* XLII (Nov. 14, 1959), 21, under the title "From Yoknapatawpha to UNESCO, the Dream."

Address upon receiving the Gold Medal for Fiction of the National Institute of Arts and Letters. Delivered in New York, May 24, 1962. Printed in *Proceedings of the American Academy of Arts and Letters and the National Institute of Arts and Letters,* Second Series, No. 13, New York, 1963, pp. 226-227.

Address Delivered by William Fulkner, An. See *Address to the annual meeting of the Delta Council* under **Addresses by Faulkner.**

After Fifty Years. A poem in *The Mississippian,* IX (Dec. 10, 1919), 4. Reprinted in Martha Mayes's "Faulkner Juvenilia," *New Campus Writing No. 2,* ed. Nolan Miller, p. 138, and in *William Faulkner: Early Prose and Poetry,* ed. Carvel Collins, p. 53.

Afternoon of a Cow. A short story in *Furiosa,* II Summer 1947), 5-17, attributed to Ernest V. Trueblood as author, who is identified as "William Faulkner's Ghostwriter." Uncollected, but reprinted in *Parodies: An Anthology from Chaucer to Beerbohm —and After,* ed. Dwight Macdonald (New York: Random House, 1960), pp. 462-473.

Ailanthia. See **Elly.**

Akers. A coon hunter bewildered by the behavior and language of Sutpen's French-speaking Negroes *(Absolom, Absolom!).*

Akron, Akrum. See **Acheron.**

Alabama Red. See **Red.**

Albert. A boy who worked in the Moseley drugstore in Mottson (i. e., Mottstown) *(As I Lay Dying).* Also the name of the British MP who took charge of the drunken Claude Hope ("Turnabout"). Also the man who drove the truck for Reverend Goodyhay *(The Mansion).*

Albert Camus. An appreciation of Camus after his death. In *The Transatlantic Review No. 6* (Spring 1961), 5.

Alec. "Unc Alec," Rider's uncle, who brought Rider something to eat. ("Pantaloon in Black" in *Go Down, Moses).*

Aleck Sander. The Negro companion of Chick Mallison. According to *Intruder in the Dust,* he was the son of Paralee, the Mallison cook. According to *The Town,* he was the son of

Guster, the Mallison cook, and of Top, and the brother of Little Top.

Alford, Doctor. The nephew of an old Jefferson resident and a doctor in Jefferson, in his thirties around 1920. Appears in *Sartoris;* referred to in *As I Lay Dying.*

Alice. The colored cook of Miss Ballenbaugh *(The Reivers).* Also a one-eyed hunting mule belonging to Major de Spain *(Intruder in the Dust).*

Alice Ben Bolt. The name of the mule Lucas Beauchamp stole from Roth Edmonds to make a payment on a divining machine ("The Fire and the Hearth" in *Go Down, Moses*).

Allanovna, Myra. A New York designer of men's expensive ties. Ratliff got two from her when he was in New York with Gavin Stevens for Linda Snopes's wedding *(The Mansion).*

Allen. A wealthy Oklahoma boy who went to Yale and ran away with a chorus girl. He was a friend of Mrs. Blair ("Fox Hunt").

Allen, Bobbie. A waitress in the restaurant owned by Mame and Max Confrey. She became Joe Christmas's first mistress *(Light in August).*

Allison, Howard I. A federal judge, a Republican, in Jefferson. He died and went to "heaven," and met several people there ("Beyond").

Allison, Howard II. The son of Judge Allison. He was born April 3, 1903, and died August 22, 1913, from a fall from a pony. (Referred to in "Beyond.")

Allison, Miss. A sixty-year-old (in 1946) retired grammar school principal in California; niece of old Major Cassius de Spain. "Allison" is probably her first name *(The Mansion).*

Allison, Sophia. The sickly mother of Judge Allison (Beyond").

All Nite Inn. An eating place in Jefferson across from the barbershop. Referred to in "Knight's Gambit."

All the Dead Pilots. A short story in *Collected Stories.* First published in *These 13.* About the death of John Sartoris III in World War I.

Alma Mater. A poem in *The Mississippian,* IX (May 12, 1920), 3. Reprinted in *William Faulkner: Early Prose and Poetry,* ed. Carvel Collins, p. 64.

Alphonse's. A restaurant in New Valois *(Pylon).*

Amboise Street. A street in New Valois *(Pylon).*

Ambuscade. The first story in *The Unvanquished.* First published in *The Saturday Evening Post,* Sept. 29, 1934.

American Drama: Eugene O'Neill. An article in *The Mississippian,* XI (Feb. 3, 1922), 5. Reprinted in *William Faulkner: Early Prose and Poetry,* ed. Carvel Collins, pp. 86-89.

American Drama: Inhibitions. An article in *The Mississippian,* XI (Mar. 17, 1922), 5 and (Mar. 24, 1922), 5. Reprinted in *William Faulkner: Early Prose and Poetry,* ed. Carvel Collins, pp. 93-97.

American Dream, The. The title given to a projected book of essays by Faulkner, of which the address given at the University of Oregon, in its published form, was to be a chapter.

American Segregation and the World Crisis. See *Address to the annual meeting of the Southern Historical Association* under **Addresses by Faulkner.**

Ames, Dalton. The father of Caddy Compson's illegitimate daughter Quentin *(The Sound and the Fury).*

Andrews. A servant, presumably a butler, of Harrison Blair ("Fox Hunt").

And Tomorrow. The fifth section of *Pylon.*

Angelique. The first name of the blind woman who insulted the wife and two sisters of the Corporal, and accused them of stealing a spoon she had thrown at them *(A Fable).*

Anse. The first name of the town marshal in the little place outside Boston where Quentin Compson went the afternoon before he killed himself *(The Sound and the Fury).*

✻ **Antonio.** The jealous·husband in "Jealousy."

Appendix to *The Portable Faulkner* (or *The Sound and the Fury*). See **Compsons, The.**

Aprés-midi d'un Faune, l'. A poem in *The New Republic,* XX (Aug. 6, 1919), 24. Reprinted in *Salmagundi* and in *William Faulkner: Early Prose and Poetry,* ed. Carvel Collins, pp. 39-40.

April.   A poem in *Contempo,* I (Feb. 1, 1932), 2. Uncollected.

✳**Armstead.**   See **Armstid.**

Armstid, Henry.   A farmer from the Frenchman's Bend region. The name was originally Armstead. He insisted, against his wife's wishes, on buying one of the spotted horses brought from Texas by Flem Snopes, and was later injured by one of them. He also, with V. K. Ratliff and Odum Bookwright, purchased the Old Frenchman's Place from Flem Snopes in order to dig for buried treasure there. He was a neighbor of the Bundren family, and gave Lena Grove a ride and let her stay overnight at his place. He ended up, we are told, in the state asylum in Jackson. (An Armstid with no given first name helped to reshingle the Whitfield church.) Appears in *The Hamlet, Light in August, As I Lay Dying,* and (possibly) "Shingles for the Lord." Is referred to in *The Town* and *The Mansion.* The name is mentioned in *Intruder in the Dust* as a family name in the Frenchman's Bend region.

Armstid, Lula.   The wife of Henry Armstid, as she is called in *As I Lay Dying.*

Armstid, Martha.   The wife of Henry Armstid, as she is called in *The Hamlet* and *Light in August.* A Mrs. Armstid with no given first name appears in "Shingles for the Lord."

Ash, Ashby.   See **Wylie, Ashby.**

As I Lay Dying.   A novel published by Jonathan Cape and Harrison Smith, New York, 1930. Dedicated to Hal (Harrison) Smith. About the death of Addie Bundren and the family's attempts to get her body to Jefferson for burial. The time is around 1930. A ballet based on the novel, with choreography by Valerie Bettis and music by Bernardo Segall, was first performed in the Hunter College Playhouse, New York, on December 19, 1948. The novel was adapted for television by John McGiffert and performed on CBS' *Camera Three* on October 7, 1956, with Mildred Dunnock. A play adapted from the novel by Robert Flynn, was first produced at Baylor University, Waco, Texas, in May 1960. A selection from the novel read by Faulkner, may be heard on Caedmon long playing record number TC-1035. The title, Carvel Collins suggests, may come from William

Marris's translation of *The Odyssey*, Bk. 11 (see *The Princeton University Library Chronicle*, XVIII [Spring 1957], 123).

Atkins, Miss. The dietician at the hospital where Joe Christmas was kept as a small boy. Joe used to eat her toothpaste, and one time saw her having an affair with an interne named Charley *(Light in August)*.

Atkinson. The partner of Matt Ord in the Ord-Atkinson Aircraft Company *(Pylon)*.

✗ **Aunt Callie.** See **Callie**.

✗ **Aunt Fittie.** See **Fittie**.

✗ **Aunt Jenny.** See **Du Pre, Mrs. Virginia**.

✗ **Aunt Tennie.** See **Tennie**.

Avant, Jim. A man from Hickory Flat who raised hounds *(The Reivers)*.

✗ **Ayers, Freddie.** The mate of the ship Diana who killed Yo Ho, the messboy ("Yo Ho and Two Bottles of Rum").

Ayers, Major. A British salesman of laxatives; one of Mrs. Maurier's guests on her yachting party *(Mosquitoes)*.

B

Backhouse, Philip St.-Just. A cousin of the Sartoris family; a lieutenant in the Confederate Army. He was in love with Cousin Melisandre, but the association of his name with an embarrassing episode prevented her from seeing him. When his name was changed to Backus she married him ("My Grandmother Millard").

Backus, Melisandre. See **Stevens, Melisandre Backus**

Backus, Philip St.-Just. See **Backhouse, Philip St.-Just**.

Baddrington, Harold. The pilot of the plane in which

Charles Mallison was bombardier. He was nicknamed Plexiglass, or Plex, because of his "obsession on the subject of cellophane" *(The Mansion)*.

Baird, Doctor. A specialist from Atlanta, called in for consultation on Donald Mahon *(Soldiers' Pay)*.

Baker, Joe. A full-blooded Chickasaw; a hermit, who lived in a little shack five miles from the McCaslin plantation. He was a hunter and fisher and associated with no one except Sam Fathers. When he died, Sam buried him and burned his hut. He called himself "Jobaker" ("The Old People" in *Go Down, Moses*).

Ballade des Femmes Perdues, Une. A poem in *The Mississippian*, IX (Jan. 28, 1920), 3. subtitled "Mais où sont les neiges d'antan." Reprinted in Martha Mayes's "Faulkner Juvenilia," *New Campus Writing No. 2*, ed. Nolan Miller, pp. 139-140, and in *William Faulkner: Early Prose and Poetry*, ed Carvel Collins, p. 54.

Ballenbaugh, Boyd. The younger brother of Tyler Ballenbaugh. He murdered Lonnie Grinnup, and was killed by Joe, the deaf-and-dumb companion of Lonnie ("Hand Upon the Waters" in *Knight's Gambit*).

Ballenbaugh, Miss. A fifty-year-old (in 1905) spinster who ran a small store at what had formerly been called Wyott's Crossing and later became Ballenbaugh's Ferry *(The Reivers)*.

Ballenbaugh, Tyler. A farmer who had taken out a five-thousand-dollar life insurance policy on Lonnie Grinnup ("Hand Upon the Waters" in *Knight's Gambit*).

Ballenbaugh's Ferry. A later name for what was once called Wyott's Crossing *(The Reivers)*.

Ballott, Mr. The stable foreman in Maury Priest's livery stable *(The Reivers)*.

Bank of Jefferson. The old bank, established in the 1830s. In 1905 Lucius Quintus Carothers (Boss) Priest was president of it *(The Reivers)*. During the 1940s a Mr. Holland was the bank's president *(The Mansion)*.

Barbour, Mr.   A boys' class Sunday School teacher in Jefferson ("Uncle Willy").

Barger, Sonny.   A storekeeper in Jefferson ("Uncle Willy").

Barker

Barn Burning.   A short story in *Collected Stories*. First published in *Harper's Magazine*, June 1939. It is reprinted in *The Faulkner Reader* and *Selected Short Stories*. About Ab Snopes's burning the barns of Mr. Harris and Major de Spain and about his son's running away. The only appearance of the boy Colonel Sartoris Snopes is in the story. The episode is retold by Ratliff in *The Hamlet*. The story was adapted for television by Gore Vidal and presented on CBS *Suspense* August 17, 1954, with E. G. Marshall, Charles Taylor, James Reese, Peter Cookson, and Beatrice Straight. The text of the television production is published in Vidal's *Visit to a Small Planet and Other Television Plays*, Boston: Little, Brown and Co., 1956, pp. 237-252.

Barricade Street.   A street in New Valois *(Pylon)*.

Barron, Homer.   A Yankee foreman on a road construction gang in Jefferson. He became Miss Emily Grierson's lover, and she killed him to keep him from leaving her ("A Rose for Emily").

Barron, Jake.   A convict at the Parchman prison farm; killed by a guard in an attempted prison break in 1943 *(The Mansion)*.

✻**Bascomb, Caroline.**   See **Compson, Caroline Bascomb**.

Bascomb, Maury L.   The shiftless brother of Mrs. Jason Compson III. Appears in *The Sound and the Fury;* referred to in the Appendix.

Basket, Herman.   An Indian, whose beautiful sister Ikkemotubbe and the white man David Hogganbeck were rivals for ("A Courtship"). In "A Justice" he told Sam Fathers the story of Sam's parenthood.

Basket, John.   An old Indian living near Major de Spain's hunting lands ("A Bear Hunt").

✻**Basket, Three.**   An old Indian, about sixty; one of those out looking for the Negro servant of the dead Issetibbeha ("Red Leaves").

Battenburg.   A town between Jefferson and Memphis where the hired killer of Judge Dukinfield was captured ("Smoke" in *Knight's Gambit*).

Bayou Street. A street in New Valois on which a police station is located (*Pylon*).

Beale, Colonel. A British colonel who came to identify the Corporal, but confused him with a British soldier named Boggan, who had been killed and buried at Mons in 1914 (*A Fable*).

Bean, Captain. A flyer at the airport in Jefferson whom Hoke Christian (Uncle Willy) tried to get to teach him to fly ("Uncle Willy").

Bear, The. The fifth story in *Go Down, Moses*. One section was originally published in *Harper's Magazine*, Dec. 1935, as "Lion"; another section was originally published in *The Saturday Evening Post*, May 9, 1942, as "The Bear." It is reprinted in *The Faulkner Reader, The Portable Faulkner,* and *Three Famous Short Novels,* and (less section four) in *Big Woods*. The story is about the capture and killing of Old Ben, the bear, by Boon Hogganbeck, and includes the death of Lion, the dog, and of Sam Fathers. The long section four recapitulates much of the history of the McCaslin family.

Bear Hunt, A. A short story in *Collected Stories*. First published in *The Saturday Evening Post*, Feb. 10, 1934. It is reprinted (much revised) in *Big Woods*. A story told by Ratliff about an episode which occurred at Major de Spain's hunting camp.

Beard, Virgil. The son of Will Beard and the writer of the anonymous letters to Narcissa Benbow for Byron Snopes (*Sartoris*).

Beard, — Mrs, —

✗ Beard, W. C. The owner of a grist mill and cotton gin in Jefferson (*Sartoris*).

Beard, Will. The owner of a boarding house in Jefferson where Byron Snopes stayed (*Sartoris*). A Mrs. Beard was running a boarding house there later at which Byron Bunch stayed (*Light in August*).

Beard's. A corner lot in Jefferson where the circus put its tents (*The Sound and the Fury*).

Beat Four. A rural pine hill country community in east

central Yoknapatawpha County, twenty-eight miles from Jefferson and four miles from the McCaslin-Edmonds plantation. It was here that Ab Snopes lived before moving to Frenchman's Bend. The McCallums, the Ingrums, the Workitts, the Frasers, and the Gowries lived in Beat Four. According to Gavin Stevens they were people who loved brawling, who preferred to make illegal whiskey from corn than to plant cotton—unlike the people of Frenchman's Bend, who liked to "raise something [they] can sell openly in daylight." Adam Fraser's store, where Lucas Beauchamp used to go, was in Beat Four. Appears in *Intruder in the Dust* and referred to in *The Hamlet*. (Mississippi counties are divided into "beats," numbered according to their survey co-ordinates. Frenchman's Bend, for example, is in Beat Two.)

Beauchamp, Bobo. One of the Yoknapatawpha County Beauchamps who worked for Mr. van Tosch in Memphis. He went into debt, stole van Tosch's horse Coppermine, and then traded it to Ned McCaslin for Mr. Priest's car, which Bobo gave to his creditor (*The Reivers*).

Beauchamp, Fonsiba (Sophonsiba). The daughter of Tomey's Turl and Tennie. Born in 1869. At the age of seventeen she married a northern Negro and moved to a small farm near Midnight, Arkansas. Appears in "The Bear"; referred to in "The Fire and the Hearth" (*Go Down, Moses*).

Beauchamp, Henry. The son of Lucas and Mollie Beauchamp. Born in 1898. Throughout his childhood he was a constant companion to Roth Edmonds ("The Fire and the Hearth" in *Go Down, Moses*).

Beauchamp, Hubert. The owner of a large plantation twenty-two miles from the McCaslin lands. His sister Sophonsiba married Theophilus (Uncle Buck) McCaslin. Appears in "Was" and "The Bear" (*Go Down, Moses*).

Beauchamp, James. A son of Tomey's Turl and Tennie and older brother of Lucas. Was known as Tennie's Jim. Born December 29, 1864. On his twenty-first birthday he fled north and disappeared. Later it was discovered that he went to Indiana. He died around 1938. A granddaughter of his had a child by

Roth Edmonds. He was also the grandfather of Bobo Beauchamp. Appears in "The Old People" and "The Bear"; is referred to in "The Fire and the Hearth" and "Delta Autumn" (*Go Down, Moses*) and *The Reivers.*

Beauchamp, Lucas. A son of Tomey's Turl and Tennie. Born March 17, 1874. His full name was originally Lucius Quintus Carothers McCaslin Beauchamp. Married Mollie Habersham (called Worsham in another place). Had three children, Henry (born 1898), an unnamed daughter (the mother of Samuel Worsham Beauchamp), and Nathalie. Lucas was arrested for the murder of Vinson Gowrie, but was freed through the activities of Chick Mallison and Eunice Habersham. Has a major role in "The Fire and the Hearth" (*Go Down, Moses*) and *Intruder in the Dust.* Appears more briefly in "The Bear." Is referred to in "Go Down, Moses," "Delta Autumn," and *The Reivers.*

Beauchamp, Mollie. The wife of Lucas. She had been, according to "Go Down, Moses," from the Worsham family of Jefferson, but acording to *Intruder in the Dust* she was from the Habersham family. She died sometime in the early 1940s. Has a major role in "The Fire and the Hearth" and "Go Down, Moses"; appears briefly in the early part of *Intruder in the Dust*; is referred to in "Delta Autumn."

Beauchamp, Nathalie. The daughter of Lucas and Mollie Beauchamp. She married George Wilkins, a shiftless laborer, and moved with him to Detroit. Appears in "The Fire and the Hearth" (*Go Down, Moses*); is referred to (but not by name) in *Intruder in the Dust.*

Beauchamp, Philip Manigault. An American private; a Negro from Mississippi. He was one of the three Americans who volunteered to act on the firing squad to execute General Gragnon (*A Fable*).

Beauchamp, Samuel Worsham. The grandson of Lucas and Mollie Beauchamp. Known as "Butch." His mother died when he was born and Mollie raised him. At the age of nineteen he went to Jefferson and at once began getting into trouble. After being put in jail for robbing a Jefferson store, he escaped and fled north. He was electrocuted at the age of twenty-six in the Illinois state prison at Joliet for killing a Chicago policeman ("Go Down, Moses").

Beauchamp, Sophonsiba (Sibbey). The sister of Hubert Beauchamp. She married Theophilus McCaslin in 1859. Was the mother of Isaac McCaslin. Appears in "Was" and "The Bear" (*Go Down, Moses*).

Beauchamp, Terrel. Known as Tomey's Turl, he was the son of Thomasina, the daughter of a Negro slave woman Eunice and old Carothers McCaslin, and, in turn, the son of McCaslin as well. Hence, McCaslin was both his grandfather and his father. Terrel fell in love with a slave named Tennie belonging to the Beauchamp family, so Uncle Buddy McCaslin played a game of poker with Hubert Beauchamp and won, thus winning Tennie. Terrel and Tennie were married in 1859. They had several children, three of whom lived: James, Fonsiba, and Lucas. Denied the name McCaslin, they took the name Beauchamp. Appears in "Was"; referred to in "The Fire and the Hearth" and "The Bear" (*Go Down, Moses*). There was in Jefferson around 1910 a fireman at the power plant named Tomey's Turl Beauchamp. He was thirty years old at the time. His relationship with the Beauchamp family is not known (*The Town*).

Bedenberry, Brother. The leader of a revival meeting in a Negro church some twenty miles from Jefferson, into which Joe Christmas broke one evening when he was in flight after killing Miss Burden (*Light in August*).

Behindman, General. An important functionary in New Valois (*Pylon*).

Benbow, Mrs. Belle. The divorced wife of Harry Mitchell and later wife of Horace Benbow. By her first husband she had a daughter, also named Belle. Appears in *Sartoris* as Mrs. Mitchell, in *Sanctuary* as Mrs. Benbow.

Benbow, Cassius Q. "Uncle Cash," a Negro. He used to drive the Benbow carriage, then ran off with the Yankees, and returned after the war to become acting marshall. He was frightened off when Colonel Sartoris shot the two Burden carpetbaggers ("Skirmish at Sartoris" in *The Unvanquished*).

Benbow, Francis. The grandfather of Horace and Narcissa Benbow. Referred to in *Sartoris*.

Benbow, Horace. The son of Will and Julia Benbow and brother of Mrs. Bayard Sartoris III. Born around 1886. He was a student at Sewanee and later at Oxford (England). Was a soldier in World War I. He became a lawyer and acted as defense attorney for Lee Goodwin. Sometime in the 1920s he married Belle Mitchell, the divorced wife of Harry Mitchell of Jefferson, and moved out of the county to Kinston to practice law. Appears in *Sartoris* and *Sanctuary*.

Benbow, Judge. The executor of Goodhue Coldfield's estate and intermediator later between Colonel Sartoris and his partner Ben J. Redmond. He had a son named Percy. His relationship with the later Benbows is not known. Appears in *Absalom, Absalom!* and "An Odor of Verbena" (*The Unvanquished*). Is mentioned in *The Hamlet*.

Benbow, Julia. The wife of Will Benbow and mother of Horace and Narcissa. She died when Narcissa was seven, about 1902. Referred to in *Sartoris*.

Benbow, Narcissa. See **Sartoris, Narcissa Benbow.**

Benbow, Percy. The son of Judge Benbow (*Absalom, Absalom!*).

Benbow, Will. The father of Horace and Narcissa Benbow. Referred to in *Sartoris*.

Berry, Ben. One of the men (perhaps a deputy) sent by the sheriff to watch over Joel Flint ("An Error in Chemistry" in *Knight's Gambit*).

Berry, Louis. One of the Indians sent out with Three Basket to hunt for the Negro body servant of old Issetibbeha ("Red Leaves").

✷ **Bessing, Mr.** The flight instructor of Cadet Thompson ("Landing in Luck").

Best, Henry. A member of the board of aldermen of Jefferson around 1912 (*The Town*).

✷ **Betsy.** Bayard Sartoris' mare, which he used to ride between Jefferson and Oxford ("An Odor of Verbena" in *The Unvanquished*).

Beulah. A cow, the "heroine" of "Afternoon of a Cow."

Beyond. A short story in *Collected Stories* about the death of Judge Allison of Jefferson. First published in *Harper's Magazine,* Sept. 1933. Reprinted in *Doctor Martino and Other Stories.* It is included in *Selected Short Stories.* Also the title of Section IV of *Collected Stories* which contains "Beyond," "Black Music," "The Leg," "Mistral," "Divorce in Naples," and "Carcassonne."

Beyond the Talking. See **Book Reviews:** "Review of *The Road Back* by Erich Maria Remarque."

Bidet, General. The group commander under whose command were Generals Lallemont and Gragnon. He was known as "Mama" Bidet (*A Fable*).

Bidwell. The name of a storekeeper in Division ("Hair").

Bienville Hotel. A hotel in New Valois (*Pylon*).

Big Bottom. The name given the hunting lands, the big woods, owned by Major de Spain ("The Old People" and "The Bear" in *Go Down, Moses*).

Biglin, Luther. The jailor in Jefferson in 1946 who took it upon himself to guard Flem Snopes's place at night. He was related to the political boss of his area and related by marriage to Sheriff Bishop (*The Mansion*).

Big Woods. A collection published by Random House, New York, 1955. Subtitled "The Hunting Stories of Willam Faulkner." Contains "The Bear" (less section four) and "The Old People" (both from *Go Down, Moses*), "A Bear Hunt" (revised from *Collected Stories*), and "Race at Morning" (revised from *The Saturday Evening Post,* Mar. 5, 1955), plus a prelude reprinted from pp. 101-105 of *Requiem for a Nun,* a first interlude revised from part of "Red Leaves," a second interlude revised from part of "A Justice," a third interlude revised from part of "Mississippi," and a postlude revised from part of "Delta Autumn" (*Go Down, Moses*).

Binford. A Binford boy with no given first name; was of the five boys who tried to court Eula Varner (*The Mansion*).

Binford, Dewitt. A resident of Frenchman's Bend, married to a Snopes girl. He took Byron Snopes's halfbreed children into his home (*The Town*).

Binford, Lucius. Reba Rivers's former landlord and former pimp. He appears (only as Mr. Binford) in *The Reivers* (1905). By the 1920s and 1930s he is dead. Is referred to (again only as Mr. Binford) in *Sanctuary,* and (as Lucius Binford) in *The Mansion.* Reba's two dogs were named Reba and Mr. Binford.

Bird, Tom Tom. A sixty-year-old Negro fireman who alternated days and nights with Tomey's Turl Beauchamp at the power plant in Jefferson (*The Town*).

Bird, Uncle. The minister of the Negro Second Baptist Church in Jefferson, of which Simon Strother was a deacon (*Sartoris*).

Birdsong. The white man Rider killed for cheating at dice ("Pantaloon in Black" in *Go Down, Moses*).

Birdsong, Preacher. A country boy from somewhere near Jefferson. He learned to box during World War I and used to box with Max Levitt (*The Town*).

✳Bishop boy. A Jefferson high school athlete who used to drink Cokes with Linda Snopes in the drugstore after school (*The Town*).

Bishop, Ephriam. The sheriff who alternated terms of office with Hubert Hampton, Jr. (*The Mansion*).

Black, Mr. The driver of the car which went to the airport when the stunt plane came in ("*Death Drag*").

✳Black John. The name of a horse belonging to Uncle Buck McCaslin ("Was" in *Go Down, Moses*).

Black Music. A short story in *Collected Stories*. First published in *Doctor Martino and Other Stories*. A non-Yoknapatawpha story about a Brooklyn architect, Wilfred Midgleston, who thought he was a faun.

Blackwater Slough. A slough near Frenchman's Bend (*The Mansion*).

Blair, Harrison. A wealthy New Yorker who had a country place in Carolina where he hunted ("Fox Hunt").

Blair, John. A young poet who visited the Roger Howes

home in Virginia and carried on a mild affair with Mrs. Howes. He died later ("Artist at Home").

Blaisedell.   The location of the Ord-Atkinson aircraft plant, near New Valois (*Pylon*).

Blake, Jim.   One of the four men who claimed Lonnie Grinnup's body ("Hand Upon the Waters" in *Knight's Gambit*).

Bland.   A Southerner, a Rhodes scholar, and a pilot in the R.A.F. He was an acquaintance of Bayard Sartoris III during the war ("Ad Astra").

Bland, Gerald.   A student at Harvard from Kentucky in 1910 (*The Sound and the Fury*).

Bland, Mrs.   Gerald's mother, an aristocratic southern lady (*The Sound and the Fury*).

Bledsoe.   A trusty or official at the Mississippi prison farm in Parchman ("Old Man" in *The Wild Palms*).

Bledsoe, Sergeant.   A British guard whom the runner knocked out when he and the Rev. Tobe Sutterfield went to get the sentry out of the guardhouse (*A Fable*).

Bleyth, Captain.   A pilot in the R.A.F. remembered by Julian Lowe (*Soldiers' Pay*).

Blizzard.   A small Arizona town near which a camp for tuberculosis patients was located ("Idyll in the Desert").

⊁**Blue.**   One of the Compson's dogs (*The Sound and the Fury*). Also one of Bayard Sartoris' hunting dogs (*Sartoris*).

Blue Goose, The.   A Negro café below the cotton gin in Jefferson (*The Town*).

Blum, Major.   A French officer who indentified the Corporal
~~Bobbie (as c-n)~~ as the leader of the mutineers (*A Fable*).

⚹ **Bobolink.**   Drusilla Hawk's horse, given her by her fiancé Gavin Breckbridge ("Raid" in *The Unvanquished*).

Bogard, Captain H. S.   A pilot in the American Army during World War I. He took Claude Hope, a British sailor, on a bombing mission, and Hope in turn took him on a torpedo boat mission ("Turnabout").

Boggan.   The name by which the British Colonel Beale identified the Corporal. But Boggan had been killed and buried at Mons in 1914 (*A Fable*).

Bolivar, Dick. Uncle Dick Bolivar, an old Negro diviner whom Ratliff got to help find out where the treasure was buried on the Old Frenchman's Place (*The Hamlet*).

Bon, Charles. The son of Thomas Sutpen and his first wife Eulalia Bon. Was born in Haiti in 1829. He later moved with his mother to New Orleans. He attended college at Oxford, Mississippi, where he met Henry Sutpen, his half brother. He had an octoroon mistress, and in 1859 a son was born to them. He was killed on May 3, 1865, by Henry Sutpen (*Absalom, Absalom!*).

Bon, Charles Etienne de Saint Velery. The son of Charles Bon and his octoroon mistress. Born 1859 in New Orleans. In 1871 he came to Sutpen's Hundred to live. In 1879 he returned to New Orleans and married a full-blooded Negro. In 1881 he returned to Sutpen's Hundred. A son, later known as Jim Bond, was born in 1882. In 1884 Charles Etienne de Saint Velery died of smallpox (*Absalom, Absalom!*).

Bon, Eulalia. The daughter of a part-French planter in Haiti, she married Thomas Sutpen in 1827. In 1829 a son Charles was born to them, and in 1831 she was divorced by Sutpen when he discovered that she had Negro blood. She later moved to New Orleans with her son (*Absalom, Absalom!*).

Bond, Jim. The son of Charles Etienne de Saint Velery Bon and his wife. Born in 1882. He stayed on the Sutpen plantation, where he was born, and in 1909 when Clytie burned the house he disappeared and was never heard of again. He was the last surviving descendant of Thomas Sutpen (*Absalom, Absalom!*).

Bonds, Jack. A man, now dead, formerly a member of the Provine gang. He appears in the original version of "A Bear Hunt" (in *Collected Stories*), but not in the revised version (in *Big Woods*).

Book Reviews:
Review of *In April Once* by W. A. Percy. In *The Mississippian*, IX (Nov. 10, 1920), 5. Reprinted in *William Faulkner: Early Prose and Poetry*, ed. Carvel Collins, pp. 71-73.

Review of *Turns and Movies* by Conrad Aiken. In *The Mississippian*, X (Feb. 16, 1921), 5. Reprinted in *William Faulkner: Early Prose and Poetry*, ed. Carvel Collins, pp. 74-76.

Review of *Aria da Capo* by Edna St. Vincent Millay. In *The Mississippian,* XI (Jan. 13, 1922), 5. Reprinted in *William Faulkner: Early Prose and Poetry,* ed. Carvel Collins, pp. 84-85.

Review of *Linda Condon, Cytherea,* and *The Bright Shawl* by Joseph Hergesheimer. In *The Mississippian,* XII (Dec. 15, 1922), 5. Reprinted in *William Faulkner: Early Prose and Poetry,* ed. Carvel Collins, pp. 101-103.

Review of *The Road Back* by Erich Maria Remarque (entitled "Beyond the Talking"). In *The New Republic,* LXVII (May 20, 1931), 23-24.

Review of *Test Pilot* by Jimmy Collins (entitled "Folklore of the Air"). In *The American Mercury,* XXXVI (Nov. 1935), 370-372.

Review of *The Old Man and the Sea* by Ernest Hemingway. In *Shenandoah.* III (Autumn 1952), 55.

Bookright. See **Bookwright.**

Bookwright, Calvin. The father-in-law of Zack (Jack) Houston. He was supposed to have made good whiskey. In *The Town* he is called "Cal" and the name is spelled "Bookright." In *The Mansion* and *The Reivers* he is Calvin Bookwright.

Bookwright, Herman. One of Eula Varna's suitors at the time she married Flem Snopes (*The Mansion*).

Bookwright, Homer. A farmer in the Frenchman's Bend region around 1940 ("Shingles for the Lord" and "Shall Not Perish"). He appears briefly in *The Mansion* around 1923.

Bookwright, Letty. The daughter of Calvin Bookwright. She married Jack Houston and within a year was killed when a stallion kicked her (*The Town*).

Bookwright, Odum. A farmer in the Frenchman's Bend region around 1900-1908. He, along with V. K. Ratliff and Henry Armstid, bought the Old Frenchman's Place from Flem Snopes. Appears in *The Hamlet;* referred to in *The Mansion.* The name "Bookwright" is mentioned in a number of the stories and novels as a family name in the Frenchman's Bend region, and in "Tomorrow" (*Knight's Gambit*) a Bookwright with no given first name is accused of murdering Buck Thorpe.

Bouc, Pierre. One of the Corporal's men. He denied the Corporal by saying that he did not belong to the group. He was let out of the cell because his name was not on the sergeant's list. He was also known by the name of Piotr, and was identified as Zsettlani (*A Fable*).

Bowden, Matt. The man who was pursuing Grumby because Grumby, by killing Granny Millard, had ruined the chances for the raiders. He gave Grumby a chance for his life and then fled to Texas ("Vendée" in *The Unvanquished*).

Bowen, Captain. A captain in the Ohio regiment which took the captured horses and mules from Sartoris ("Raid" in *The Unvanquished*).

Boy and Eagle. The title given to *A Green Bough*, XVIII when it was reprinted in *Mississippi Verse*, edited by Alice James.

Boyd, Amy. The wife of Howard Boyd. She used to go out dancing on Saturday nights while her husband stayed home and read ("The Brooch").

Boyd, Howard. The son of a demanding mother and the husband of a girl who went out to dances without him. When his wife left, after being ordered out by his mother, he committed suicide ("The Brooch").

Bradley. The name of a man who lived in the cottage next to the one Harry and Charlotte stayed in on a Wisconsin lake (*The Wild Palms*).

Brandt, Doctor. A specialist from Memphis who removed the spot from Bayard Sartoris' face (*Sartoris*).

Breckbridge, Gavin. Drusilla Hawk's fiancé, who was killed in the war at Shiloh ("Raid" in *The Unvanquished*).

Bridesman, Major. The flight commander of the group to which Lieutenant Levine belonged (*A Fable*).

Bridger. One of Major Grumby's men who fled with Matt Bowden to Texas ("Vendée" in *The Unvanquished*).

Briggins, Lycurgus. The grandson of Parsham Hood (*The Reivers*).

Briggins, Mary. The mother of Lycurgus, and a daughter of Parsham Hood (*The Reivers*).

Brooch, The. A short story in *Collected Stories*. First published in *Scribner's Magazine,* Jan. 1936. A non-Yoknapatawpha story about Howard Boyd, who lived with his wife and mother in a "little lost Mississippi hamlet." The story was adapted by Faulkner for television, and was first produced on April, 2, 1953, on the Lux Video Theater, starring Dan Duryea, Sally Forrest, and Mildred Natwick.

Broussard
(as person)

Broussard's. A restaurant in New Orleans where Talliaferro and Fairchild used to eat (*Mosquitoes*).

Brown, Joe. The name assumed by Lucas Burch when he went to Jefferson (*Light in August*).

Brownlee, Percival. A twenty-six-year-old Negro bought on March 3, 1856, by Theophilus McCaslin from General Forrest. Theophilus wanted to use him as a bookkeeper, but he could not keep books. Neither could he plow, nor take care of cattle, so McCaslin tried to get rid of him by freeing him, but he refused to leave. In October of the same year McCaslin renamed him Spintrius. He later disappeared, reappeared in 1862 and conducted some revival meetings among the Negroes on the plantation, and disappeared again when the Union Army came through. He reappeared again in 1866 with an army paymaster, but ran away when McCaslin encountered him. He was last heard of twenty years later as a prosperous owner of a house of prostitution in New Orleans ("The Bear" in *Go Down, Moses*).

Brummage, Judge. The judge at the trial of Mink Snopes (*The Mansion*).

Brzewski. Presumably an American soldier from Pittsburg who had died at sea and was buried by Captain Middleton. But he was confused with Boggan, a British soldier who had been killed in 1914, and with the Corporal, the leader of the mutiny which led to the false armistice in 1918 (*A Fable*).

✗ Brzonyi. The name, mentioned only once (by Captain Middleton), apparently by which the Corporal was known in the French Army (*A Fable*).

Buchwald. An American private from Brooklyn who later became a millionaire bootlegger during the 1920s. He was one of the three American soldiers who volunteered to act as the firing *Buck* squad to execute General Gragnon (*A Fable*).

Buckner, Billie. The wife of the manager of the Callaghan mine in Utah. Harry Wilbourne performed an abortion on her (*The Wild Palms*).

Buckner, "Buck." The manager of the Callaghan mine (*The Wild Palms*).

Bucksnort. The nickname of Buck Thorpe ("Tomorrow" in *Knight's Gambit*).

Buckworth. The deputy warden at the prison farm at Parchman. He was later transferred to the highway patrol ("Old Man" *Bud, Uncle* in *The Wild Palms*).

Buffaloe, Joe. The city electrician in Jefferson who in 1904 built an automobile, the first in Jefferson. Appears in *The Town* and *The Reivers;* is referred to in *The Mansion*.

Buford. "Bufe." A deputy sheriff in Yoknapatawpha County during the 1920s (*Light in August*).

Bullitt, Bob. A stunt flyer at the dedication airshow at the *Bullitt, Mrs.* Feinman Airport (*Pylon*).

Bunch, Byron. A laborer at the sawmill in Jefferson. His name was confused with Burch, the man Lena Grove was looking for. When he saw Lena he fell in love with her and looked after *Bundren, Mrs.* her and her baby (*Light in August*).

Bundren, Addie. The wife of Anse Bundren. She had been a schoolteacher. After her marriage she had an affair with the minister, Whitfield. Jewel, her favorite son, was his child. When she died her family took her to Jefferson for burial (*As I Lay Dying*).

Bundren, Anse. The father of the Bundren family and husband of Addie. He insisted on carrying out his wife's wishes that she be buried with her family in Jefferson, despite flooded conditions. After the funeral he remarried immediately, taking the money Dewey Dell's boy friend had given her for an abortion (*As I Lay Dying*).

Bundren, Cash. The eldest son of Anse and Addie Bundren. He was a carpenter, and built his mother's coffin. On the trip to

Jefferson he injured his leg and they set it in cement (*As I Lay Dying*).

Bundren, Darl (Darrell). The second son of Anse and Addie Bundren. On the trip to Jefferson he set fire to the Gillespie barn. Later he was taken to the asylum in Jackson (*As I Lay Dying*). His being taken to the asylum is referred to in "Uncle Willy."

Bundren, Dewey Dell. The fourth child and only daughter of Anse and Addie Bundren. She was seventeen. She was pregnant by a boy named Lafe, who gave her ten dollars for an abortion. When she tried to get something at a Mottson drugstore, the druggist refused to help her, and when she tried to get something at a Jefferson drugstore, the clerk, Skeet MacGowan, seduced her by pretending that the act would "cure" her. When her father saw the ten dollars he took it away from her (*As I Lay Dying*).

Bundren, Jewel. The third son of the Bundrens, he was actually the child of Addie Bundren and the Reverend Whitfield. When he was fifteen he spent his nights working for Lon Quick, a neighbor, cleaning a field so he could earn enough money to buy a horse (*As I Lay Dying*).

Bundren, Vardaman. The youngest child of Anse and Addie Bundren. He could not understand his mother's death, and when they put her in the coffin and nailed it shut he bored some holes in the top so she could breathe (*As I Lay Dying*).

Burch, Lucas. The father of Lena Grove's child. He had moved away from Doane's Mill and gone to Jefferson. There, under the name of Joe Brown, he worked for a while at the sawmill and then, with Joe Christmas, turned to bootlegging (*Light in August*).

Burchett. The name of the family that raised the orphan Susan Reed ("Hair").

Burden, Beck (Rebecca?). A daughter of Calvin Burden I, and sister of Nathaniel Burden, and therefore an aunt of Joanna Burden (*Light in August*).

Burden, Calvin I. An adventurer from Missouri, originally of a New England family named Burrington. He became a carpetbagger in Jefferson, and along with his grandson was shot and killed by Colonel Sartoris. Appears in "Skirmish at Sartoris" (*The Unvanquished*); referred to in *Light in August* and (but not by name) in *Sartoris*.

Burden, Calvin II.   A grandson of Calvin I, a son of Nathaniel Burden, and a half-brother of Joanna Burden. With his grandfather he was shot and killed by Colonel Sartoris. Appears in "Skirmish at Sartoris" (*The Unvanquished*); referred to in *Light in August* and (but not by name) in *Sartoris*.

Burden, Evangeline.   The wife of Calvin Burden I and the mother of Nathaniel Burden (*Light in August*).

Burden, Joanna.   A spinster living in Jefferson around 1930, a descendant of the carpetbaggers whom Colonel Sartoris shot. She became the mistress of Joe Christmas and he murdered her when she became too demanding. Appears in *Light in August*; is referred to in *The Mansion*.

Burden, Juana.   The Mexican first wife of Nathaniel Burden (*Light in August*).

Burden, Nathaniel.   The son of one Calvin Burden and the father of another, and the father of Joanna Burden (*Light in August*).

Burden, Sarah.   One of the three daughters of Calvin Burden I (*Light in August*).

Burden, Vangie (Evangeline?).   One of the three daughters of Calvin Burden I. (*Light in August*).

✱ **Burgess, Mr. and Mrs.**   The parents of a girl Benjy Compson molested (*The Sound and the Fury*).

Burk.   A member of the flight squadron commanded by Major Bridesman (*A Fable*).

Burke.   An Irish maid of Mrs. Harrison Blair. She was a friend of Ernie's, ("Fox Hunt").

Burney, Dewey.   A young man from Charlestown, Georgia, killed during the war. He had enlisted after having been suspected of stealing (*Soldiers' Pay*).

Burney, Mrs.   The mother of Dewey Burney. A woman of lower class (*Soldiers' Pay*).

Burnham, Lieutenant Frank. A stunt flyer who was killed in a crash during the airshow at the dedication of the Feinman Airport (*Pylon*).

Burrington, Nathaniel. A New England minister, the father of Calvin Burden. Referred to in *Light in August*.

✶**Burrington, Nathaniel II.** Joanna Burden's nephew, living in New Hampshire. Referred to in *Light in August*.

Burt. The boatswain's mate on the vessel manned by Claude Hope and Ronnie Smith ("Turnabout").

Burtsboro Old Town. A settlement in the Frenchman's Bend region (*The Hamlet*).

Bush, Lem. A neighbor of the Hineses with whom Milly rode to the circus (*Light in August*).

Butch. One of the boys at the barbershop who wanted to go out and lynch Will Mayes ("Dry September").

✶ **Butler, Joe.** One of the two "code" names used by Byron Snopes so his young amanuensis Virgil Beard would not know the purpose of the letters he was writing (*Sartoris*).

By the People. A short story in *Mademoiselle*, Oct. 1955. It was rewritten for Chapter 13 of *The Mansion*.

C

✶**Caesar.** Major Saucier Weddel's horse ("Mountain Victory").

Cain's Store. A farmer's supply store in Jefferson where Ab Snopes bought the cream separator for his first wife (*The Hamlet*).

Caldwell, Sam. A flagman for the railroad who helped Ned McCaslin load the stolen racehorse in a boxcar for its trip from Memphis to Parsham (*The Reivers*).

Caledonia Chapel. A small rural church in the Beat Four region where Vinson Gowrie was buried (*Intruder in the Dust*). It is referred to in *The Mansion*.

Callaghan. A New York riding stable man who tried to teach Mrs. Blair to ride ("Fox Hunt").

Callaghan Mines. A mine in Utah where Harry Wilbourne worked as a doctor. The owner, a man named Callaghan, lived in Chicago (*The Wild Palms*).

Callaghan, Miss. A grade school teacher in Jefferson ("Uncle Willy").

Callicoat, David. The English name by which Ikkemotubbe was called ("A Justice"). *"Callie"*

Callie. Aunt Callie, the colored woman who took care of the Priest children (*The Reivers*).

Canova, Signor. The stage name of Joel Flint ("An Error in Chemistry" in *Knight's Gambit*).

Carcassonne. A short story in *Collected Stories*. First published in *These 13*. A non-Yoknapatawpha story about a man who wanted to write poetry and who lived in a garret (apparently the Wilfred Midgleston of "Black Music," although he is unnamed here). Carcassonne is a city in southern France and is used by Faulkner as a symbol of the imagination. There is a possible pun on the word, the word *carcasse* meaning skeleton, since the character's skeleton appears in the story in contradistinction to his imagination. *Captain / Captain of / Yacht*

Carl. An eighteen-year-old messboy from Philadelphia who lost his virginity in Naples when his ship docked there ("Divorce *somethers, miss*) in Naples").

Carter. The family name of old Anse McCallum's mother *✶*("The Tall Men"). Also the architect for whom Wilfred Midgleston worked ("Black Music").

Cartoons. Among known cartoons done by Faulkner are the following: *Ole Miss 1916-1917*, XXI, p. 163; *Ole Miss 1917-1918*, XXII, p. 113; *Ole Miss 1919-1920*, XXIV, pp. 105, 155, 157; *Ole Miss 1920-1921*, XXV, pp. 131, 137; *Ole Miss 1921-1922*, XXVI, p. 188; and *The Scream*, I (May 1925), 11, 14, and 15. These, plus some other drawings, are reproduced in *William Faulkner: Early Prose and Poetry,* ed. Carvel Collins.

Caruthers, Miss.   A former organist in the Reverend Gail Hightower's church in Jefferson (*Light in August*).

Caspey.   The son of Simon and Euphronia. He had been in World War I and sometime during the 1920s he was sent to the penitentiary for stealing. In *Sartoris* he is called Elnora's brother; in "There Was a Queen" he is referred to as her husband.

Casse-tête.   The "good" thief who was executed with the Corporal. Called "Horse" by Lapin and sometimes known as "Dimwit." He wanted to go to Paris (*A Fable*).

Catalpa Street.   The street in Memphis where Miss Reba's place of business was located (*The Reivers*). In *Requiem for a Nun* it is called Manuel Street.

Cathay.   A poem in *The Mississippian,* IX (Nov. 12, 1919), 8. Reprinted in *William Faulkner: Early Prose and Poetry,* ed. Carvel Collins, p. 41.

Cavalcanti.   The name of a wineshop on the outskirts of a small Italian village near Milan. Also the family name of the aunt of Giulio Farinzale ("Mistral").

Cayley Girl, The.   The daughter of Hence Cayley and a woman named Mossop. She was courted by Max Harriss, who gave her a diamond ring ("Knight's Gambit").

Cayley, Hence.   The father of the girl to whom Max Harriss gave a ring ("Knight's Gambit").

Centaur in Brass.   A short story in *Collected Stories*. First published in *The American Mercury,* Feb. 1932. Rewritten as Chapter I of *The Town*.

Chance.   A sketch in the New Orleans *Times-Picayune* Sunday section, May 17, 1925, p. 7. Reprinted in *New Orleans Sketches* (ed. Collins).

Chance, Vic.   An airplane maker from whom Roger Shumann wanted to get a plane (*Pylon*).

Charlestown, Georgia.   The setting of *Soldiers' Pay*.

Charley.   The name of the interne with whom Joe Christmas saw Miss Atkins having an affair (*Light in August*). Also a railroad man in Memphis (*The Reivers*).

Charlie. One of Caddy Compson's boy friends (*The Sound and the Fury*).

Cheest! A sketch in the New Orleans *Times-Picayune* Sunday section, Apr. 5, 1925, p. 4. Reprinted in *New Orleans Sketches* (ed. Collins).

Child Looks from His Window, A. A poem in *Contempo*, II (May 25, 1932), 3. Uncollected.

Chlory. A colored servant in Judge Allison's home ("Beyond").

Christian, Hoke. A sixty-year-old drugstore proprietor in Jefferson. He was a dope addict whom the people of the church tried to cure ("Uncle Willy"). In *The Town* he is known only as Uncle Willy. His death (before 1938) is referred to in *The Mansion*. The drugstore is referred to in *The Reivers*.

Christian, Walter. The Negro janitor of the Christian drugstore. He used to drink the alcohol in the prescription case (*The Town*).

Christmas, Joe. The illegitimate son of Milly Hines and a part-Negro carnival man. His mother died when he was born and he was put by his grandfather on the steps of a hospital. He was named Christmas by the staff because he had been found on Christmas day. He was raised by a farmer named Simon McEachern. After several adventures he ran away and ended up in Jefferson, where he worked for a while at the sawmill and then went into bootlegging. He lived in a cabin on the Burden place and became the lover of Joanna Burden, a middle-aged spinster. He killed her, was put in jail but escaped, and was caught hiding in Hightower's house by Percy Grimm, who castrated and then shot him (*Light in August*).

Church, Mrs. A lady in Mottstown who called on Mrs. Pruitt ("That Will Be Fine").

Cinthy. A Negro slave belonging to Hightower's grandfather (*Light in August*).

Claire de Lune. A poem in *The Mississippian*, IX (Mar. 3,

1920), 6. Reprinted in *William Faulkner: Early Prose and Poetry,* ed. Carvel Collins, p. 58.

Clapp, Walter. The horse trainer at Colonel Linscomb's (*The Reivers*).

Clay, Beulah. A woman whose funeral Frony refers to at which the mourners mourned for two days (*The Sound and the Fury*).

Clefus. A janitor who swept out Gavin Stevens' office (*The Town*).

Cobbler, The. A sketch in the New Orleans *Times-Picayune* Sunday section, May 10, 1925, p. 7. Reprinted in *New Orleans Sketches* (ed. Collins).

Co-Education at Ole Miss. A poem in *The Mississippian,* X (May 4, 1921), 5. Reprinted in *William Faulkner: Early Prose and Poetry,* ed. Carvel Collins, p. 77.

Cofer. The agent for the doctor who rented the beach house on the Mississippi gulf coast to Harry and Charlotte (*The Wild Palms*).

Colbert, David. Referred to as the "chief Man of all the Chickasaws in our section" sometime around 1800. His wife was distantly related to Herman Basket's aunt ("A Courtship").

Coldfield, Ellen. The daughter of Goodhue Coldfield, born in Tennessee on Oct. 9, 1817. She married Thomas Sutpen in 1838. They had two children, Henry and Judith. She died on Jan. 23, 1863, while her husband was away at war (*Absalom, Absalom!*).

Coldfield, Goodhue. A Methodist merchant from Tennessee who settled in Jefferson in 1828. He was the father of Ellen and Rosa Coldfield. When the war came he locked himself up in the attic of his home and was fed by his daughter Rosa, who hauled up food to him in a pail outside the window. He died in his self-imprisoned room in 1864. Appears in *Absalom, Absalom!*; is referred to in *Requiem for a Nun*.

Coldfield, Rosa. The daughter of Goodhue Goldfield and a sister of Mrs. Thomas Sutpen. Born in 1845. In 1865 she went to live at Sutpen's Hundred to be with her niece Judith. She became engaged to Sutpen, but when he wanted to try to produce a male heir before marriage, she went back to Jefferson. In 1909 she got Quentin Compson to go out to the old place with her, where she discovered her nephew Henry Sutpen. She died on January 8, 1910 (*Absalom, Absalom!*).

Coleman, Mrs. A lady mentioned by Mrs. Saunders at whose home she is going to pay a call (*Soldiers' Pay*).

Collected Stories of William Faulkner, The. Published by Random House, New York, 1950. Contains 42 stories, divided as follows: *The Country:* "Barn Burning," "Shingles for the Lord," "The Tall Men," "A Bear Hunt," "Two Soldiers," and "Shall Not Perish"; *The Village:* "A Rose for Emily," "Hair," "Centaur in Brass," "Dry September," "Death Drag," "Elly," "Uncle Willy," "Mule in the Yard," "That Will Be Fine," and "That Evening Sun"; *The Wilderness:* "Red Leaves," "A Justice," "A Courtship," and "Lo!"; *The Wasteland:* "Ad Astra," "Victory," "Crevasse," "Turnabout," and "All the Dead Pilots"; *The Middle Ground:* "Wash," "Honor," "Dr. Martino," "Fox Hunt," "Pennsylvania Station," "Artist at Home," "The Brooch," "My Grandmother Millard," "Golden Land," "There Was a Queen," and "Mountain Victory"; and *Beyond:* "Beyond," "Black Music," "The Leg," "Mistral," "Divorce in Naples," and "Carcassonne." All 42 stories had received previous publication.

Collier. An airman in the squadron of which Captain Bogard was a member ("Turnabout").

Collyer. A British flyer who, after he was shot down, became a squadron adjutant (*A Fable*).

Commercial Hotel. A sidestreet hotel in Jefferson, known as Rouncewell's because of the family which owned it. In 1910 or thereabout it was taken over by Flem Snopes and renamed the Snopes Hotel. Sometime in the 1920s it was taken over by Dink Quistenberry and renamed the Jefferson Hotel (*The Town* and *The Mansion*). Referred to in *The Reivers* as the place where Boon Hogganbeck stayed.

Compson. A Compson with no given first name was locked up during the period of the Civil War because he was insane. He had a wife who was one of the social leaders of Jefferson dur-

Compson,
Mrs.

ing that time. Rosa Millard borrowed her hat and parasol when she visited the Yankee troops ("Skirmish at Sartoris" in *The Unvanquished*).

Compson, Benjamin. The youngest son of Jason Compson III. Born April 7, 1895. When it was discovered that he was an idiot his name was changed from Maury (after his uncle Maury L. Bascomb) to Benjamin. In 1913, after molesting some girls, he was castrated. In 1933 he was put away in the asylum in Jackson. According to *The Sound and the Fury* and Appendix this occurred after Mrs. Compson died, but according to *The Mansion* it occurred before she died and his brother Jason had to have him released at her insistence. Then two years later he set fire to the house and burned himself to death and destroyed the house.

Compson, Candace (Caddy). The daughter of Jason Compson III. Born around 1891. In 1910, after becoming pregnant by a man named Dalton Ames, she married an Indiana banker named Sydney Herbert Head. He divorced her in 1911. In 1920 she married a motion picture executive in Hollywood and was divorced in Mexico in 1925. In 1940 she was in Paris, and was reported to have become the mistress of a Nazi occupation general. Appears in *The Sound and the Fury* and the Appendix to it, "That Evening Sun," and "A Justice." Is referred to in *The Mansion*.

Compson, Caroline Bascomb. The wife of Jason Compson III, and mother of Quentin, Caddy, Jason, and Benjy. Is reported to have died in 1933. Appears in *The Sound and the Fury* and Appendix and "That Evening Sun." Is referred to in *The Mansion*.

Compson, Charles Stuart. The son of Quentin MacLachan Compson I. He fought the American rebels in Georgia during the Revolution, was wounded and left for dead, but managed four years later to reach Kentucky, where his aged father and son were. He wanted to be a schoolteacher, but gave that up and turned to gambling. He participated in the plot to seize the Mississippi Valley and turn it over to the Spanish. When that failed he fled. Appears in the Appendix to *The Sound and the Fury*.

Compson, Jason Lycurgus I. The son of Charles Stuart Compson, he was taken as an infant by his grandfather from Carolina to Kentucky in 1779. He is next heard of in 1811, when he appeared at the Chickasaw Agency in Okataba County, and soon became the agent's partner. In 1813 the Chickasaw chief Ikkemotubbe traded him a square mile of land in central Yoknapatawpha County for a racing mare, and he built the Compson home there. He had much to do with the founding and early development of Jefferson. He was the father (or grandfather, according to another account), of General Compson. Appears in *Requiem for a Nun* and the Appendix to *The Sound and the Fury*.

Compson, Jason Lycurgus II. He was, according to *Requiem for a Nun,* the son of Jason Lycurgus Compson I; according to the Appendix to *The Sound and the Fury,* he was his grandson, with Quentin MacLachan Compson II, a governor, coming between. He was a young man around Jefferson in 1838, and became a friend of Thomas Sutpen. During the war he was a brigadier general. He was the father of Jason Richmond Compson. He spent most of his last years hunting with Major de Spain on the Major's hunting grounds on the old Sutpen place. He died there in 1900. *The Town* substantiates the *Requiem for a Nun* account by saying that he was both the governor and the general. Appears in "The Old People" and "The Bear" (in *Go Down, Moses*), *Absalom, Absalom!,* and the Appendix to *The Sound and the Fury*. Is referred to in "Delta Autumn" (in *Go Down, Moses*), *Requiem for a Nun,* "My Grandmother Millard," the revised version of "A Bear Hunt," "An Odor of Verbena" (in *The Unvanquished*), *The Town,* and *The Reivers*.

Compson, Jason Richmond. The son of General Compson and the father of Quentin, Caddy, Jason, and Benjy. He was trained as a lawyer but dissipated his life away by drinking. He died in 1912. Appears in *The Sound and the Fury* and Appendix, "That Evening Sun," "A Justice," and *Absalom, Absalom!* Is referred to (as General Compson's son) in "The Bear" (in *Go Down, Moses*).

Compson, Jason IV. The son of Jason Richmond Compson. Born in 1893. He went to a school in Memphis, where he learned

cotton grading, and then opened a cotton buying and selling
office in the farmers' supply store in Jefferson where he worked.
He embezzled the money his sister Candace sent for the support
of her daughter, who, in turn, stole the money from him. According to the Appendix to *The Sound and the Fury,* when his
mother died in 1933 he sent his younger brother to the asylum
and sold the Compson property and moved into a room above
the store where he worked. But according to *The Mansion* he
mortgaged the place and built a house for his mother and himself in downtown Jefferson. This latter account relates that he
bought back the land sold to the golf club, and then in 1943 sold
the entire estate to Flem Snopes, who turned it into a housing
development. Appears in *The Sound and the Fury* and Appendix,
"That Evening Sun," "A Justice," and *The Mansion.* Is referred
to in *The Town.*

Compson, Quentin MacLachan I.   The first of the American
Compsons. Born in 1699 in Glasgow; raised in the Scottish highlands by his mother's people. He participated in the Jacobite
uprising of 1745 and fled to America to Carolina. In 1779 he fled
from Carolina to Kentucky, taking his infant grandson with him.
He died around 1784 and was buried in Harrodsburg, Kentucky.
Appears in the Appendix to *The Sound and the Fury.*

Compson, Quentin MacLachan II.   His place in the Compson
line is not clear. According to the Appendix to *The Sound and
the Fury* he was the son of Jason Lycurgus Compson I and the
father of Jason Lycurgus Compson II and was governor of the
state. Another account (*Requiem for a Nun*) ignores him altogether, and calls Jason II the son of Jason I. A third account
(*The Town*) says that Jason II was the governor.

Compson, Quentin III.   The son of Jason Richmond Compson. Born around 1889 (the chronology to *Absalom, Absalom!*
says 1891, however). Was sent to Harvard, where he committed
suicide in June 1910. Appears in *The Sound and the Fury* and
Appendix, *Absalom, Absalom!,* "That Evening Sun," and "A
Justice." He relates parts of the first two and all of the second two
of these. A story, "Lion," later rewritten as part of "The Bear,"

was originally a story related by Quentin. The revised version of "A Bear Hunt" is apparently related by him. He is referred to in *The Mansion*.

Compson, Quentin IV.   The illegitimate daughter of Candace Compson and Dalton Ames. Born in 1911, and raised by her grandmother. On the night of April 7, 1928, she stole almost seven thousand dollars from her uncle Jason and ran away with a carnival pitchman already under sentence for bigamy. She was not heard of again. Appears in *The Sound and the Fury* and Appendix. Is referred to in *The Mansion*.

Compsons, The.   The title given to the Appendix to *The Portable Faulkner*. This has been included in all reprints of *The Sound and the Fury* after 1946. It covers information about the Compson family from 1699 to 1945.

Comyn.   An Irish aviator in World War I. Appears in "Ad Astra." Is referred to in *Sartoris*.

Confrey, Mame.   The wife of Max Confrey (*Light in August*).

Confrey, Max.   The owner of the restaurant where Bobbie Allen worked (*Light in August*).

Connor (or Connors), Buck.   The town marshall in Jefferson. Called Buck Connor in *Light in August*, Buck Connors in *The Town*, and just Buck in *Sartoris*. There was also a Buck Connors of the same age as Charles Mallison, Jr., who used to play with Charles and Aleck Sander and some of the other boys (*The Town*).

Contalmaison.   The Mississippi plantation home of Major Saucier Weddel ("Mountain Victory").

Conventicle, Flight Sergeant.   A Welshman; a member of Major Bridesman's command (*A Fable*).

Cook, Celia.   A young girl from Oxford who scratched her name on the window pane with a diamond ring ("Ambuscade" in *The Unvanquished*).

Coon Bridge.   A bridge a few miles down the river from Major de Spain's hunting camp. Young Ike McCaslin was sent there with the team to meet the men who were bringing Sam Fathers back to camp ("The Bear" in *Go Down, Moses*).

Cooper.   A fellow reporter of the Reporter (*Pylon*).

Cooper, Minnie.   A forty-year-old spinster in Jefferson who said she had been attacked by the Negro Will Mayes ("Dry September").

Coppermine.   The real name of the horse Bobo Beauchamp stole from Mr. van Tosch and which Ned McCaslin renamed Lightning (*The Reivers*).

Corporal, The.   See **Stefan.**

Corrie.   See **Hogganbeck, Everbe Corinthia.**

Cotton, Ernest.   The killer of Houston in the story "The Hound." The revised version, in *The Hamlet,* makes Mink Snopes the killer. Cotton does not appear in the novel.

Country, The.   Section I of *Collected Stories.* Contains "Barn Burning," "Shingles for the Lord," "The Tall Men," "A Bear Hunt," "Two Soldiers," and "Shall Not Perish."

Country Mice.   A sketch in the New Orleans *Times-Picayune* Sunday section, Sept. 20, 1925, p. 7. Reprinted in *New Orleans Sketches* (ed. Collins).

Courtesan Is Dead, The.   The title given to *A Green Bough,* XXXV when it was reprinted in *Mississippi Verse,* edited by Alice James.

Courthouse, The.   The prose introduction to "Act One" of *Requiem for a Nun.* Subtitled "(A Name for the City)." It is reprinted in *The Faulkner Reader.* Under the title, "A Name for the City" it was published first as a short story in *Harper's Magazine,* Oct. 1950, and revised for the novel.

Courtship, A.   A short story in *Collected Stories.* First published in *The Sewanee Review,* Oct. 1948. About the Indians.

Cousin Melisandre.   A cousin of Bayard Sartoris II who stayed at the Sartoris plantation during the Civil War. She was embarrassed when the federal troops tipped over an outdoor privy in which she was sitting guarding the family silver. She married Philip St.-Just Backhouse after his name was changed to Backus ("My Grandmother Millard").

Cowan, Mrs.   A lady with whom Hawkshaw the barber boarded in Jefferson ("Hair").

Cowrie, Captain. A British flight officer who shared a hut with Major Bridesman (*A Fable*).

Crack. The first sergeant of the company known as the Sartoris Rifles organized by McLendon in 1917 (*The Mansion*).

Crain, Amos. A farmer neighbor of Roger Howes in Virginia ("Artist at Home"). *Crain, mrs. —*

Cranston, Lily. The proprietress of the resort Cranston's Wells, Mississippi ("Doctor Martino").

Cranston, Lucy. The maiden name of the wife of John Sartoris II, and the mother of the twins Bayard III and John III. Her death is not recorded, but she died sometime before 1919 (*Sartoris*).

Cranston's Wells. A Mississippi summer resort run by Miss Lily Cranston ("Doctor Martino").

Crawford. A shortened form of Crawfish-ford, who, according to one account ("A Justice"), was the father of Sam Fathers. But in "The Old People" and "The Bear" (in *Go Down, Moses*), Sam is called the son of Ikkemotubbe.

Crawford, Doctor. The doctor at Hoke's sawmill. He sewed up Lion after his foray with Old Ben ("The Bear" in *Go Down, Moses*).

Crenshaw, Jack. A Revenue Department field agent who hunted whiskey stills in Yoknapatawpha County (*The Town*).

Crevasse. A short story in *Collected Stories*. First published in *These 13*. A non-Yoknapatawpha story about a group of soldiers caught in a cave-in.

Crossman County. A county bordering Yoknapatawpha County, probably to the north. Has two small towns, Glasgow and Hollymount (*Intruder in the Dust*).

Crowe. A painter at whose house Harry met Charlotte (*The Wild Palms*).

Crump, Lucas. A mail carrier out of Blizzard, Arizona; the narrator of the story to the "I" who reports it ("Idyll in the Desert").

Cumberland County. The home of the sister of Colonel

Devries (*The Mansion*). In the original version of the story ("By the People") it was called Minton County.

Cunninghame, Sergeant. The sergeant in charge of the troops when Alec Gray was a private. He was ordered by the sergeant-major to report Gray for not shaving before inspection ("Victory").

D

Dad. A man who worked for Brother Goodyhay and robbed Mink Snopes of his ten dollars (*The Mansion*).

Daingerfield, Miss. One of the girls Gerald and Mrs. Bland were taking on a picnic the day Quentin Compson committed suicide. (*The Sound and the Fury*).

Daisy. The wife of Uncle Ash Wylie. Referred to in "The Bear" (*Go Down, Moses*).

Damon and Pythias Unlimited. A sketch in the New Orleans *Times-Picayune* Sunday section, Feb. 15, 1925, p. 7. Reprinted in *New Orleans Sketches* (ed. Collins).

Damuddy. The name which the Compson children called their grandmother. She died around 1898 (*The Sound and the Fury*).

Dan. One of Roth Edmonds' lotmen ("The Fire and the Hearth" in *Go Down, Moses*). The horse on the store wagon driven by Uncle Job (*The Sound and the Fury*). A hunting dog belonging to the McCallums (*Sartoris*). One of the Compson's dogs (*The Sound and the Fury*). A horse owned by Mister Ernest ("Race at Morning"). And a horse owned by Faulkner ("Afternoon of a Cow").

Dandridge, Margaret. The maiden name of Judge Stevens'

wife, the mother of Gavin Stevens and Mrs. Charles Mallison, and the grandmother of Chick Mallison. Referred to in *Intruder in the Dust*.

Davy. An American student at Oxford who went into the army and lost a leg. He wanted his dead friend George to find the leg because he thought it might be doing harm. He was attacked by Jotham Rust, the brother of Everbe Corinthia ("The Leg").

Deacon. The colored porter in Cambridge to whom Quentin Compson gave some letters to be delivered after his suicide (*The Sound and the Fury*).

Death Drag. A short story in *Collected Stories*. First published in *Scribner's Magazine*, Jan. 1932, under the title "Death-Drag." Reprinted in *Doctor Martino and Other Stories*. It is included in *The Portable Faulkner*. About the visit of some stunt flyers to Jefferson.

Dedication of an Airport. Section I of *Pylon*.

Delta Autumn. The sixth story in *Go Down, Moses*. First published in *Story*, May-June 1942. It is included in *The Portable Faulkner*. Part was revised for the postlude of *Big Woods*. About the aged Ike McCaslin's last hunting trip with Roth Edmonds, at which time we learn of Roth's having fathered a child of the grandniece of Lucas Beauchamp.

Demarchi. A member of the flight squadron commanded by Major Bridesman (*A Fable*).

Demont. See **Dumont.**

de Montigny. See **Montigny, de.**

Depre, Mrs. Virginia. See **Du Pre, Mrs. Virginia.**

de Spain, Lula. The wife of Major de Spain I. It was her one-hundred-dollar rug that Ab Snopes ruined. Appears in "Barn Burning." Is referred to in *The Hamlet*.

de Spain, Major Cassius I. A member of one of the old important families of Jefferson. He had been a major in the Civil War, and shortly after became sheriff of Yoknapatawpha County. It was he who went after Wash Jones when Wash killed Sutpen. After Sutpen's death he bought part of the hundred acres in northwestern Yoknapatawpha County and turned it into a hunting ground. After Old Ben the bear was killed and Sam Fathers died, he sold the timber rights of the land to a sawmill. He was involved in litigation with Ab Snopes when Ab ruined an expensive rug belonging to his wife, after which Ab burned down his barn. He was a cousin of Chick Mallison's grandfather. Appears in "The Old People" and "The Bear" (in *Go Down, Moses*), *Absalom, Absalom!*, "Barn Burning," and "Wash." Is referred to in "A Bear Hunt," "Delta Autumn" (in *Go Down Moses*), *The Hamlet, Intruder in the Dust,* "Shall Not Perish," *The Town* and *The Reivers.*

de Spain, Major Cassius II.   Not a major, but so called out of respect for his father. He was a wealthy Jefferson banker and a powerful political figure. His twenty-three-year-old son, an aviator, was killed fighting the Japanese in World War II ("Shall Not Perish"). This is apparently the de Spain of "A Bear Hunt" also, for he too was a married man. He has probably been superseded by Manfred de Spain.

de Spain, Manfred.   A son of Major Cassius de Spain, sometimes called Major, but actually a lieutenant, a West Point man who had been in the Spanish-American War. In 1904 he became mayor of Jefferson. He was a bachelor, and after Flem Snopes moved to Jefferson in 1909 he began having an affair with Flem's wife, the former Eula Varner. In 1919 or 1920 he became president of the Sartoris (Merchants and Farmers) Bank and remained so until 1927, when Mrs. Snopes committed suicide, after which he left town and was not heard of again. Appears in *The Town.* Is referred to in *The Mansion* and *The Reivers.*

Despleins, Jules.   A French flyer who took part in the dedication of the Feinman Airport (*Pylon*).

de Vitry.   See **Vitry, de.**

Devries, Colonel.   A wounded veteran and hero of World War II, holder of the Congressional Medal of Honor, who ran against Clarence Snopes for United States representative (*The Mansion*). In the original version ("By the People") he was also a veteran of the Korean War.

Diana. The ship which was the setting of "Yo Ho and Two Bottles of Rum."

Dicey. The Negro woman who took care of Milly Jones when Milly's baby was born ("Wash").

Dick, Colonel. The Yankee colonel from an Ohio regiment with whom Granny Millard dealt concerning the return of the horses and mules taken from Sartoris ("Raid" in *The Unvanquished*).

Dilazuck's. A livery stable in Jefferson in 1917 (*The Mansion*).

Dilsey. The wife of Roskus and mother of Versh, Frony, and T. P. She was a cook at the Jason Richmond Compson home. When Mrs. Compson died in 1933 she moved to Memphis and lived with her daughter Frony. She was still living in 1943. The family name of Dilsey and Roskus is Gibson. Appears in *The Sound and the Fury* and Appendix and "That Evening Sun."

Dilsey. The title given to part of section four of *The Sound and the Fury* reprinted in *The Portable Faulkner.*

✳**Dimwit.** See **Casse-tête.**   *District Attorney*

Division. A small town on the state line between Mississippi and Alabama where the Starnes family lived ("Hair").

Divorce in Naples. A short story in *Collected Stories*. First published in *These 13*. A non-Yoknapatawpha story about two American sailors in Naples, involving the loss of virginity by the younger. This incident leads to a breech of friendship between the two, which is later patched up on the return trip to the United States.

Dixie Café. An eating place in Jefferson (*The Town*).

Doane's Mill. A small pine sawmill village in Alabama where Lena Grove lived, and where Lucas Burch, her seducer, worked (*Light in August*).

Doc. A friend of the newspaperman McCord. He, along with McCord and a man named Gillespie, owned a cottage on a Wisconsin lake where Charlotte and Harry went (*The Wild Palms*). Also a student at the University of Mississippi who told Gowan Stevens where he could buy liquor (*Sanctuary*).   "Doc" (2) "Doctor Jones" (as is)

Doctor Martino. A short story in *Collected Stories*. First published in *Harper's Magazine,* Nov. 1931. Reprinted in *Doctor Martino and Other Stories.* A non-Yoknapatawpha story about an old doctor who had a strange power over the girl Louise King.

Doctor Martino and Other Stories.   A volume of 14 short stories published by Harrison Smith and Robert Haas, New York, 1934. Contains "Doctor Martino," "Fox Hunt," "The Hound," "Death Drag," "There Was a Queen," "Smoke," "Turn About," "Beyond," "Wash," "Elly," "Black Music," "Leg," "Mountain Victory," and "Honor." All but two were reprinted in *Collected Stories. "Smoke"* was reprinted in *Knight's Gambit;* "The Hound" was rewritten for inclusion in *The Hamlet.*

Dodge, Granby.   A stock trader and lay preacher; a cousin of the mother of the Holland twins. He killed Anselm Holland, Sr., and hired a Memphis gangster to shoot Judge Dukinfield ("Smoke" in *Knight's Gambit*).

Dollar.   A storekeeper in Mottstown (*Light in August*).

Don.   A young American tourist in Italy; a companion of the narrator of the story ("Mistral").

Doom.   *Du homme,* the name given Ikkemotubbe by his French friend, the Chevalier Soeur-Blonde de Vitry ("Red Leaves"). Is referred to as Doom in *The Reivers.*

Doshey.   Mentioned in *The Hamlet* as one of the old family names of the Frenchman's Bend region. A Calhoun County Doshey was Eustace Grimm's wife.

Dough, James.   Mrs. Wardle's nephew, who was visiting her. He had been a corporal-pilot in a French escadrille and had lost a leg in the war (*Soldiers' Pay*).

Downs, Mrs.   A white woman fortune teller in the Negro section of Jefferson (*Intruder in the Dust*). An unnamed woman bearing the same general description, having the same profession, and living in the same locality appears in *Sanctuary.*

Drake, Hubert.   Temple Drake's brother, the youngest of four, called Buddy by her. A student at Yale (*Sanctuary*).

Drake, Judge.   Temple Drake's father, a judge in Jackson (*Sanctuary*).

Drake, Temple. See **Stevens, Temple Drake.**

Dry September. A short story in *Collected Stories*. First published in *Scribner's Magazine,* Jan. 1931. Reprinted in *These 13.* ~~Drummer~~ It is included in *The Faulkner Reader* and *Selected Short Stories.* About the lynching of a Negro in Jefferson.

Du homme. See **Doom.**

Dukinfield, Emma. Judge Dukinfield's daughter, who had brought him a brass box from Europe which always sat on his desk ("Smoke" in *Knight's Gambit*).

Dukinfield, Judge. A Jefferson judge. He was to try the case of Gavin Stevens against Manfred de Spain (brought on when Gavin used Flem Snopes's having taken the brass from the valves in the power plant as a pretext to impeach the mayor), but he turned the case over to Judge Stevens, Gavin's father. He later became the executor of the estate of Anselm Holland, Sr., and while in the process of probating it he was shot to death in his office. Appears in *The Town* and "Smoke" (in *Knight's Gambit*). Is referred to in *The Mansion*.

Dumont, Mme. The married name of Marthe (or Magda), *(as C-17)* the half-sister of Stefan, the Corporal. In one place the name is spelled Demont (*A Fable*). *[Marthe's husband]*

Duncan, Demon. See **Ginsfarb.**

Du Pre, Virginia. Known as Miss Jenny or Aunt Jenny, she was a sister of Colonel Sartoris. She came from Carolina in 1869 to live with the family. She died in 1930. Appears in "An Odor of Verbena" (in *The Unvanquished*), *Sartoris, Sanctuary,* and "There Was a Queen." Is referred to in *Requiem for a Nun* (as Mrs. Virginia Depre), "All the Dead Pilots" (as Mrs. Virginia Sartoris), *The Town,* and *The Mansion*.

Dying Gladiator. A poem in *The Double Dealer,* VII (Jan.-Feb. 1925), 85. Reprinted in *Salmagundi* and in *William Faulkner: Early Prose and Poetry,* ed. Carvel Collins, p. 113.

E

Eagle. A hunting dog owned by Mister Ernest ("Race at Morning").

Earl. See **Triplett, Earl.**

Ed. The name Pete heard called to mysteriously on the yacht. Possibly the Captain's name (*Mosquitoes*). Also the judge at the race at Parsham (*The Reivers*).

Edmonds, Carothers McCaslin (Cass). The grandson of old Lucius Quintus Carothers McCaslin and the son of Carolina McCaslin. Born in 1850. He raised Ike McCaslin, and Ike turned over the McCaslin lands to him. He was the father of Zachary Taylor Edmonds. Appears in "Was," "The Old People," and "The Bear" (in *Go Down, Moses*). Is referred to in "The Fire and the Hearth" and "Delta Autumn" (in *Go Down, Moses*), "A Bear Hunt," *The Town,* and (as McCaslin Edmonds) *The Reivers.*

Edmonds, Carothers (Roth). The son of Zachary Edmonds and great-great-grandson of old Lucius Quintus Carothers McCaslin. He was born in 1898. He attended the state university at Oxford around 1920. The last white descendant of the family, he maintained the old McCaslin plantation. He fathered illegitimately around 1940, a child born to the granddaughter of James Beauchamp. Has a major role in "The Fire and the Hearth" and "Delta Autumn" (in *Go Down, Moses*), and appears briefly or is merely referred to in "Go Down Moses," *Intruder in the Dust,* "Race at Morning," *The Town* and *The Reivers.*

Edmonds, Louisa. The wife of Zachary Taylor Edmonds (*The Reivers*).

Edmonds, Sarah. The maiden name of Grandfather (Boss) Priest's wife. She was born in 1854, and was probably a sister of Carothers McCaslin Edmonds (*The Reivers*).

Edmonds, Zachary Taylor (Zack). The son of McCaslin Edmonds and father of Roth Edmonds. Appears in "The Fire and the Hearth" (in *Go Down, Moses*) and *The Reivers* (where he is called McCaslin Edmonds' nephew). Charles Mallison, Jr., in *The Town*, calls McCaslin Edmonds Roth's father, and does not mention Zach. *[Edmonds' boy]*

Education of Lucius Priest, The. The title given to pp. 95-115, 132-133, 139-143, and 152-161 of *The Reivers* when they were preprinted in *Esquire*, May 1962. (The paging is not exact, for the selections were edited for continuity.) *[Eggleston, "Buzzard"]*

Ek. The liar in "The Liar."

Ellen. A tame fox belonging to the MacCallums (*Sartoris*).

Elly. An eighteen-year-old girl from a Jefferson family. Her real name was Ailanthia, the same as her grandmother's. She deceived her parents by taking Paul de Montigny on a trip with her, and when her grandmother threatened to tell her father, and Paul refused to marry her, she forced the car off the road at a dangerous curve, apparently killing both of them and seriously injuring herself ("Elly").

Elly. A short story in *Collected Stories*. First published in *Story*, Feb. 1934. Reprinted in *Doctor Martino and Other Stories*. A story about modern Jefferson, but containing no characters from the other stories and novels.

Elma, Miss. The office deputy in the sheriff's office, the widow of a former sheriff (*The Town*).

Elnora. A Negro cook at the Sartoris home. She is mentioned in *Sartoris* as the daughter of Simon Strother and the sister of Caspey. In "There Was a Queen" she is called the daughter of Simon's wife and Colonel Sartoris, and the wife of Caspey. She is referred to in "All the Dead Pilots." *[Emma, Miss (as c-r)]*

Emmeline. The nurse of Aunt Louisa's children, Cousin Louisa and Cousin Fred, in Mottstown ("That Will Be Fine").

Emmy. The daughter of a drunken housepainter. The Reverend Joseph Mahon took her into his home as housekeeper after he discovered that she had had an affair with his son Donald (*Soldiers' Pay*).

Emmy's Father

Ephriam. Paralee's father and Aleck Sander's grandfather, no longer living (*Intruder in the Dust*).

Ephum. A colored worker at Miss Ballenbaugh's place (*The Reivers*).

Episode. A sketch in the New Orleans *Times-Picayune* Sunday section, Aug. 16, 1925. Reprinted in *New Orleans Sketches* (ed. Collins).

Ernest. See **Mister Ernest.**

✱**Ernest be Toogood.** See **Trueblood, Ernest V.**

Ernie. The "secretary or valet" (probably bodyguard) of Harrison Blair ("Fox Hunt").

Error in Chemistry, An. The fifth story in *Knight's Gambit.* First published in *Ellery Queen's Mystery Magazine,* June 1946, where it won a second prize in a mystery story contest. About the murder of Joel Flint's wife and her father, Wesley Pritchel. The story was adapted for television and presented on CBS, "Climax," December 2, 1954, with Edmund O'Brien.

Eula. Book II of *The Hamlet.*

Eula (1)
Eula (2)

Eula Acres. The name Flem Snopes gave to the housing subdivison he made out of the old Compson plantation (*The Mansion.*)

Eunice. A slave bought by Carothers McCaslin in 1807 and married to Thucydides in 1809. In 1810 she gave birth to a girl, Thomasina, whose father was McCaslin himself. Eunice drowned herself on Christmas day, 1832, when she discovered that her daughter was pregnant by her own father ("The Bear" in *Go Down, Moses*). There was another colored woman named Eunice, who was Horace Benbow's cook (*Sartoris*).

Euphronia. The wife (now dead) of Simon Strother and mother of Caspey and Elnora (*Sartoris*). See also **Frony.**

Eustace. A young lawyer in Jefferson with no given last name (*Sartoris*). He may be the Eustace Graham of *Sanctuary.*

Evening in New Valois, An. The second section of *Pylon.*

Everbe Corinthia. See **Hogganbeck, Everbe Corinthia.**

Ewell, Bryan. A deputy sheriff of Yoknapatawpha County. He was sent to watch over Mr. Pritchel (actually Joel Flint in disguise); ("An Error in Chemistry" in *Knight's Gambit*).

Ewell, Walter. A friend of Major de Spain's who always went hunting with the major and General Compson and Ike McCaslin. Appears in "The Old People" and "The Bear" (in *Go Down, Moses*) and "Race at Morning." Is referred to in "Delta Autumn" (in *Go Down, Moses*), "A Bear Hunt," *The Mansion,* and *The Reivers.*

Ewing, Ira I. A Nebraska wheat farmer and Cambellite preacher, the father of Ira Ewing II ("Golden Land").

Ewing, Ira II. A wealthy California realtor who lived in Beverly Hills. At fourteen he ran away from his Nebraska home. He married and was the father of two children. He became a drunkard and kept a mistress ("Golden Land").

Ewing, Mitch. The depot freight agent in Jefferson. He boarded at Mrs. Cowan's ("Hair"). In *Sartoris,* where he is known only as Mitch, he went with Bayard Sartoris and Hub on their second drinking spree on the evening of the day Bayard was hurt when he was thrown by a stallion he tried to mount. *Ewing, Mrs. —*

Ewing, Samantha. The mother of Ira Ewing II ("Golden Land").

Ewing, Samantha II. The movie actress daughter of Ira Ewing II. She went by the screen name of April Lalear ("Golden Land").

Ewing, Voyd. The homosexual son of Ira Ewing II ("Golden Land").

F

Fable, A. A novel published by Random House, New York, 1954. Dedicated to his daughter Jill. A non-Yoknapatawpha novel concerning the execution of a corporal in the French Army during World War I for his part as leader of a mutiny of thirteen soldiers during May 1918, thus leading to the "false" armistice. The time of the action covers one week, and the novel is a symbolic parallel with Passion Week. One section (pp. 151-189) was published separately (and in a somewhat different form) in 1950 under the title *Notes on a Horsethief*, and the same (as it appeared in the novel) was printed in *Vogue*, July 1954. A selection from the novel may be heard by Faulkner on the Caedmon long playing record number TC-1035.

Fairchild, Dawson.   A novelist; a guest of Mrs. Maurier on her yachting party (*Mosquitoes*). Presumably based upon Sherwood Anderson.

Faith or Fear.   See *Address to the graduating class of Pine Manor Junior College, Wellesley, Massachusetts,* under **Addresses by Faulkner.**

Falls, Will.   Known as Old Man Falls, almost ninety-four, an inmate of the poorhouse. He had once been an acquaintance of Colonel Sartoris' and brought Bayard a pipe which had belonged to the Colonel. He later tried to cure a blemish on Bayard's face with an old home-remedy ointment (*Sartoris*).

⚹**Fancy.**   A pony belonging to the Compson family (*The Sound and the Fury*).

Fantouches [sic].   A poem in *The Mississippian,* IX (Feb. 25, 1920), 3. Subtitled "à Paul Verlaine." Reprinted in Martha Mayes's "Faulkner Juvenilia," *New Campus Writing No. 2,* ed. Nolan Miller, p. 141, and in *William Faulkner: Early Prose and Poetry,* ed. Carvel Collins, p. 57.

Farinzale, Giulio.   A young Italian soldier in love with the ward of the village priest. ("Mistral").

Farmer.   The jailor in Jefferson during the Civil War (*Requiem For a Nun*).

Farmer, Cecilia.   The jailor's daughter who scratched her name and the date on the window pane with a diamond ring (*Requiem For a Nun*). See also **Cook, Cecilia.**

Farr, George.   The young man who married Cecily Saunders (*Soldiers' Pay*).

Fathers, Sam.   The son of Ikkemotubbe, the Chickasaw chief, and a a quadroon slave, sold by his father to old Carothers McCaslin in 1809. Versed in woodlore, he taught Ike McCaslin the knowledge of the woods and initiated him into the rites of hunting. He was called Fathers as a short form of Had-Two-Fathers, because his natural father and his mother's husband were not the same person. He died after Old Ben, the bear, was killed by Boon Hogganbeck in 1883. Appears in "The Old People" and "The Bear," and is referred to in "Delta Autumn" (in *Go Down, Moses*), *Intruder in the Dust*, and *The Reivers*. Appears anachronistically in "A Justice," a story related by Quentin Compson.

Faulkner. A "funny man . . . little kind of black man . . . a white man, except he was awful sunburned and kind of shabby dressed—no necktie and hat. . . . Not dangerous: just crazy." Met by Jenny and Pete and their friends Thelma and Roy (*Mosquitoes*).

Faulkner at Nagano. A book of interviews and other miscellaneous pieces published by Kenkyusha, Ltd., Tokyo, 1956. Contains, besides interviews and the "Colloquies at Nagano Seminar," "Message Given at Nagano," "Impressions of Japan," "To the Youth of Japan," and the Nobel Prize Address. Edited by Robert A. Jelliffe.

✱ Faulkner, Bill. The owner of the farm and the person involved most directly in the incident with Beulah, the cow ("Afternoon of a Cow").

Faulkner in the University. Published by the University of Virginia Press, Charlottesville, 1959. Subtitled "Class Conferences at the University of Virginia, 1957-1958." Besides the class conferences, the book contains two addresses: "Address to the Raven, Jefferson, and ODK Societies" and "Address to the English Club of the University of Virginia." Edited by Frederick L. Gwynn and Joseph L. Blotner.

Faulkner Reader, The. A collection published by Random House, New York, 1954. Contains, besides a "Foreword" by Faulkner, the Nobel Prize Address, *The Sound and the Fury* (complete, with the "Appendix"), "The Bear" (*Go Down, Moses*),

"Old Man" (*The Wild Palms*), "Spotted Horses" (*The Hamlet*), "A Rose for Emily," "Barn Burning," "Dry September," "That Evening Sun," "Turnabout," "Shingles for the Lord," "A Justice," "Wash," "An Odor of Verbena" (*The Unvanquished*), "Percy Grimm" (*Light in August*), and "The Courthouse" (*Requiem for a Nun*).

Faun, The. A poem in *The Double Dealer*, VII (Apr. 1925), 148. Reprinted in *Salmagundi* and in *William Faulkner: Early Prose and Poetry,* ed. Carvel Collins, p. 119.

Feinman, Colonel H. I. The chairman of the sewage board of New Valois. The local airport was named for him (*Pylon*).

Feinman Airport. The airport in New Valois (*Pylon*).

Female Academy, The. See **Academy, The.**

Fentry, G. A. The father of Stonewall Jackson Fentry ("Tomorrow" in *Knight's Gambit*).

Fentry, Jackson and Longstreet. The name given the son of the Thorpe girl and an unknown father by Stonewall Jackson Fentry, who took care of the baby until his relatives came and took it away from him. When the baby grew up he was called Buck Thorpe ("Tomorrow" in *Knight's Gambit*).

Fentry, Stonewall Jackson. A member of the jury who refused to acquit Bookwright for killing Buck Thorpe. He had married a Thorpe girl and had started to raise her illegitimate son after she died in childbirth until the Thorpes came along and took the baby away from him. The reason he held out against Bookwright was that Buck Thorpe was the baby he had started to raise ("Tomorrow" in *Knight's Gambit*).

Ffollansbye. An officer in the R.A.F. who first recommended MacWyrglinchbeath for a commission. He was killed during the war ("Thrift"). He also appears briefly in "All the Dead Pilots" as an acquaintance of John Sartoris.

Fibby. See **Phoebe.**

Fire and the Hearth, The. The second story in *Go Down, Moses.* One section was published originally in *Collier's Magazine,* June 22, 1940, under the title "A Point of Law"; another section was published originally in *The Atlantic Monthly,* Nov.

1940, under the title "Gold Is Not Always." A story about Lucas Beauchamp.

⚹Fite. The family name of Eustace Grimm's father's second wife (*The Hamlet*).

Fittie, Aunt. The madame of a house of prostitution in Kiblett, Arkansas, who took Miss Corrie (Everbe Corinthia, later Mrs. Boon Hogganbeck) into her place after Corrie's mother died (*The Reivers*).

Flem. Book I of *The Hamlet* and Book III of *The Mansion*.

Flint. The name of the interne who took Harry Wilbourne to the party where he met Charlotte (*The Wild Palms*).

Flint, Ellie Pritchel. The daughter of Wesley Pritchel and wife of Joel Flint. She was killed by her husband ("An Error in Chemistry" in *Knight's Gambit*).

Flint, Joel. A Yankee pitchman who married Ellie Pritchel and then murdered her and her father so he could get control of Pritchel's property ("An Error in Chemistry" in *Knight's Gambit*).

Flowers That Died, The. A poem in *Contempo*, III (June 25, 1933), 1. Uncollected.

Folklore of the Air. See **Book Reviews:** "Review of *Test Pilot* by Jimmy Collins." *Tonsiba*

Fonzo. See **Winbush, Fonzo.**

Fool About a Horse. A short story in *Scribner's Magazine*, Aug. 1936. Rewritten for *The Hamlet*.

Foote. The night marshal in Jefferson in 1942 ("Two Soldiers").

Foreword to *Sherwood Anderson & Other Famous Creoles: A Gallery of Contemporary New Orleans* (which see).

Foreword to *The Faulkner Reader* (which see).

Forrest, General Nathan Bedford. General Forrest (1821-1877), famous for his cavalry raids on the Union forces and for the phrase "to get there fustest with the mostest," is one of the few actual historical persons to appear under his own name in the Yoknapatawpha County stories. Appears in "My Grandmother Millard" and is referred to frequently elsewhere.

Fortinbride, Brother. A private in Colonel Sartoris' regiment until he was wounded and returned home to become a Methodist lay preacher. He preached Granny Millard's funeral sermon ("Riposte in Tertio" in *The Unvanquished*).

Fothergill, Zeb. An acquaintance of Colonel Sartoris'. He used to steal horses from the federal troops during the Civil War. Is referred to in *Sartoris*.

Fox Hunt. A short story in *Collected Stories*. First published in *Harper's Magazine,* Sept. 1931. Reprinted in *Doctor Martino and Other Stories*. A non-Yoknapatawpha story about a man named Harrison Blair of New York who owned a summer place in Carolina, where he went hunting.

Fox, Matt. A barber in Maxey's barbershop in Jefferson ("Hair").

Franciana. The name of the state in which New Valois is located (*Pylon*).

Frank. A boy friend of Ruby Lamar. He was shot by her father (*Sanctuary*).

Frankie. A young lady who used to play tennis at the Mitchell home (*Sartoris*).

Fraser. A childless widower who took care of Monk after Monk's mother (or grandmother) died. Monk lived with him until Fraser died ("Monk" in *Knight's Gambit*).

Fraser, Adam. The owner of a store in Beat Four where Lucas Beauchamp used to go (*Intruder in the Dust*).

Fraser, Doyle. The son of Adam Fraser. He worked in his father's store (*Intruder in the Dust*).

Fraser, Mr. A guest of Major de Spain at the major's hunting grounds ("A Bear Hunt").

Frazier, Judge. The judge in the case in which Bookwright was tried for the murder of Buck Thorpe ("Tomorrow" in *Knight's Gambit*). The name "Frazier" is mentioned by Gavin Stevens as a family name in east central Yoknapatawpha County. It may be the same name as "Fraser" (*The Town*).

Fred. The first name of both the uncle and cousin of the narrator of "That Will Be Fine." Uncle Fred was the husband of Aunt Louise. They lived in Mottstown.

Freedmantown. The Negro section of Jefferson (*Intruder in the Dust*).

Freeman. One of the men who used to sit on the gallery of the Littlejohn Hotel (*The Hamlet*).

French Architect

Frenchman's Bend. A small rural settlement in southeastern Yoknapatawpha County, twenty-two miles from Jefferson, in the county division known as "Beat Two." Gavin Stevens said of it: ". . . in the valleys along the rivers, the broad rich easy land where a man can raise something he can sell openly in daylight, the people named Littlejohn and Greenleaf and Armstead and Millingham and Bookwright [live]." The place was named Frenchman's Bend because all the land in that part of the county had once been owned by Louis Grenier, one of the first settlers in the county, and the first slave owner and planter there. It was in Frenchman's Bend that the Snopeses got their first real start. From the 1890s up through the 1940s the most important man in Frenchman's Bend was Will Varner, who owned the store there and had mortgages on most of the farms. Frenchman's Bend is the setting for *The Hamlet,* "Shingles for the Lord," "Two Soldiers," "Shall Not Perish," and parts of "Hand Upon the Waters" and "Tomorrow" (both in *Knight's Gambit*), *Sanctuary, The Town,* and *The Mansion.*

From Yoknapatawpha to UNESCO, the Dream. See *Address to the seventh national conference of the U. S. National Commission for UNESCO* under **Addresses by Faulkner.**

Frony (Euphronia). The daughter of Roskus and Dilsey. She married around 1910, and her son Luster was born in 1911. She married (probably a second time) a Pullman porter and moved to St. Louis, but later moved back to Memphis to provide a home for her mother. Appears in *The Sound and the Fury* and Appendix. Is referred to in "That Evening Sun."

Frost, Mark. A poet; the guest of Mrs. Maurier on her yachting party (*Mosquitoes*).

G

Gabe. The blacksmith in Jefferson in 1905 (*The Reivers*).

Gambrell, C. L. The warden at the state prison farm who was shot by Monk ("Monk" in *Knight's Gambit*).

Gant, Eunice. The clerk in the luggage department at Wildermark's department store (*The Town*).

Gant, Jim. A stock trader who left his wife and two-year-old daughter and ran away to Memphis with a Mrs. Vinson. His wife followed them and shot them ("Miss Zilphia Gant").

Gant, Zilphia. A girl who, when she was growing up, was kept isolated from others of her age by her mother, but who nevertheless found a man and married him. Her mother succeeded in separating them, however, and he disappeared. Through the services of a detective agency Zilphia discovered that he had remarried, and after he and his second wife died she took their child and raised it as her own ("Miss Zilphia Gant").

Gargne, M. and Mme. The patron and patronne of the place in Paris where the Rev. Tobe Sutterfield stayed (*A Fable*).

Garraway, Mr. The keeper of a small store on Seminary Hill who moved his money from the Sartoris bank because he did not like the adulterous activities of de Spain and Mrs. Flem Snopes (*The Town*).

Gary, Doctor. The family physician in Charlestown, Georgia, who looked after Donald Mahon (*Soldiers' Pay*).

Gatewood, Jabbo. The son of Uncle Noon Gatewood. He was a drunkard who was constantly being put in jail and just as constantly being released because in those days (1910-1912) he was the only one in Jefferson who could fix an automobile (*The Town*).

Gatewood, Noon. The owner of a blacksmith shop on the edge of Jefferson (*The Town*).

Gawtrey, Steve. An acquaintance of Harrison Blair whom Blair invited to his country home in Carolina ("Fox Hunt").

Gayoso Feed Co. A feed company in Memphis where the McCallums bought feed ("The Tall Men").

Gene. The fat bootlegger who provided liquor and other forms of celebration for Red's funeral (*Sanctuary*).

General. A dog belonging to the MacCallums (*Sartoris*). *General,*

General, The. An acquaintance of Jean-Baptiste ("Home"). *American British German Generalissimo*

George. The first name of the narrator's father in "That Will Be Fine." He ran a livery stable in Jefferson. The boy's *George (2)* name was the same as his father's. Also the name of a waiter at Broussard's in New Orleans (*Mosquitoes*). Also an English student at Oxford, a friend of Davy. He was killed early in World War I, and used to return to his friend in dreams ("The Leg"). Also the second cook on the ship, a big black Greek with eyebrows that "looked like two crows in overlapping flight." A friend of the messboy Carl ("Divorce in Naples").

Georgie. The seven-year-old narrator of "That Will Be *Georgie's* Fine." He used to help his Uncle Rodney by standing watch *mother* and notifying him when the husbands of his paramours came *German, The* along.

Gibson. The family name of Roskus, Dilsey, Versh, T. P., and Frony (*The Sound and the Fury*).

Gibson, Will. The owner of a country store on whose porch the men would sit and talk ("The Liar").

Gihon. A federal agent who was investigating Linda Snopes Kohl (*The Mansion*).

Gihon County. The Alabama county in which Hawkhurst was located ("Skirmish at Sartoris" in *The Unvanquished*).

Gihon, Danny. The son of Mrs. Margaret Noonan Gihon and nephew of the narrator of the story. He took the money his mother had been paying in installments for her coffin ("Pennsylvania Station").

Gihon, Mrs. Margaret Noonan. The mother of Danny Gihon.

She used to pay Mr. Pinckski a certain amount of money each month for her coffin ("Pennsylvania Station").

Gillespie. A friend of the newspaperman McCord, who, along with McCord and a man called Doc, owned a cottage on a Wisconsin lake where Charlotte and Harry stayed (*The Wild Palms*).

Gillespie, Mack. The son of the farmer whose barn Darl Bundren set on fire (*Light in August*).

Gilligan, Joe. A thirty-two-year-old private who met Donald Mahon on the train and who helped Margaret Powers take care of him until he died (*Soldiers' Pay*).

Gillman, Mr. The owner of the mill where Uncle Doc Hines worked (*Light in August*).

Gilman. A justice of the peace in a small New England village, who, with his twin sons, worked a "law and order" deal on some bigtime bootleggers ("Country Mice").

Ginger. One of Bayard Sartoris' hunting dogs (*Sartoris*).

Ginotta, Joe. The brother of Pete and a restaurant owner in New Orleans (*Mosquitoes*).

Ginotta, Pete. The boy friend of Jenny Steinbauer and an uninvited guest on Mrs. Maurier's yachting party (*Mosquitoes*).

Ginsfarb. The man who did stunt flying under the name of Demon Duncan ("Death Drag").

Glasgow. A small town in Crossman County (*Intruder in the Dust*).

Go Down, Moses. The seventh and last story in *Go Down, Moses*. First published in *Collier's Magazine,* Jan. 25, 1941. The story is about Molly Beauchamp's attempts to recover the body of her grandson electrocuted for the murder of a Chicago policeman. The title is that of a well-known Negro spiritual.

Go Down, Moses. A collection of related stories published by Random House, New York, 1942. Dedicated to "Mammy," Caroline Barr. Contains seven stories about the McCaslin-Edmonds-Beauchamp families: "Was," "The Fire and the Hearth," "Pantaloon in Black," "The Old People," "The Bear," "Delta Autumn," and "Go Down, Moses." All except "Was" had received previous publication, but all were revised (some rewritten) for the book. The first edition was called *Go Down, Moses and Other Stories*.

Gold Is Not Always. A short stort in *The Atlantic Monthly*, Nov. 1940. Later incorporated into "The Fire and the Hearth" in *Go Down, Moses*.

Golden Dome, The. The prose introduction to "Act Two" of *Requiem for a Nun*. Subtitled "(Beginning Was the Word)," it is about the state capital of Mississippi: Jackson.

Golden Land. A short story in *Collected Stories*. First published in *The American Mercury*, May 1935. A non-Yoknapatawpha story about Ira Ewing, a wealthy California realtor, and his family.

Gombault. The town marshal of Jefferson in 1942. He went to see the McCallums about the two boys not registering for the draft ("The Tall Men"). Also a United States marshal who came to Jefferson in 1923 because of the Montgomery Ward Snopes affair (*The Town*).

✻ Gombault, Pete. "Uncle Pete" Gombault, an old Negro who used to be the United States marshal during Reconstruction days. He was known as "Mulberry" because he sold illegal whiskey which he hid in the roots of a mulberry tree behind the drugstore where he had worked before the war. He later became a janitor and furnace attendant for several doctors and lawyers and one of the banks (*Requiem for a Nun*). The sketch of his activities sounds a great deal like that of Cassius Q. Benbow's as related in "Skirmish at Sartoris" in *The Unvanquished*.

Goodwin, Lee. A bootlegger who lived in the deserted house on the Old Frenchman's Place in 1930. He was arrested for the murder of the halfwit Tommy, was defended by Horace Benbow, and then was lynched by a mob in Jefferson because they thought that he, and not Popeye, had raped Temple Drake with a corncob (*Sanctuary*).

Goodyhay, J. C. An ex-Marine of the Pacific war who was in a landing barge explosion and who turned preacher after he found out he was not dead. Mink Snopes helped work for a few days on the church he was building (*The Mansion*).

Gordon. A red-headed sculptor: a guest of Mrs. Maurier's on her yachting party (*Mosquitoes*).

Gowan, Judge. A Jefferson judge before whom Lucas Beauchamp and George Wilkins were brought for making illegal whiskey ("The Fire and the Hearth" in *Go Down, Moses*).

Gower. The district attorney at Harry Wilbourne's trial (*The Wild Palms*).

Gowrie. A Mr. Gowrie with no given first name used to supply whiskey to the people of Jefferson (*The Town*).

Gowrie, Amanda Workitt. The deceased wife of Nub Gowrie (*Intruder in the Dust*).

Gowrie, Bilbo. A thirty-year-old twin (with Vardaman) of Nub Gowrie. He spent most of his nights hunting and most of his days sleeping, and let his older brother Bryan take care of the farm (*Intruder in the Dust*).

Gowrie, Bryan. The third son of Nub Gowrie, the hard-working one who ran the Gowrie farm and supported the others (*Intruder in the Dust*).

Gowrie, Crawford. The second son of Nub Gowrie. He had been drafted on Nov. 2, 1918, and deserted on Nov. 10, and after hiding out for several months was captured and sent to Leavenworth for a year. He was reportedly a whiskey smuggler and/or strike breaker in Memphis after his release. He later returned home and began stealing lumber from his brother Vinson. He killed Vinson and Jake Montgomery and later, after his capture, shot himself while in his jail cell awaiting trial (*Intruder in the Dust*).

Gowrie, Forrest. The eldest son of Nub Gowrie. He was married and had been away from home for twenty years, the manager of a delta cotton plantation above Vicksburg (*Intruder in the Dust*).

Gowrie, N. B. Forrest (Nub). A one-armed shiftless farmer from Beat Four. He was the father of six sons. Appears in *Intruder in the Dust*. Is referred to in *The Mansion*.

Gowrie, Vardaman. A twin (with Bilbo) son of Nub Gowrie. Like Bilbo, he spent most of his nights hunting and most of his days sleeping, and let his older brother Bryan take care of the farm (*Intruder in the Dust*).

Gowrie, Vinson. The youngest son of Nub Gowrie. He was about twenty-eight years old. He was hard working, and was engaged in the lumber business with his great uncle Sudley Workitt. He was shot by his brother Crawford because Crawford had been stealing lumber from him and was discovered (*Intruder in the Dust*).

Graduation Dress, The. A piece written especially for television by Faulkner. Produced on the General Electric Theater, Oct. 30, 1960. It was adapted for television by William R. Cox, and starred Hugh O'Brian, Stella Stevens, Tommy Nolan, Ellen Corby, and Buddy Ebsen. A rural Mississippi story about the Jerico family and the travelling photographer Sam Sharp.

Grady. A newspaper reporter in New Valois (*Pylon*).

Gragnon, General Charles. The division commander under whose command the Corporal and his men mutinied. He was executed by an American sergeant named Buchwald (*A Fable*).

Graham, Eustace. The district attorney who prosecuted the case against Lee Goodwin (*Sanctuary*). In *Sartoris* there is a young Jefferson lawyer known only by the first name of Eustace.

Grandilieu Street. A street in the French Quarter of New Valois (*Pylon*).

Grant, Joe. A stunt flyer at the dedication airshow at the Feinman Airport (*Pylon*).

Gratton. A man who had been in the army and who wanted to meet Bayard Sartoris, and whom Bayard insulted by refusing to shake hands with him (*Sartoris*).

Gray, Alec I. A Scottish shipbuilder, the grandfather of Captain Alec Gray ("Victory").

Gray, Alec II. A private in the army in World War I from Scotland. He was disciplined for not shaving before inspection and killed the sergeant-major who had ordered his discipline. He was given a medal for heroism after the sergeant-major's death.

He became a captain, and at the war's end settled in London. His fortunes sank lower and lower and he finally ended up selling matches on Piccadilly ("Victory").

Gray, Annie. The wife of Matthew Gray and mother of Captain Alec Gray ("Victory").

Gray, Elizabeth. The baby sister of Captain Alec Gray ("Victory").

Gray, Jessie. A sister of Captain Alec Gray ("Victory").

✗**Gray, Johnny.** A young gangster who met death in the guise of an attractive girl ("The Kid Learns").

Gray, John Wesley. A brother of Captain Alec Gray ("Victory").

Gray, Matthew I. A Scottish shipbuilder, the father of Captain Alec Gray ("Victory").

Gray, Matthew II. A brother of Captain Alec Gray ("Victory").

Gray the Day. A poem in *The New Republic*, LXXIV (Apr. 12, 1933), 253. Reprinted as *A Green Bough*, XXX.

Green, Captain. A local National Guard man in Charlestown, Georgia, who recruited soldiers from the neighborhood during World War I. He was killed in the war (*Soldiers' Pay*).

Green Bough, A. A book of poems published by Harrison Smith and Robert Haas, New York, 1933. Contains forty-four poems, none titled, twelve reprinted from magazines and one reprinted from *Mosquitoes*.

Greenbury Hotel. A hotel in Memphis where people from Jefferson and most of northern Mississippi always stayed ("Knight's Gambit"). Probably the Peabody Hotel.

Green Is the Water. The title given to *A Green Bough*, XIX, when it was reprinted in *Mississippi Verse*, edited by Alice James.

✗**Greenleaf.** Mentioned by Gavin Stevens in *Intruder in the Dust* as a family name in the Frenchman's Bend region.

Grenier County. A neighboring county to Yoknapatawpha County, where the Mr. Harris whose barn Ab Snopes burned lived (*The Hamlet*).

Grenier, Louis. A French architect and dilettante who came, around 1800, with Doctor Samuel Habersham and Alexander Holston to the settlement which was to become Jefferson. He bought land in the southeastern part of Yoknapatawpha County (and beyond), and established the first cotton plantation and had the first slaves in that part of the state. He died in 1837. His place later became known as the Old Frenchman's Place, and the small settlement as Frenchman's Bend. His last descendant was known as Lonnie Grinnup a feeble-minded man in his middle thirties sometime around the first quarter of the twentieth century, although his real name was the same as that of his first Yoknapatawpha County ancestor. The first Grenier appears in *Requiem for a Nun* and is referred to in *Intruder in the Dust,* "Hand Upon the Waters" (*Knight's Gambit*), *The Town,* and *The Reivers.* A Grenier County is mentioned in *The Hamlet,* and a Grenier Weddel appears in *The Town.*

Grier, Eck. An unidentified Grier spoken of by the dogs, according to Ratliff ("By the People"). In the revised version, in *The Mansion,* the name is changed to Res Grier.

Grier, Pete. The nineteen-year-old son of Res Grier. He joined the army after Pearl Harbor and was killed when the ship carrying him across the Pacific was sunk. Appears in "Two Soldiers." Is referred to in "Shall Not Perish."

Grier, Res. A farmer in the Frenchman's Bend region around 1940. He was the father of Pete Grier. Appears in "Shingles for the Lord," "Two Soldiers," and "Shall Not Perish." Is referred to in *The Mansion.*

Grierson, Emily. A Jefferson spinster who died at the age of seventy-four. She had killed her lover, Homer Barron, and then fixed up a bridal suite where she slept with the body ("A Rose for Emily").

Grimm, Eustace. A young farmer who lived on the Snopes place. His father's first wife had been Ab Snopes's sister. Appears in *The Hamlet* and *As I Lay Dying.*

Grimm, Percy. A young man about twenty-five around 1930, too young to have been in World War I. He resented the fact, and to compensate he joined the National Guard. He castrated and then shot Joe Christmas (*Light in August*).

Grinnup, Dan. A descendant of Louis Grenier's who, when he was not too drunk, drove the livery stable hack to meet the incoming trains (*The Reivers*).

Grinnup, Lonnie. A man in his middle thirties and feeble minded. He was actually the sole surviving descendant of Louis Grenier—which was Lonnie's own name as well—one of the three original settlers in Jefferson. Lonnie drowned, and it was discovered that he had been murdered. Appears in "Hand Upon the Waters" (in *Knight's Gambit*). Is referred to in *Intruder in the Dust* and (but not by name) in *The Reivers*. There is a chronological discrepancy here. We are told that Lonnie was still alive at the time of *Intruder in the Dust* (*circa* the 1940s), and Gavin Stevens (who was born *circa* 1890) was involved in investigating his murder. Yet Dan Grinnup in 1905 "had no family save an idiot nephew or cousin or something still living in a tent in the river jungle beyond Frenchman's Bend. . . ." This may *not* be Lonnie, but he is the only person the description is known to fit.

Groom

✷Griselda. A mare belonging to Thomas Sutpen which gave birth to a colt the same day Milly Jones gave birth to Sutpen's daughter ("Wash").

Grotto. A nightclub on the edge of Memphis where Temple Drake and Red went (*Sanctuary*).

Grove, Lena. A twenty-year-old girl from Doane's Mill, Alabama, who walked and hitchhiked to Jefferson in search of Lucas Burch, the father of her unborn child (*Light in August*).

Grove, McKinley. The forty-year-old brother of Lena Grove, who kicked her out of his home when he discovered that she was pregnant (*Light in August*).

✷ Grover. The son of Faulkner's cook, called "Rover" by the Faulkner boys ("Afternoon of a Cow").

Grumby, Major. The leader of a group of fifty or sixty raiders known as Grumby's Independents. He shot and killed Granny Millard and was in turn killed by Bayard Sartoris and Ringo.

Appears in "Riposte in Tertio" and "Vendée" (in *The Unvanquished*). Is referred to in *The Hamlet*.

Grummet's. A hardware store in Mottson (Mottstown) (*As I Lay Dying*).

Gualdres, Captain Sebastian. An Argentine house guest of the Harriss' and a great horseman. He married the Harriss girl and joined the American Army as a private after Pearl Harbor ("Knight's Gambit").

Guest's Impression of New England, A. A short descriptive article in *New England Journeys No. 2* (*Ford Times* Special Edition), 1954.

Gus. The brother of the bootlegger who told the story of their encounter with the Gilman family ("Country Mice").

Guster. The mother of Top and Aleck Sander, as she is called in *The Town*. In *Intruder in the Dust* Aleck Sander's mother is called Paralee.

H

Habersham, Emily. A social worker in Jefferson in 1929 who took charge of having Byron Snopes's halfbreed children sent back to him (*The Town*). Although she is called Miss Habersham here, she may be the same person as the Mrs. Habersham who was also a social worker in Jefferson in 1942 ("Two Soldiers").

Habersham, Eunice. A seventy-year-old spinster (in 1941 or so), a descendant of one of the oldest families in Jefferson. Because Lucas Beauchamp's wife Mollie had come from her family, she helped Chick Mallison and Aleck Sander try to solve the murder for which Lucas was arrested (*Intruder in the Dust*). In *The Town*, where she is merely referred to, she is called a granddaughter of Doctor Habersham.

Habersham, Martha. A social leader in Jefferson around the time of the Civil War. She had much to do with forcing Drusilla Hawk to marry Colonel Sartoris. Her husband was a banker who signed the Colonel's peace bond after the Colonel had killed the two carpetbaggers. Appears in "Skirmish at Sartoris" and "An Odor of Verbena" (both in *The Unvanquished*).

Habersham, Mrs. See **Habersham, Emily.**

Habersham, Doctor Samuel. The first agent of the Chickasaw Agency which later became Jefferson. He died sometime before 1833. His son, who was eight years old in 1800, reportedly married a Chickasaw and went with the Indians in the 1830s to Oklahoma. Yet during the Civil War there was a banker in Jefferson named Habersham, and we hear elsewhere that Miss Eunice Habersham of Jefferson was his granddaughter. Whether the social worker, Emily Habersham, was a relative is not known. The doctor appears in *Requiem for a Nun* and is referred to in *Intruder in the Dust* and *The Town*.

Had-Two-Fathers. It is not clear whether this is another name for Three Basket or another Indian, but from the context it seems to be another name for Three Basket ("Red Leaves"). Elsewhere the name is given as the original last name of Sam Fathers ("A Justice").

Hagood. The editor for whom the Reporter worked (*Pylon*).

Hair. A short story in *Collected Stories*. First published in *The American Mercury*, May 1931. Reprinted in *These 13*. About a barber in Jefferson named Henry Stribling and nicknamed Hawkshaw.

Hait, Lonzo. An employee of I. O. Snopes who was killed when he was struck by a freight train when he was tying some mules to the tracks in order to have them killed so Snopes could collect damages from the railroad. Referred to in *The Town* and *The Mansion*.

Hait, Mannie. The wife and then widow of Lonzo Hait. She collected damages from the railroad on her husband and the mules. It was an altercation with her that led to the elimination of I. O. Snopes from Jefferson by Flem (*The Town*).

✳**Haley, Lem.** A back country farmer who owned hunting hounds. Referred to in "The Liar." (Of all the sketches in the *Times-Picayune*, "The Liar," and possibly "Sunset," are the closest to the later Yoknapatawpha stories. In *The Hamlet* Haley is mentioned as one of the old family names in the Frenchman's Bend region). *Half-Wit, A*

Halladay, Jim. The district attorney around 1940, who resided in Harrisburg (*Intruder in the Dust*).

Halliday. A man from Mottstown who recognized Joe Christmas (*Light in August*).

Hamblett, Jim. The justice at the courthouse at the time Charles Bon's son was arrested for disorderly conduct (*Absalom, Absalom!*).

Hamlet, The. A novel published by Random House, New York, 1940. Dedicated to Phil Stone. This, since the publication of *The Town* and *The Mansion,* would apparently by subtitled *Snopes,* Vol. I. Several parts were originally short stories which were rewritten for the novel. Contains four sections: "Flem," "Eula," "The Long Summer," and "The Peasants." About the arrival of the Snopes family in Frenchman's Bend. The time is 1902-1908. In 1958 the third section of the novel was turned into a motion picture by 20th Century-Fox under the title "The Long, Hot Summer," directed by Martin Witt, and starring Paul Newman, Joanne Woodward, Anthony Franciosa, Orson Welles, Lee Remick, and Angela Lansbury.

✳ **Hamp.** The name or nickname (possibly "Hampton") of the warden at the Mississippi prison farm in Parchman in 1927 ("Old Man" in *The Wild Palms*).

Hampton, Hope. See **Hampton, Hubert, Jr.**

Hampton, Hubert (Hub). The sheriff of Yoknapatawpha County during the first two decades or so of the twentieth century. Appears in *The Town* and *The Mansion* by that name. In *The Hamlet* and *The Reivers* he is known only as Hampton.

Hampton, Hubert, Jr. The son of Hubert Hampton and sheriff of Yoknapatawpha County during the 1940s. He is apparently the Hope Hampton of *Intruder in the Dust* and possibly the Hub of "An Error in Chemistry" (in *Knight's Gambit*), since both were sheriff, and the time element seems to apply more accurately to him than to his father. Appears in *The Mansion*. Another Hub Hampton, known as the grandson of the first, "is sheriff now, or will be again next year," the time of the statement being 1961 (*The Reivers*).

✳ **Hampton, Sally.** The maiden name of Mrs. Maurice Priest (*The Town*).

Hand Upon the Waters. The third story in *Knight's Gambit*. First published in *The Saturday Evening Post,* Nov. 4, 1939. About the drowning of Lonnie Grinnup, who was really Louis Grenier, the last descendant of one of the founders of Jefferson.

Hanley. A member of the flight squadron commanded by Major Bridesman (*A Fable*).

Hardwick. A small Tennessee town where Boon Hogganbeck, Butch Lovemaiden, Miss Reba, and Miss Corrie were taken to jail because Parsham had no jail (*The Reivers*).

Harker, Mr. A former sawmill engineer who ran the Jefferson power plant at night around 1912 or so (*The Town*).

Harker, Otis. The nephew ("or cousin or something") of the Mr. Harker of the power plant. He took over the sawmill when Mr. Harker moved on to the power plant and used to come in evenings when Mr. Harker wanted to be off. He later succeeded Grover Cleveland Winbush as night marshal of Jefferson (*The Town*).

✗**Harmon, Mrs.** A woman whose house Mr. Mitchell was supposed to have run into when the hill people, frightened by the train, frightened his horse ("The Liar").

Harper. A gunner on the airship piloted by Captain Bogard ("Turnabout").

Harris. The man who owned the circus in which Howard Rogers and Buck Monaghan did stunt flying ("Honor").

Harris, Elmer. The chief of police in the small Virginia village near the spot where Carleton Van Dyming had his country place ("Black Music").

Harris, Melony. A maid at the Harry Mitchell home who was given money by Simon Strother to open a beauty shop. Simon was killed at her place (*Sartoris*).

Harris, Mr.   The man on whose farm Ab Snopes lived and whose barn Ab burned. He lived in Grenier County. Appears in "Barn Burning." Is referred to in *The Hamlet*. Also the man in Jefferson from whom the stunt flyers rented a car ("Death Drag"). He is possibly the same Mr. Harris who used to run a livery stable in Jefferson (*Sanctuary*), and may be the father of the seven-year-old narrator of "That Will Be Fine," for his father, George (with no last name given) owned a livery stable in Jefferson. Also the neighbor and bitter enemy of Juan Venturia ("The Rosary").

Harris, Mrs. Plurella.   One of the names used by Rosa Millard on the forged orders she used to get horses back from the federal troops ("Riposte in Tertio" in *The Unvanquished*).

Harrisburg.   The city where the district attorney for Yoknapatawpha County is located (Jefferson has only a county attorney.) (*Intruder in the Dust*).

Harrison, Sergeant.   A Yankee soldier who came to investigate the shooting of a horse by Bayard and Ringo ("Ambuscade" in *The Unvanquished*).

Harriss Girl, The.   The sister of Max Harriss and later the stepdaughter of Gavin Stevens. She married Captain Gualdres ("Knight's Gambit").

Harriss, Max.   The son of a wealthy Yoknapatawpha County widow. He tried to kill Captain Gualdres by substituting an unmanageable horse for the one the Captain always rode nightly. When his attempt was foiled by Gavin Stevens he enlisted in the army ("Knight's Gambit").

Harriss, Mrs.   See **Stevens, Melisandre Backus.**

Harrykin Creek.   The local way of pronouncing Hurricane Creek ("My Grandmother Millard," *The Town,* and *The Reivers*).

Hatcher, Louis.   An old country Negro with whom Quentin Compson and Versh used to go hunting 'possum (*The Sound and the Fury*).

Hatcher, Martha.   The wife of Louis Hatcher (*The Sound and the Fury*).

Haven Hill Store.   A country store some thirty miles from Frenchman's Bend ("Tomorrow" in *Knight's Gambit*).

Hawk, Dennison I.   An uncle by marriage of Bayard Sartoris II. He married a sister of Colonel Sartoris' wife. He was killed during the civil war. Referred to in "Ambuscade" and "Raid" (*The Unvanquished*).

Hawk, Dennison II.   The son of Uncle Dennison and Aunt Louise. He was known as Cousin Denny. He later married and studied law in Montgomery, Alabama. Appears in "Raid." Is referred to in "An Odor of Verbena" (*The Unvanquished*).

Hawk, Drusilla.   The daughter of Uncle Dennison and Aunt Louise. She was engaged to Gavin Breckbridge, who was killed in the war, so she dressed herself like a soldier and went fighting the Yankees along with Colonel Sartoris. She was forced into marrying him by the ladies of Jefferson because she had been living with him. After he was killed she returned to Alabama to live with her brother ("Raid," "Skirmish at Sartoris," and "An Odor of Verbena" in *The Unvanquished*).

Hawk, Louise.   Aunt Louise (sometimes called Louisa), the mother of Denny and Drusilla. Appears in "Raid" and "Skirmish at Sartoris" (*The Unvanquished*).

Hawkhurst.   The name of the plantation in Gihon County, Alabama, where Bayard Sartoris' Uncle Dennison and Aunt Louise lived ("Ambuscade," "Raid," and "Skirmish at Sartoris" in *The Unvanquished*).

Hawkshaw.   See **Stribling, Henry.**

Head, Sydney Herbert.   An Indiana banker whom Caddy Compson married in April 1910. He divorced her in 1911 (*The Sound and the Fury*).

Hell Creek.   A swampy creek on the road between Jefferson and Memphis (*The Reivers*).

Hell Creek Crossing.   The title given to pages 75-91 of *The Reivers* when they were preprinted in *The Saturday Evening Post*, Mar. 31, 1962.

Henderson, Mrs. A lady on the train, an acquaintance of Margaret Powers', who was worried about Donald Mahon (*Soldiers' Pay*).

Henry. A gradeschool classmate of Quentin Compson's who answered the question Quentin had not heard because he was daydreaming (*The Sound and the Fury*). Also the first name of the Governor of Mississippi in 1938 (*Requiem for a Nun*). Also the Negro porter on the New York to Chicago train on which Julian Lowe and Joe Gilligan were riding to Buffalo (*Soldiers' Pay*). Also one of the sharecroppers on the Sartoris plantation (*Sartoris*). Also Jack Houston's Negro farmhand (*The Mansion*).

Here He Stands. The title given to *A Green Bough*, XX when it was reprinted in *Mississippi Verse*, edited by Alice James.

Hermaphroditus. A poem read by Dawson Fairchild from a volume called *Satyricon in Starlight* (*Mosquitoes*). It became *A Green Bough*, XXXVIII.

Het. Old Het; a seventy-year-old inmate of the poorhouse who used to come to see Mannie Hait (*The Town*).

Hickahala Bottom. A place near Jefferson and the Sartoris plantation where Ab Snopes hid the mules and horses stolen from the federal troops ("Riposte in Tertio" in *The Unvanquished*).

Highboy. The name of Chick Mallison's pony (*Intruder in the Dust*).

Hightower, Gail. A retired Presbyterian minister living in Jefferson. He had been forced to resign from his church after his wife committed suicide. Joe Christmas was killed in his house (*Light in August*).

Hightower, Hiram. A Baptist minister who, in 1886, came to the small settlement run by Ballenbaugh and "with his fists" converted the whole settlement (*The Reivers*).

Hill, The. A sketch in *The Mississippian*, XI (Mar. 10, 1922), 1-2. Reprinted in *William Faulkner: Early Prose and Poetry*, ed. Carvel Collins, pp. 90-92.

Hilliard. A livery stable man in Oxford in 1875 from whom Ringo got a fresh horse on which to ride back to Jefferson after

Hinds, Gen. ~~Thomas~~

Hines, Mrs.

he had come to tell Bayard of Colonel Sartoris' death ("An Odor of Verbena" in *The Unvanquished*).

Hines, Euphues. Uncle Doc Hines, the grandfather of Joe Christmas. He got a job in the hospital where he had abandoned Joe, and after Joe was adopted he went back to Mottstown. When Joe was arrested for killing Miss Burden he wanted—as the "hand of God's justice"—to kill Joe (*Light in August*).

Hines, Milly. The daughter of Euphues Hines and the mother of Joe Christmas. She died when Joe was born (*Light in August*).

Hipps, Buck. The man from Texas who brought the spotted horses and auctioned them off to the farmers of Frenchman's Bend in front of the Littlejohn Hotel (*The Hamlet*).

His Name Was Pete. A short article by Faulkner on the death of his daughter's dog, which had been run over and killed by a speeding motorist. In the Oxford *Eagle,* Aug. 15, 1946. Reprinted in *Magazine Digest,* Jan. 1953.

Hoake

Hoake, Alison. The maiden name of the mother of Hoake McCarron (*The Hamlet*).

Hog Bayou. A hunting camp near the camp where Roth Edmonds and Ike McCaslin went hunting every fall ("Race at Morning").

Hogben. The man who ran the ore train for the Callaghan Mines (*The Wild Palms*).

Hogganbeck, Boon. The grandson of a Chickasaw woman and a whiskey trader. Boon was a hunter who trained the dog Lion to hunt Old Ben, the great bear. He killed the bear during a hunt in 1883. After that Major de Spain got him a job of town marshal at Hoke's, a local sawmill town. Later, around 1905, he worked in Maury Priest's livery stable in Jefferson, and was involved in the escapade to Memphis with Ned McCaslin and young Lucius Priest. He married one of Miss Reba Rivers' "girls," and became the father of Lucius (Priest) Hogganbeck. Appears in "The Old People," "The Bear," and *The Reivers*. Is referred to in "Delta Autumn," "A Bear Hunt," and *The Town*.

Hogganbeck, David. A white man who was a rival of Ikkemotubbe for Herman Basket's sister around 1798 ("A Courtship"). Although it is not mentioned in any of the stories, he was, according to Faulkner, the grandfather of Boon (see *Faulkner in the University,* p. 261).

Hogganbeck, Everbe Corinthia. The wife of Boon Hogganbeck. She was originally from Kiblett, Arkansas, where she learned the profession of prostitution after her mother died, and then moved on to Memphis to Miss Reba Rivers' place, because there was more money to be made in Memphis. She became known as Miss Corrie there, and it was there that Boon met her. They were married in 1905 (*The Reivers*). The name "Everbe Corinthia" was also used by Faulkner in another (a non-Yoknapatawpha) story. See **Rust, Everbe Corinthia.**

Hogganbeck, Lucius Priest. The son of Boon Hogganbeck. He bought a Model T Ford, one of the first in Jefferson, and started a passenger hauling business. He was once the butt of a practical joke played on him by Ratliff to frighten him enough to get rid of his hiccups. Appears in *The Town* and "A Bear Hunt," and is referred to in *The Mansion* only as Lucius Hogganbeck. In *The Reivers,* where he is born, we discover that he is named for young Lucius Priest. There is apparently some time discrepancy among all three of the works in which he appears.

Hogganbeck, Melissa. A history teacher in the Academy ("Knight's Gambit" and *The Town*).

Hoke's. A small settlement with a sawmill, a commissary, and two stores, a railroad junction near Major de Spain's hunting lands ("The Bear" in *Go Down, Moses*).

Holcomb, Ashley. A boy of the same age as Chick Mallison who used to go rabbit hunting with Chick and Aleck Sander (*The Town*).

Holcomb, Beth. A countrywoman, one of Brother Goodyhay's flock (*The Mansion*).

Holland, Anselm, Jr. (Anse). The "younger" of twin sons of Anselm Holland, Sr. He left home while still in his teens, and returned ten years later and tried to get his share of the Holland land. His father refused to give it to him, so he lived alone in the backwoods in a two-room cabin. He later confessed to having killed his father (which he did not do) ("Smoke" in *Knight's Gambit*).

Holland, Anselm, Sr. A man who married a woman named Cornelia Mardis, whose father had a large farm which Anselm took over when his wife died. They had twin sons, Virginius and Anselm, Jr. Mr. Holland was found dead, supposedly fallen from a horse but actually murdered by Granby Dodge ("Smoke" in *Knight's Gambit*). It was on his farm that Ab Snopes had lived before moving to Frenchman's Bend (*The Hamlet*).

Holland, Mr. The foreman of the jury in the trial of Book-wright for the murder of Buck Thorpe ("Tomorrow" in *Knight's Gambit*). In the early 1940s the president of the Bank of Jefferson was a Mr. Holland (*The Mansion*).

Holland, Virginius. The "elder" of twin sons of Anselm Holland, Sr. He stayed with his father and helped run the farm until his father kicked him out. Then he went to stay with a cousin named Granby Dodge ("Smoke" in *Knight's Gambit*).

Hollyknowe. A hunting camp near Van Dorn ("Race at Morning"). Also a small town in Mississippi compared to Jefferson and Mottstown ("Knight's Gambit").

Hollymount. A small town in Crossman County (*Intruder in the Dust*).

Holmes, Jack. The jumper in the stunt flying team with Roger Shumann (*Pylon*).

Holmes, Miss. One of the girls Gerald and Mrs. Bland took on a picnic the day Quentin Compson committed suicide (*The Sound and the Fury*).

Holston, Alexander. One of the three original settlers in the region which became Yoknapatawpha County. He arrived around 1800 with Doctor Samuel Habersham and Louis Grenier. He was part-groom and part-bodyguard to the Doctor, and part-nurse, part-tutor to the Doctor's eight-year-old son. He established the first public house in Jefferson, which later became known as the Holston House. He died in 1839. Although in *Requiem for a Nun* he is called a "childless bachelor," in "Skirmish at Sartoris" (*The Unvanquished*) there is a Mrs. Holston runing the hotel, and as late as the 1940s the hotel is being run by two sisters, the "last descendants" of Alexander Holston (*The Mansion*). He is referred to in *Intruder in the Dust*, "Hand Upon the Waters" (*Knight's Gambit*), and *The Town*, as well as in *Requiem for a Nun* and *The Mansion*.

Holston, Doctor. The man who sent his colored boy to warn General Compson's wife that the Yankee troops were in Jefferson ("My Grandmother Millard").

Holston House. Jefferson's original hotel, established by Alexander Holston. It is mentioned often in the stories and novels.

Home. A sketch in the New Orleans *Times-Picayune* Sunday section, Feb. 22, 1925, p. 3. Reprinted in *New Orleans Sketches* (ed. Collins).

Honor. A short story in *Collected Stories*. First published in *The American Mercury*, July 1930. Reprinted in *Doctor Martino and Other Stories*. It is included in *Selected Short Stories*. A non-Yoknapatawpha story about a test pilot and stunt flyer, Buck Monaghan.

Hood, Parsham. An elderly Negro resident of Parsham, Tennessee, at whose home young Lucius Priest stayed (*The Reivers*).

Hooper. A kind of travelling evangelist who ate at Broussard's with Talliaferro and Fairchild (*Mosquitoes*).

Hope, L. C. W. (Claude). A midshipman in the British Navy who manned a torpedo boat, and who invited Captain Bogard, an American pilot, to ride with him after the Captain had taken him on a bombing mission ("Turnabout").

Hopkins. One of the men who used to hang around the telegraph office to wait for stock reports on cotton (*The Sound and the Fury*).

Horn, Corporal. A British guard whom the runner knocked out and whose uniform the Negro Sutterfield wore to get the sentry out of the guardhouse (*A Fable*).

✳Horse. See **Casse-tête.**

Hound, The. A short story first published in *Harper's Magazine*, Aug. 1931. Reprinted in *Doctor Martino and Other Stories*. It was later rewritten for inclusion in *The Hamlet*. About the murder of Jack Houston, although here the killer is a man named Ernest Cotton, not Mink Snopes, as in the revised version.

Houston. A Negro waiter in Rogers' Café (*Sartoris*).

Houston, Jack. A farmer in the Frenchman's Bend region. He married a local girl called Lucy Pate (in *The Hamlet*) or Letty Bookwright (in *The Mansion*), who, within a year of their marriage, was kicked by a stallion and killed. He owned a cow which the idiot Ike Snopes fell in love with and he gave the cow to Ike. He impounded a stray cow belonging to Mink Snopes and Mink killed him. Appears in *The Hamlet* and *The Mansion*. In *The Town* Ratcliff calls him Zack Houston. A Houston with no given first name attended Addie Bundren's funeral (*As I Lay Dying*), but the time sequence would prevent his being Jack Houston.

Houston, Zack. See **Houston, Jack.**

Hovis, Mr. The cashier in the Sartoris (de Spain) bank (*The Town*).

Hovis, Mrs. A church woman in Jefferson who worked with Mrs. Merridew in the attempt to reform Hoke Christian ("Uncle Willy").

Howes, Anne. The wife of the novelist Roger Howes. She was involved in an affair with the poet John Blair ("Artist at Home").

Howes, Darrel. A tuberculosis patient at Sivgut ("Idyll in the Desert").

Howes, Roger. A forty-year-old novelist who was born in Mississippi, became an ad writer in New York, and then turned novelist and settled in Virginia. He had a wife and two children ("Artist at Home").

Hoxey, Major. A middle-aged bachelor who became mayor of Jefferson and then gave Flem Snopes the position of super-intendent of the municipal power plant ("Centaur in Brass"). He was superseded by Manfred de Spain in the revised version (in *The Town*).

Hub. The name of the young man who went with Suratt

(Ratliff) to take Bayard Sartoris home after Bayard had been thrown by a stallion. They stopped at his farm home for a drink (*Sartoris*). See also **Hampton, Hubert.**

Hughes, Manny. A postal clerk at the Blizzard, Arizona, post office ("Idyll in the Desert").

Hule. Vatch's younger brother. He tried to warn Major Weddel to escape from Vatch's plot to kill him ("Mountain Victory").

Hulett, Mr. The court clerk at the Jefferson courthouse when Mollie went to get her divorce from Lucas Beauchamp ("The Fire and the Hearth" in *Go Down, Moses*).

Hume. A British soldier referred to in "Ad Astra" as a man who made a comment about Bayard Sartoris' sorties after his brother had been killed.

Hurricane Bottoms. A swamp four miles from Jefferson where the bandits who broke out of the jail were captured (*Requiem for a Nun*).

Hurricane Creek. A creek which ran through the back pasture of the Sartoris plantation. Called Harrykin Creek locally ("My Grandmother Millard," *The Town*, and *The Reivers*).

Hurtz. The name of the man the Reporter's mother married (*Pylon*).

I

Idyll in the Desert. A short story published by Random House, New York, 1931, in a limited edition of 400 copies. Not published elsewhere. A non-Yoknapatawpha story about some tuberculosis patients on the Arizona desert.

If I Were a Negro. An article published in *Ebony*, XI (Sept. 1956), 70-73.

If There Be Grief. The title given to *A Green Bough*, XLIV when it was reprinted in *Mississippi Verse*, edited by Alice James. This is the same poem as "My Epitaph" and *This Earth*.

Ike. One of the four men who claimed Lonnie Grinnup's body after he was drowned ("Hand Upon the Waters" in *Knight's Gambit*).

Ikkemotubbe. According to the most trustworthy reports, he was the son of Mohataha, sister of the Chickasaw chief Issetibbeha. In 1800 he left the tribe and went to New Orleans. There he met a Chevalier Soeur-Blonde de Vitry, who called Ikkemotubbe Du Homme, which was later anglicized into Doom. Eight years later Ikkemotubbe returned home. He poisoned his cousin Moketubbe's son, after which Moketubbe abdicated and Ikkemotubbe became chief. In 1813 he traded a square mile of land in Yoknapatawpha County to Jason Compson for a racing mare, and in the 1830s sold a hundred acres of land in the northwest part of the county to Thomas Sutpen. In the middle 1830s he moved to Oklahoma, taking the Chickasaws with him. He was the father of Sam Fathers. According to one report ("Red Leaves"), Ikkemotubbe was Issetibbeha's father and the grandfather of Moketubbe. In still another report ("A Justice"), he was known in New Orleans as David Callicoat and was a Chocktaw chief. The suffix "tubbe" is a Chickasaw word for "chief." He appears in "A Justice," "A Courtship," *Requiem for a Nun*, and the Appendix to *The Sound and the Fury*. He is referred to in several of the stories in *Go Down, Moses*, in *Absolom, Absolom!*, in *The Town*, and (but not by the name Ikkemotubbe) in "Red Leaves" and *The Reivers*.

Impressions of Japan. A short descriptive and comparative article published in the Memphis *Commercial-Appeal*, Sept. 26, 1955. It was reprinted in *Esquire*, Dec. 1958, and in *Faulkner at Nagano.*

Ingrum, Willy. The town marshall of Jefferson around 1941. The name was probably originally Ingraham (*Intruder in the Dust*).

Innocent at Rinkside, An. A piece of reportage in *Sports Illustrated,* Jan. 24, 1955, on a hockey game.

Insignificant Fyce Baits a Bear, An. The title given a fragment from the second section of "The Bear" when it was reprinted in *Life*, XXXIX (Nov. 14, 1955), 194.

Introduction to Sanctuary. In the Modern Library reprint of *Sanctuary,* first issued in 1932, Faulkner contributed an introduction containing some significant autobiographical material.

Intruder in the Dust. A novel published by Random House, New York, 1948. About the arrest of Lucas Beauchamp for the murder of Vinson Gowrie and the attempts of Chick Mallison, Eunice Habersham, and Aleck Sander to free him. In 1949 the novel was made into a motion picture by Metro-Goldwyn-Mayer, directed by Clarence Brown and starring David Brian, Claude Jarman, Jr., and Juano Hernandez. Most of the setting was filmed in Oxford, Mississippi.

Inverness. A small settlement near Frenchman's Bend (*As I Lay Dying*).

Irey (Ira). The first name of the turnkey in the small Missouri town where the Rev. Tobe Sutterfield and his grandson were detained (*A Fable*).

Isham. An elderly Negro who accompanied Roth Edmonds on hunting trips ("Delta Autumn" in *Go Down, Moses*).

Isom. The son of Elnora, grandson of Simon, and great-great-grandson of old Joby, Colonel Sartoris' body servant. Isom, who was born in 1904, was the gardener at the Sartoris place, and later became Narcissa's driver. Appears in *Sartoris, Sanctuary,* and "There Was a Queen." Is referred to in "All the Dead Pilots."

Issetibbeha. The father of Moketubbe, brother of Sometimes-Wakeup and Mohataha, and uncle of Ikkemotubbe, and formerly chief of the Chickasaws. He died sometime between 1800 and 1808 and was succeeded by his son Moketubbe. *Requiem for a Nun,* "The Old People" (in *Go Down, Moses*), "A Courtship," and *The Town* all refer to him as Ikkemotubbe's uncle, as does "A Justice," without calling him by name. In "Red Leaves,"

[margin handwritten note: Jesetablbehd s Body servant]

however, he is known as Doom's (Ikkemotubbe's) son. He is referred to in *The Reivers*.

Ivory Tower, The. An article in *The Mississippian*, IX (Mar. 17, 1920), 4. Reprinted in Martha Mayes's "Faulkner Juvenilia," *New Campus Writing No. 2*, ed. Nolan Miller, pp. 142-143.

I Will Not Weep for Youth. A poem in *Contempo*, I (Feb. 1, 1932), 1. Uncollected.

J

[margin handwritten note: Jabbo]

Jabbo, Captain. The guard who shot Jake Barron in a break from the state prison in 1943 (*The Mansion*).

Jack. A mutual friend of Buck Monaghan and Howard Rogers, who introduced them to each other ("Honor").

✗ Jackie. One of Miss Reba Rivers' girls (*The Reivers*).

Jackson, Al. The subject of a tall story told to Major Ayers by Dawson Fairchild. He was supposed to be descended from *[margin handwritten note: Jackson, Andrew]* Andrew Jackson. He ran a sheep farm in Louisiana, and the sheep turned into fish (*Mosquitoes*).

Jackson, Arthur. The flyer for whom Jiggs went to work after Roger Shumann was killed (*Pylon*).

[margin handwritten note: Jackson, ESen, Jackson, Old man]

Jackson, Claude. The brother of Al Jackson. He was supposed to have turned into a shark (*Mosquitoes*).

Jail, The. The prose introduction to "Act III" of *Requiem for a Nun*. Subtitled "(Not Even Yet Quite Relinquish—)," it continues the story of the origins of Jefferson begun in "The Courthouse." It was preprinted in *The Partisan Review*, Sept-Oct. 1951.

Jake. The third man in the flying circus which visited Jefferson. He drove the car upon which Ginsfarb was supposed to jump ("Death Drag"). Also the Negro servant in Judge Allison's house ("Beyond"). Also the name of the mule which Tomey's Turl rode to the Beauchamp plantation ("Was" in *Go Down, Moses*).

James. Mr. Faulkner's brother's son ("Afternoon of a Cow").

James, Lieutenant Colonel. The commander of the battalion to which the runner was sent after he gave up his commission to became a private (*A Fable*).

Jameson, Dorothy. A painter, a guest of Mrs. Maurier's on her yachting party (*Mosquitoes*).

Jealousy. A sketch in the New Orleans *Times-Picayune* Sunday section, Mar. 1, 1925, p. 2. Reprinted in *New Orleans Sketches* (ed. Collins).

Jealousy and Episode. A limited edition of 500 copies of two sketches from the New Orleans *Times-Picayune* Sunday section, published by Faulkner Studies, Minneapolis, 1955.

Jean. One of the twelve followers of the Corporal. He sat on the Corporal's immediate left (*A Fable*).

Jean-Baptiste. A French immigrant who was about to join a gang of bank robbers until he heard a man playing on a musical saw a song from his old homeland ("Home").

Jefferson. The county seat of Yoknapatawpha County, situated in almost the exact geographical center of the county. It is seventy-five miles southeast of Memphis and forty miles from Oxford, Mississippi. It originated around 1800 as a Chickasaw Agency trading post. A Doctor Samuel Habersham was the agent, and the place was originally called Habersham's or simply Habersham. After the doctor and the two others who had come with him died, the leaders of the community became Jason Lycurgus Compson, the post trader Ratcliffe, and Doctor Peabody. They were instrumental in getting the courthouse built. In 1833 the settlement was named Jefferson, after the mail rider Thomas Jefferson Pettigrew, to appease him for the so-called theft of a lock removed from the mailpouch to put on the jail door. Most of the early history of Jefferson is to be found in the first and third prose sections of *Requiem for a Nun*.

Jefferson Hotel. The name given the former Commercial Hotel (and later the Snopes Hotel) when it was run by Dink Quistenberry in the late 1920s (*The Town*).

Jerico, Buddy. The young brother and self-appointed guardian of Laura Jerico ("The Graduation Dress").

Jerico, Laura. A high school graduate in a rural Mississippi settlement who wanted a new dress for the graduation exercises but was too shiftless to work for it. When a travelling photographer for a mail-order house appeared with a dress and proposed that she join up with him to model the dress at various places between there and New Orleans, she willingly agreed. The photographer's plot was foiled by Buddy Jerico, who ran to the fields to fetch his father and mother, who scared the photographer off ("The Graduation Dress").

Jerico, Ma. The mother of Laura Jerico ("The Graduation Dress").

Jerico, Pa. The father of Laura Jerico ("The Graduation Dress").

Jerrod, Hubert. A wealthy Oklahoma student at Yale who was engaged to Louise King ("Doctor Martino").

Jerry. The first name of an American pilot ("Turnabout").

Jesus. The husband of Nancy, the Compson washerwoman. He was jealous and threatened to kill her because she consorted with white men ("That Evening Sun").

Jiggs. The mechanic for Roger Shumann's plane (*Pylon*).

Jingus. A slave belonging to the Hawk family at Hawkhurst ("Raid" in *The Unvanquished*).

Job. The Negro helper at the farmers' supply store where Jason Compson worked (*The Sound and the Fury*). Also the Negro servant of Judge Dukinfield ("Smoke" in *Knight's Gambit* and *The Town*.

Jobaker. See **Baker, Joe.**

Joby. Colonel Sartoris' body servant brought with him from Carolina. He was the husband of Louvinia, and the father of Simon and Loosh, and the grandfather of Ringo and Simon Strother. Appears in *The Unvanquished* and "My Grandmother

Millard," and is referred to in *Sartoris*. Also his great-great-grandson, Elnora's son, who had gone to Memphis to wear fine clothes on Beale Street ("There Was a Queen").

Jock. The pilot of the stunt plane which visited Jefferson. He had been a flyer in World War I, and was an acquaintance of Captain Warren ("Death Drag").

Jody. The boy who worked at the drugstore in Jefferson with Skeet MacGowan (*As I Lay Dying*).

Joe. The deaf-and-dumb companion of Lonnie Grinnup. He killed Boyd Ballenbaugh, the murderer of Lonnie ("Hand Upon the Waters" in *Knight's Gambit*). Also the man who hired the boat to seek the buried treasure. He was the thirty-five-year-old brother of Pete ("Once Aboard the Lugger"). Also the blind aged husband of the woman Spratling sketched ("Epsiode"). Also the partner of the bootlegger ("Country Mice").

Joe's. The bar where the men on Hagood's paper went to drink (*Pylon*).

John Henry. A country Negro who, with his father, pulled Bayard Sartoris from his wrecked car and took him home (*Sartoris*). Also the name given by the tall convict to his mule on the prison farm ("Old Man" in *The Wild Palms*).

John Paul. The driver of the carriage for the family of the narrator ("That Will Be Fine").

Jonas. A slave belonging to the McCaslin's ("Was" in *Go Down, Moses*).

Jones. The secretary of the Fair Association in Jefferson ("Death Drag").

Jones, Doctor. The old janitor at the Sartoris bank (*Sartoris*).

Jones, Herschell. A young man of Jefferson who used to go out to the Sartoris place to see Narcissa (*Sanctuary*).

Jones, Januarius. A fat young teacher of Latin who pursued Cecily Saunders and Emmy, the Mahon cook (*Soldiers' Pay*).

Jones, Melicent. The daughter of Wash Jones. In 1853 she gave birth to a daughter Milly by an unknown father. She was rumored to have ended up in a brothel in Memphis (*Absalom, Absalom!*).

Jones, Milly. The daughter of Melicent Jones and grand-daughter of Wash Jones. She was born in 1853. In 1869 she gave birth to a daughter fathered by Thomas Sutpen. He spurned her when he discovered that the baby was not a boy. Jones then killed Sutpen and when he was about to be arrested he killed Milly and the baby ("Wash" and *Absalom, Absalom!*).

Jones, Wash. A squatter on the Sutpen land who arrived in 1850 with a daughter Melicent. In 1853 she gave birth to an illegitmate daughter Milly. Jones took care of the Sutpen property while Sutpen was away at war. In 1869 the granddaughter Milly gave birth to Sutpen's child, and when Sutpen spurned her because the child was not male, Wash killed him, and when the sheriff came after him he killed Milly and the baby and then died resisting arrest ("Wash" and *Absalom, Absalom!*).

Jordan, Mrs. A neighbor of Aunt Louise's in Mottstown where the narrator Georgie was sent to sleep on the night his Uncle Rodney was captured trying to flee ("That Will Be Fine").

Jubal. Major Saucier Weddel's Negro body servant ("Mountain Victory").

Jug. The name or nickname of the photographer on Hagood's paper (*Pylon*).

Julio. The brother of the little girl who followed Quentin Compson all over the countryside outside Boston. He wanted to have Quentin arrested for trying to kidnap the girl (*The Sound and the Fury*).

Julius. The "Semitic man," the brother of Mrs. Eva Wiseman, and a guest of Mrs. Maurier's on her yachting party. His last name may be Kauffman, for his grandfather was named Julius Kauffman (*Mosquitoes*).

Junkin, Professor. The principal of the Jefferson high school who called Mrs. Compson to tell her that Quentin (Caddy's daughter) was not attending classes (*The Sound and the Fury*).

Jupiter. Colonel Sartoris' horse which he rode during the war (*The Unvanquished*). Also a horse belonging to Harrison Blair ("Fox Hunt").

Justice, A. A short story in *Collected Stories*. First published in *These 13*. It is included in *The Faulkner Reader* and *The Portable Faulkner*. Part was revised for the second interlude of *Big Woods*. An anachronistic story about Sam Fathers related by Quentin Compson.

Justice of the Peace (1)
Justice of the Peace (2)

K

Kate. One of the girl friends of Dewey Dell Bundren (*As I Lay Dying*).

Katie. Major de Spain's mule which the men rode when they went hunting ("The Bear" in *Go Down, Moses*).

Kauffman, Julius. The grandfather of Julius, the "Semitic man," and of Eva Wiseman. He knew the background history of Mrs. Maurier's family (*Mosquitoes*).

Kaye, C. A major in the R.A.F. squadron to which John Sartoris belonged ("All the Dead Pilots").

Kazimura. The Japanese gardener for old Mrs. Ewing ("Golden Land").

Kemp, Beasley. The man to whom Ab Snopes traded a straight stock and a worn-out sorghum mill for a horse (*The Hamlet*).

Kennedy, Watt. The sheriff of Yoknapatawpha County around 1930 (*Light in August*). *Kenny*

Kentucky: May: Saturday. A piece of reportage by Faulkner in *Sports Illustrated*, May 16, 1955. About the Kentucky Derby.

Ketcham. The jailer at the time Rider was taken to the Jefferson jail ("Pantaloon in Black" in *Go Down, Moses*).

Kiblett. The town in Arkansas where Miss Corrie (Mrs. Boon Hogganbeck) came from and where her nephew Otis lived (*The Reivers*).

Kid Learns, The. A sketch in the New Orleans *Times-Picayune* Sunday section, May 31, 1925, p. 2. Reprinted in *New Orleans Sketches* (ed. Collins).

Killebrew, Miss. The teller at the Sartoris (de Spain) bank (*The Town*).

Killegrew. An elderly farmer in the Frenchman's Bend region in the 1930s and 1940s. He had machinery which the poorer farmers borrowed. He also had a radio which the Grier boys would listen to outside the window at night ("Shingles for the Lord" and "Two Soldiers").

Killegrew, Hampton. A night watchman in Jefferson, called "Hamp" ("Knight's Gambit").

Killigrew, Hunter. A deputy in Jefferson around 1923 (*The Mansion*).

King, Mrs. Alvina. The mother of Louise King ("Doctor Martino").

King, Louise. A young lady born in Mississippi and living in St. Louis, who was under the strange influence of Dr. Jules Martino ("Doctor Martino").

"Kingdom of God, The." A sketch in the New Orleans *Times-Picayune* Sunday section, Apr. 26, 1925, p. 4. Reprinted in *New Orleans Sketches* (ed. Collins).

Kingston. See **Kinston.**

Kinston. A neighboring town to Jefferson in another county. Horace Benbow moved there after he married the divorced wife of Harry Mitchell and took up law practice (*Sanctuary*). In "That Will Be Fine" the place is called Kingston.

Kitchener (Kit). The nickname of the English girl John Sartoris and Spoomer fought over. So called "because she had such a mob of soldiers" (Lord Kitchener was a famous British general.) ("All the Dead Pilots").

Kneeland, Mr. A tailor in Jefferson around 1912 (*The Town*).

Knew I Love Once. A poem in *Contempo*, I (Feb. 1, 1932), 1. Reprinted as *A Green Bough*, XXXIII.

Knight's Gambit. The sixth and last story in *Knight's Gambit*. Not previously published. About the Harriss family

of Jefferson and Captain Sebastian Gualdres, and about the
marriage of Gavin Stevens to Mrs. Harriss. The title is from
chess, and is explained by Gavin Stevens on pp. 218-219 of the
book. The story was adapted for television and performed on
CBS, "Climax," July 7, 1955, under the title *Wild Stallion*, with
Paul Henreid, Evelyn Keyes and Mary Astor.

Knight's Gambit. A cycle of six related stories published by
Random House, New York, 1949. About Gavin Stevens, the
Jefferson lawyer. Contains: "Smoke," "Monk," "Hand Upon
the Waters," "Tomorrow," "An Error in Chemistry," and
"Knight's Gambit." Three of the stories ("Monk," "Tomorrow,"
and "An Error in Chemistry") are related by Chick Mallison.
One ("Knight's Gambit") is related in the third person from
Chick's point of view.

Kohl, Barton. A sculptor, a Jew, and a Communist who lived
in Greenwich Village. After living with Linda Snopes for some
time he married her and they went to Spain in 1936 to fight
on the side of the Loyalists. He was killed in a plane crash
there (*The Mansion*).

Kohl, Linda Snopes. See **Snopes, Linda.**

Kyerling, R. A flyer who was in the same sortie in which
John Sartoris was killed ("All the Dead Pilots").

L

Labove. The law student schoolteacher in Frenchman's Bend
whose sexual desire for Eula Varner was so strong that he
tried to assault her (*The Hamlet*).

Lafe. The young man who was the father of Dewey Dell
Bundren's unborn child. He gave her ten dollars to get "fixed

up" (*As I Lay Dying*). Also the sitter on Will Gibson's store porch who kept interrupting Ek ("The Liar").

Lalear, April.   The screen name of Samantha Ewing ("Golden Land").

Lallemont, General.   The corps commander, a superior to General Gragnon (*A Fable*).

Lamar, Ruby.   The common-law wife of Lee Godwin. She tried to protect Temple Drake but was unsuccessful (*Sanctuary*).

Landing in Luck.   A story in *The Mississippian*, IX (Nov. 26, 1919), 2 and 7. Reprinted in *William Faulkner: Early Prose and Poetry*, ed. Carvel Collins, pp. 42-50. Faulkner's first published short story. About a young flying cadet named Thompson and his first solo flight.

Land of the Pharaohs.   A motion picture released by Warner Brothers, produced and directed by Howard Hawks in 1954. The dialogue was written by Faulkner.

Landry, Sergeant.   The sergeant in charge of the detachment sent to Valaumont Fortress to bring back to Paris the body of an unidentified soldier for the Tomb of the Unknown Soldier (*A Fable*).

Lanier Street.   A street in New Valois (*Pylon*).

Lao T'se.   A Pekinese belonging to a Mrs. Widrington which the halfbreed children of Byron Snopes apparently killed and ate (*The Town*).

Lapin.   The "bad" thief who was executed with the Corporal (*A Fable*).

Laura, Miss.   Quentin Compson's grade school teacher (*The Sound and the Fury*).

Lawington, Miss.   The cateress or baker in Jefferson who bought cakes from Mrs. Bundren and Mrs. Tull (*As I Lay Dying*).

Leblanc.   A policeman in New Valois (*Pylon*).

Ledbetter, Mrs.   A lady in Rockyford who bought a sewing machine from Ratliff (*The Town* and *The Mansion*).

Leg, The.   A short story in *Collected Stories*. First published in *Doctor Martino* and *Other Stories* as "Leg." A non-Yoknapatawpha story about a soldier in World War I who had his leg amputated and whose dismembered leg got him into trouble.

Legate, Bob. A Legate older than Will, apparently, for he used to go hunting with McCaslin Edmonds, General Compson, and Major de Spain. Referred to in *The Reivers*.

Legate, Will. An excellent shot and deer hunter who used to go hunting with Ike McCaslin and Roth Edmonds ("Delta Autumn" in *Go Down, Moses* and "Race at Morning"). He was appointed by the sheriff to guard Lucas Beauchamp at the county jail. (*Intruder in the Dust*).

Legendre, Doctor. A doctor in New Valois (*Pylon*).

Lena. A slave of the Hawk family at Hawkhurst ("Raid" in *The Unvanquished*).

Leonard. Mentioned in *The Hamlet* as one of the old family names of the Frenchman's Bend region.

Leonora. The Negro woman who took care of the Reporter and cleaned his living quarters (*Pylon*).

Lessep, Alison. The maiden name of Mrs. Maury Priest (*The Reivers*).

Letter to the North. An article in *Life*, XL (Mar. 5, 1956), 51-52. On the problem of segregation in the South.

Letters written by Faulkner [for more complete information see the bibliography to the "Nonfiction Prose" section]:

To *The Mississippian*, IX (Apr. 7, 1920), 1.

To *The Forum*, LXXXIII (Apr. 1930), lvi.

To Maurice Edgar Coindreau, *The Princeton University Library Chronicle*, XVIII (Spring 1957), Pl. 2.

To Maurice Edgar Coindreau, *The Princeton Unversity Chronicle*, XVIII (Spring 1957), Pl. 2.

To the President of the League of American Writers, *Writers Take Sides*, New York, The League of American Writers, 1938, p. 23.

To the Memphis *Commercial-Appeal*, July 12, 1941, p. 4.

To the Oxford *Eagle*, Mar. 13, 1947, p. 5.

To the Memphis *Commercial-Appeal*, Mar. 26, 1950, Sec. IV, p. 4.

To the Memphis *Commercial-Appeal,* Apr. 9, 1950, Sec IV, p. 4.

To the Oxford *Eagle,* Sept. 14, 1950, p. 13.

To *Time,* LVI (Nov. 13, 1950), 6.

To the Secretary of the American Academy of Arts and Letters, *Proceedings of the American Academy of Arts and Letters and the National Institute of Arts and Letters,* Second Series, No. 1, 1951, p. 19.

To Richard Walser, *The Enigma of Thomas Wolfe,* ed. Richard Walser, Cambridge: Harvard University Press, 1953, p. vii.

To *The New York Times,* Dec. 26, 1954, Sec. IV, p. 6.

To the Memphis *Commercial-Appeal,* Feb. 20, 1955, Sec. V, p. 3.

To the Memphis *Commercial-Appeal,* Mar. 20, 1955, Sec. V, p. 3.

To *The New York Times,* Mar. 25, 1955, p. 22.

To the Memphis *Commercial-Appeal,* Apr. 3, 1955, Sec. V, p. 3.

To the Memphis *Commercial-Appeal,* Apr. 10, 1955, Sec. V, p. 3.

To the Memphis *Commercial-Appeal,* Apr. 17, 1955, Sec. V, p. 3.

To *Life,* XL (Mar. 26, 1956), 19.

To *The Reporter,* XIV (Apr. 19, 1956), 7.

To *Time,* LXVII (Apr. 23, 1956), 12.

To *Time,* LXVIII (Dec. 10, 1956), 6 and 9.

To *The New York Times,* Dec. 16, 1956, Sec. IV, p. 8.

To *Time,* LXIX (Feb. 11, 1957), 8.

To *The New York Times,* Oct. 13, 1957, Sec. IV, p. 10.

To *The New York Times,* Aug. 28, 1960, Sec. IV, p. 10.

To Sherwood Anderson. Reproduced in facsimile in James B. Meriwether, *The Literary Career of William Faulkner,* Princeton University Library, 1961, Pls. 27, 28, and 29.

Levine, Gerald David. An eighteen-year-old Jewish pilot, a second lieutenant in Major Bridesman's command. He committed suicide (*A Fable*).

Levitt, Matt. A twenty-one-year-old mechanic and former Golden Gloves champion from Ohio who courted Linda Snopes. After striking Gavin Stevens and getting into a fight with young Anse McCallum, he was fired from the garage in Jefferson where he worked, and left town (*The Town*).

Lewis, Matt. The owner of the livery stable in Blizzard, Arizona ("Idyll in the Desert").

Liar, The. A sketch in the New Orleans *Times-Picayune* Sunday section, July 26, 1925, pp. 3 and 6. Reprinted in *New Orleans Sketches* (ed. Collins).

Light in August. A novel published by Harrison Smith and Robert Haas, New York, 1932. Pages 425-440 were reprinted in *The Faulkner Reader* and *The Portable Faulkner* under the title "Percy Grimm." The time of the novel is 1929-1932. About Joe Christmas, the Reverend Gail Hightower, Byron Bunch, Lena Grove, Joanna Burden, and Percy Grimm. Two selections from the novel are read by Faulkner on MGM long playing record number E3617 ARC. The title, according to Malcolm Cowley, refers to the countryman's saying about pregnant stock. To be "light" means to have given birth. According to Faulkner, however, the title refers to the "peculiar quality of light" in Mississippi in August (*Faulkner in the University*, pp. 74 and 199).

* Lightning. The name Ned McCaslin gave to the stolen horse Coppermine. Ned first called him Forkid Lightning (*The Reivers*).

Lilacs, The. A poem in *The Double Dealer*, VII (June 1925), 185-187. Reprinted in *Salmagundi* and as *A Green Bough*, I. The poem is subtitled "To A. . . and H. . ., Royal Air Force, August, 1925."

Lilley. The owner of a small store in Jefferson, a shabby side-street grocery patronized mostly by Negroes (*Intruder in the Dust*).

Linda. Book II of *The Mansion*.

Linscomb, Colonel. A resident of Parsham, Tennessee, whose horse Acheron raced against Lightning (Coppermine) (*The Reivers*).

* Lion. The dog specially trained by Boon Hogganbeck to catch

Old Ben, the bear. He was killed by the bear at the time Boon killed the bear. Appears in "The Bear" (*Go Down, Moses*). Is referred to in *The Town*.

Lion. A short story in *Harper's Magazine*, Dec. 1935. It was rewritten for part of "The Bear" (*Go Down, Moses*).

Little Chicago. The only name known for a woman who ran Mrs. Rouncewell's boarding house for a short time in the mid-1930s. Referred to in *The Reivers*.

Littlejohn's Hotel. A boardinghouse in Frenchman's Bend, run by a Mrs. Littlejohn. It was there that Ratliff always stayed when he was in the neighborhood, and it was there also that Buck Hipps auctioned off the spotted horses. Mrs. Littlejohn kept the idiot Ike Snopes to help her. The hotel is mentioned in both *The Hamlet* and *The Town*, and *The Hamlet* and *Intruder in the Dust* both mention the name Littlejohn as an old family name of the region. A man named Littlejohn attended Addie Bundren's funeral (*As I Lay Dying*).

Little Top. See **Top.**

Lizards in Jamshyd's Courtyard. A short story in *The Saturday Evening Post*, Feb. 27, 1932. Rewritten for the last episode in *The Hamlet*. (Jamshyd is a character in Persian mythology, the king of the peris, elves descended from evil angels).

Lizzie. The first name of Mrs. Ab Snopes's widowed sister ("Barn Burning").

Lo. A short story in *Collected Stories*. First published in *Story*, Nov. 1932. It is included in *Selected Short Stories*. About the visit of Francis Weddel to President Jackson.

Log-in-the-Creek. A lazy young Indian who lay on his back and played the harmonica. He married Herman Basket's sister ("A Courtship").

Long, Hot Summer, The. The title of the motion picture made from Book III of *The Hamlet*.

Long, Judge. The federal judge for the Yoknapatawpha County district in 1923. He would have tried Montgomery Ward Snopes on a pornography charge if Flem had not arranged it so

Montgomery Ward would be tried on an illegal whiskey charge instead (*The Town* and *The Mansion*).

Long Summer, The. Book III of *The Hamlet*. In 1958 this was published separately in a paperback Signet book in conjunction with the motion picture made from it.

Loosh. See **Lucius.**

Lord-to-God. A big woodpecker in the woods of Major de Spain's hunting grounds ("The Bear" in *Go Down, Moses*).

Lorraine. The Memphis prostitute who was Jason Compson's lady friend (*The Sound and the Fury*). She could quite possibly be the Miss Lorraine who was a guest with a Miss Myrtle of Reba Rivers after Red's funeral (*Sanctuary*).

Louisa. The name of both the aunt and cousin of seven-year-old Georgie. They lived in Mottstown ("That Will Be Fine"). Also the name of the maid in the San Antonio brothel where Harry Wilbourne went to get help about Charlotte's pregnancy (*The Wild Palms*).

Louvinia. The wife of Joby and mother of Loosh and Simon, and the general housekeeper at the Sartoris plantation. Appears in *The Unvanquished* and "My Grandmother Millard."

Lovelady, Mr. The man in Jefferson who collected insurance money from the Negroes ("That Evening Sun").

Lovemaiden, Butch. A deputy from Hardwick who got in a fight with Boon Hogganbeck because Boon resented his calling Corrie a whore (*The Reivers*).

Lovesong of J. A. Prufrock. Section VI of *Pylon*.

Lowe, Julian. A flying cadet, too young to have been in the war. He thought he was in love with Margaret Powers, but after she sent him home to his mother in San Francisco he soon turned to other interests (*Soldiers' Pay*).

Lucius. "Loosh," the son of Joby and Louvinia, and husband of Philadelphia. He was a slave on the Sartoris plantation. When the Yankee soldiers came through he got ideas of freedom and decided to leave, but he soon returned to the plantation. Appears in *The Unvanquished* and "My Grandmother Millard."

Ludus. The husband of Minnie, Reba Rivers' Negro maid.

He used to steal money from Minnie and give it to other women (*The Mansion*). Also a driver for the Priest livery stable whom Boon Hogganbeck chased across the Square and shot at because he had lied about why the team he had out was not in (*The Reivers*).

Luke. The name of a bootlegger in Oxford (*Sanctuary*).

Luluque. A Midian, one of the twelve followers of the Corporal (*A Fable*).

Lumpkin, Mathilda. The maiden name of Mrs. Carleton Van Dyming ("Black Music").

Luster. The son of Frony and the caretaker of Benjy Compson during the 1920s. He was born around 1911 (*The Sound and the Fury*). In *Absalom, Absalom!* Quentin Compson refers to a Luster who used to go hunting with him and his father, which would be chronologically impossible, unless he were a different person. In *The Sound and the Fury* it was Versh, Luster's uncle, who went hunting with them. Also a colored worker in the Priest livery stable (*The Reivers*).

M

MacCallum. See **McCallum.**

MacCallum, Virginius. See **McCallum, Anse I.**

MacGowan, Skeet. See **McGowan, Skeets.**

MacKenzie, Shreve. See **McCannon, Shrevlin.**

MacWyrglinchbeath, Wully (Mac). A Scottish airplane mechanic in World War I who used his army leave to join another outfit so he could draw double pay. He became a pilot so he could earn more money ("Thrift").

Madden, Rufus. A man from Charleston, Georgia, who became Captain Green's first sergeant during World War I. He was with Richard Powers when his own men shot Powers. Later Madden worked in a store in Charlestown (*Soldiers' Pay*).

Magda. See **Marthe.**

Mahon, Donald. A blinded and wounded pilot who returned from World War I to his home in Charlestown, Georgia, to die (*Soldiers' Pay*).

Mahon, Joseph. An Episcopal minister, the father of Donald Mahon (*Soldiers' Pay*).

Malcolm. Mr. Faulkner's son ("Afternoon of a Cow").

Mallison, Charles, Jr. (Chick). The son of Charles, Sr., and Margaret Stevens Mallison, and a nephew of Gavin Stevens. When he was sixteen he worked to find the murderer of Vinson Gowrie so that the accused Lucas Beauchamp would be freed. Later he attended Harvard University and then started law school. In 1942 he joined the Air Force and became a bombardier. He was shot down over Germany and spent ten months in a prison camp. He returned to Jefferson in the fall of 1945. He appears in and narrates "Monk," "Tomorrow," and "An Error in Chemistry" (*Knight's Gambit*), and parts of *The Town* and *The Mansion*. He also narrated the original versions of "A Name for the City" (later rewritten for *Requiem for a Nun*) and "By the People" (later rewritten for *The Mansion*). The story "Knight's Gambit" and the novel *Intruder in the Dust* are third-person narratives from his point of view.

Mallison, Charles, Sr. The father of Chick Mallison. Appears in "Knight's Gambit," *Intruder in the Dust, The Town,* and *The Mansion.*

Mallison, Margaret Stevens. The mother of Chick Mallison and the twin sister of Gavin Stevens. Appears in "Knight's Gambit," *Intruder in the Dust, The Town,* and *The Mansion.* Is referred to in *Requiem for a Nun.*

Manassas. A racing horse which belonged to Colonel Linscomb (*The Reivers*).

Man Comes, Man Goes. A poem in *The New Republic,* LXXIV (May 3, 1933), 339. Reprinted as *A Green Bough,* VI.

Mandy. The cook at the home of Georgie's grandfather ("That Will Be Fine"). Also the MacCallum's cook (*Sartoris*).

Mannie. The young wife of Rider, a renter from Roth Edmonds. She died after they were married six months and Rider became crazed with grief ("Pantaloon in Black" in *Go Down, Moses*).

Mannigoe, Nancy. A Negro woman who used to help out at the Compsons when Dilsey was sick. She was a cocaine addict. She had an affair with a Mr. Stovall, a white man, and when she ask him publicly to pay her he kicked her teeth out. She was pregnant (perhaps by him; certainly not by her husband) and she was frightened of her husband, Jesus, who was jealous. Later she became the nurse of the two Stevens children, and when she discovered that Temple was planning to run away from home with another man she killed the six-months-old Stevens baby, for which she was hanged. The name was originally Manigault. Appears (as Nancy only) in "That Evening Sun" and (as Nancy Mannigoe) in *Requiem for a Nun*.

Mannock [margin handwritten note]

Mansion, The. A novel published by Random House, New York, 1959. Dedicated to Phil Stone. Subtitled *Snopes*, Vol. III. The third (with *The Hamlet* and *The Town*) volume of the trilogy devoted to the Snopes family. Contains a "Note" by Faulkner. It covers action between 1908 and 1946, with emphasis on 1908 and 1938-1946. Pages 294-321 are a rewritten version of the story "By the People." Pages 3-51 were preprinted in *Esquire*, Dec. 1959, under the title "Mink Snopes." The title refers to the old de Spain house, which Flem Snopes remodeled into a Southern mansion when he moved into it.

Man's Responsibility to Fellow Man. See *Address to the annual meeting of the Delta Council* under **Addresses by Faulkner.**

Manuel Street. A street in Memphis where Miss Reba Rivers' house of prostitution was located (*Requiem for a Nun*). In *The Reivers* it is called Catalpa Street.

Marble Faun, The. A long cyclic pastoral poem published by the Four Seas Company, Boston, 1924. Dedicated to his mother. Contains a preface by Phil Stone. Faulkner's first published volume.

Marchand. The manager of the Ord-Atkinson Aircraft plant (*Pylon*).

Marders, Sarah. A friend of Belle Mitchell's who used to play tennis with her (*Sartoris*).

Mardis, Cornelia. The maiden name of the wife of Anselm Holland, Sr. ("Smoke" in *Knight's Gambit*).

Marengo. See **Ringo.**

Marionettes. A play in one act, illustrated and bound by Faulkner himself. An unpublished work, but included here because it exists in more than one copy.

Markey, Robert. A Memphis lawyer who had been a Heidelberg friend of Gavin Stevens ("Knight's Gambit").

Marowitz. A talkative Jew, a kind of minor confidence man ("Damon and Pythias Unlimited").

Marsh. Mrs. Grier's brother, who had been in World War I. Referred to in "Two Soldiers."

Martha. The wife of the doctor who rented Harry and Charlotte the cottage on the Mississippi gulf coast (*The Wild Palms*).

Marthe. The younger of the two half-sisters of the Corporal. Before going to France she was known as Magda. She married a French farmer named Dumont in order to get a passport for herself, her sister, and her half-brother (*A Fable*).

Martel, General. The "Grand Commander" of the French Armies (*A Fable*).

Martino, Dr. Jules. A St. Louis doctor who spent his summers at Cranston's Wells, Mississippi. He exerted a strange influence over Louise King ("Doctor Martino").

Marya. The elder of the two half-sisters of the Corporal. She was an idiot (*A Fable*).

Matthew. One of the four men who claimed Lonnie Grinnup's body after he was found drowned ("Hand Upon the Waters" in *Knight's Gambit*).

Maurier, Harrison. A young man from Atlanta who liked Cecily Saunders (*Soldiers' Pay*).

Maurier, Mrs. Patricia. A wealthy New Orleans woman, owner of the yacht Nausikaa (*Mosquitoes*).

Maxey, Mr. The owner of the barbershop in Jefferson where Henry Stribling (Hawkshaw) worked. Appears in "Hair" and *Light in August.*

Maycox, Judge. The judge before whom Lucas Beauchamp was to be tried (*Intruder in the Dust*).

Maydew. The sheriff who went out after Rider ("Pantaloon in Black" in *Go Down, Moses*).

Mayes, Will. The Negro night watchman at the ice plant in Jefferson, whom Minnie Cooper falsely accused of attacking her. He was lynched by a mob led by John McLendon ("Dry September").

McAndrews. The foreman at the sawmill where Rider worked ("Pantaloon in Black" in *Go Down, Moses*).

McCallum, Anse I. The father of the six McCallum brothers. He was sixteen when the Civil War broke out, and walked to Virginia to join the army. He died around 1925 or 1926. Appears in *Sartoris* as Virginius MacCallum. Is referred to in *The Hamlet* and "The Tall men." In *The Hamlet* there is also a man referred to as "Old Man Hundred-and-One McCallum." McCallum is a name mentioned as being from both the Frenchman's Bend and Beat Four regions.

McCallum, Anse II. One of the twin sons of Buddy McCallum. He and his brother had not registered for the draft in 1940, and a U. S. marshal came to arrest them. Their father sent them to Memphis to enlist ("The Tall Men"). In *The Town*, in a time shift (back to around 1925), he gets in a fight with Matt Levitt.

McCallum, Buddy. The youngest son of Anse McCallum I, and a half-brother to the other five. He had been in World War I and had been decorated by both the French and American governments. He brought home a German Luger which he traded to the Gowries for some hounds. Right after returning home he married and then had twin sons—Anse and Lucius. On the day the U. S. marshal came to arrest his sons for draft evasion he injured his leg in an accident and had to have it amputated. Appears in *Sartoris* and "The Tall Men." Is referred to in *Intruder in the Dust*. He appears also in *The Town* in an apparent time shift.

McCallum, Henry. The second son of old Anse McCallum. He was reputed to have made good whiskey (McCallum whiskey is mentioned in *The Hamlet*). Appears in *Sartoris*. Henry is the only one of the brothers not mentioned in "The Tall Men."

McCallum, Jackson. The eldest son of old Anse McCallum. Appears in *Sartoris* and "The Tall Men."

McCallum, Lee. The fifth son of old Anse McCallum. Appears in *Sartoris* and "The Tall Men."

McCallum, Lucius. One of the twin sons of Buddy McCallum. He and his brother had not registered for the draft in 1940 and a U. S. marshal came to arrest them. Their father sent them to Memphis to enlist ("The Tall Men").

McCallum, Raphael Semmes (Rafe). One of the twin sons of old Anse McCallum. According to *Sartoris* he was forty-one in 1920, but according to "The Tall Men" he was forty-five in 1940 or 1941. It was from him that Max Harriss got the horse which he hoped would throw and kill Captain Gualdres. Appears in *Sartoris*, "Knight's Gambit," and "The Tall Men." Is referred to in *As I Lay Dying* and *The Mansion*.

McCallum, Stuart. One of the twin sons (with Rafe) of old Anse McCallum. Appears in *Sartoris*, "The Tall Men," and (only as Rafe McCallum's twin brother) *As I Lay Dying*.

McCannon, Shrevlin (Shreve). Quentin Compson's roommate at Harvard. He was born in Edmonton, Alberta, Canada, in 1890, and attended Harvard from 1909 to 1914. He was in the Canadian Medical Corps in France from 1914 to 1919. Later he became a surgeon in Edmonton. Appears in *Absalom, Absalom!* and (as Shreve MacKenzie) in *The Sound and the Fury*.

McCarron, Hoake. A wealthy young man from away who succeeded in taking Eula Varner's virginity and became the father of her child (Linda Snopes). Appears in *The Hamlet* and *The Mansion*. Is referred to in *The Town*.

McCaslin,
Mu, —

McCaslin, Amodeus (Uncle Buddy). A son of old Lucius Quintus Carothers McCaslin and a twin of Theophilus (Uncle Buck) McCaslin. He was born around 1800 in Carolina. Some ten years before the Civil War he and his brother embarked on a project to free their slaves. When the war came he played a game of poker with his brother to see who would enlist and who would stay home. He won, so he became a sergeant in Colonel Sartoris' regiment. He was never married. He died around 1870. Appears in "Was" (*Go Down, Moses*) and "Retreat" (*The Unvanquished*), and is referred to in most of the other stories in *Go Down, Moses*.

McCaslin, Delphine. The wife of Ned William McCaslin and cook for Grandmother Priest (*The Reivers*).

McCaslin, Isaac (Uncle Ike). The son of Theophilus McCaslin and Sophonsiba Beauchamp. He was born in 1867 and was raised by his cousin McCaslin Edmonds, to whom he gave the McCaslin lands. He married a Jefferson girl and moved to Jefferson, where he became a carpenter and opened a hardware store (where Jason Compson later worked). He was taught woodlore and hunting by Sam Fathers. He died in 1947. Appears in most of the stories in *Go Down, Moses*, "A Bear Hunt," "Race at Morning," and *The Reivers*. Is referred to in *The Hamlet, The Town,* and *The Mansion*.

McCaslin, Lucius Quintus Carothers. The father of the McCaslin twins and a daughter who married an Edmonds. He was the first of the McCaslins in Yoknapatawpha County, arriving there from Carolina around 1800 (although in *The Reivers* the date is set at 1813). He fathered, through a Negro slave and her daughter, the branch of the family which became known as the Beauchamps. He died in 1837. He appears in none, but is referred to throughout most of the stories in *Go Down, Moses* and in *The Reivers*. He is mentioned in *Intruder in the Dust*.

McCaslin, Ned William. The Negro coachman for Grandfather Priest. He was born on the McCaslin lands in 1860 and claimed to be a grandson of old Lucius Quintus Carothers McCaslin (although the Negro descendants of McCaslin were known as Beauchamps). It was Ned who traded Grandfather

Priest's automobile for the stolen racehorse. He died in 1934 (*The Reivers*).

McCaslin, Theophilus (Uncle Buck).   A son of old Lucius Quintus Carothers McCaslin and a twin brother of Amodeus (Uncle Buddy) McCaslin. He was born around 1800 in Carolina. He stayed at home during the war and let his brother enlist. Around 1859 he married Sophonsiba Beauchamp. They had one son, Isaac. Uncle Buck helped Bayard Sartoris and Ringo hunt down Grumby, the man who killed Granny Millard. He died around 1870, three years after his son was born. Appears in "Retreat" and "Vendée" (*The Unvanquished*), and in "Was" (*Go Down, Moses*), and is referred to throughout most of the other stories in *Go Down, Moses* and in *The Hamlet* and *The Reivers*.

McCord, "Mac."   A Chicago newspaperman who was a friend of Harry and Charlotte. He had worked on a New Orleans paper with Charlotte's brother (*The Wild Palms*).

McDiarmid, Mr.   The man who ran the depot eating room in Parsham, and who, according to report, "could slice a ham so thin that his entire family had made a summer trip to Chicago on the profits from one of them. . . ." He acted as one of the judges in the race between Acheron and Lightning (*The Reivers*).

McEachern, Simon.   The farmer who adopted and raised Joe Christmas. He was a harsh, narrow, religious man who punished Joe frequently (*Light in August*).

McGinnis, Lieutenant Darrel (Mac).   The co-pilot of the airship piloted by Captain Bogard ("Turnabout").

McGowan, Skeets.   The clerk and soda jerker in Uncle Willy Christian's drugstore. He seduced Dewey Dell Bundren in the basement of the store on the pretense that the act would cause an abortion. Appears in *Intruder in the Dust, The Town, The Mansion,* and (as Skeet MacGowan) in *As I Lay Dying*. In *The Sound and the Fury* the drugstore clerk is known as Mac.

McKellog, Colonel.   A United States Army colonel stationed in Memphis. His car and driver took the nine-year-old Grier boy back home to Frenchman's Bend ("Two Soldiers").

McKie. The name of the man the captain asked about after his men were lost in a cave-in ("Crevasse").

McLean, Private. A private in Captain Alec Gray's regiment whose discipline the captain ordered because his rifle was dirty ("Victory").

McLendon, Jackson. See **McLendon, John.**

McLendon, John. A resident of Jefferson who had organized a regiment and became a captain in World War I. He led the mob which lynched Will Mayes. Appears in "Dry September," *Light in August,* and (as Captain McLendon only) in *The Mansion.* In *The Town* he is called Jackson McLendon.

McNamara, Mr. A young ex-jockey, a "cousin" of Marowitz, and something of a minor con man ("Damon and Pythias Unlimited").

McWilliams, Mr. The conductor on the train between Jefferson and Memphis ("Knight's Gambit").

McWillie. The son of Colonel Linscomb's chauffeur, and the jockey of Acheron (*The Reivers*).

Meadowfill, Essie. The daughter of old man Meadowfill. In 1942 she graduated as valedictorian from the Jefferson High School and was given a five-hundred-dollar scholarship, which she refused. She then got a job in the Bank of Jefferson. After the war she met and married an ex-Marine named McKinley Smith (*The Mansion*).

Meadowfill, Old Man. He owned a small house and plot of land on the corner of the old Compson place which Flem Snopes wanted. When he refused to sell (the title was actually in his daughter's name), Snopes tried to drive him out by annoying him, and finally Gavin Stevens stepped in and got the land plus a strip of Flem's land, on which an oil company wanted to build a filling station, sold it, and gave the money to Essie so she and her Marine corporal husband would have enough money to buy a farm (*The Mansion*).

Meek, Melissa. The librarian in Jefferson in 1943. She found the picture of Caddy Compson and a Nazi general in a magazine (the Appendix to *The Sound and the Fury*).

Meeks, Doc.   A peddler for Watkins Products (*The Mansion*).

Melisandre.   See **Cousin Melisandre.**

Meloney

Merchants and Farmers Bank.   The real name of the bank founded by Bayard Sartoris II and of which Manfred de Spain and later Flem Snopes became president (*The Mansion* and *The Reivers*). In *The Sound and the Fury* it is stated that the Merchants and Farmers Bank had failed (that was where Jason Compson got the checks on out-of-town banks so he could juggle the money sent by Caddy for the support of young Quentin).

Merridew, Mrs.   A church woman who took it upon herself to reform Hoke Christian ("Uncle Willy").

Message Given at Nagano.   A statement to the people of Nagano. Printed in *Faulkner at Nagano*.

Metal-Detector Salesman

Metcalf.   The jailer in Mottstown (*Light in August*).

Meyers, Al.   One of the stunt fliers at the dedication airshow at the Feinman Airport (*Pylon*).

Middle Ground, The.   Section V of the *Collected Stories*. Contains "Wash," "Honor," "Dr. Martino," "Fox Hunt," "Pennsylvania Station," "Artist at Home," "The Brooch," "My Grandmother Millard," "Golden Land," "There Was a Queen," and "Mountain Victory."

Middleton, Captain.   The American captain who came to identify the Corporal and confused him with an American soldier named Brzewski, who had died at sea in 1917 (*A Fable*).

Midgleston, Martha.   Wilfred Midgleston's wife ("Black Music").

Midgleston, Wilfred.   A Brooklyn architect's draftsman who was sent to Virginia with the plans for Carleton Van Dyming's house. On the trip he had the illusion that he was a faun, and frightened Mrs. Van Dyming by gamboling on the green ("Black Music"). Although no name is given the character, he is apparently the person in "Carcassonne."

Midnight.   A small town in Arkansas where Fonsiba Beauchamp moved after she was married ("The Bear" in *Go Down, Moses*).

Millard, Rosa. The mother-in-law of Colonel Sartoris and grandmother of Bayard Sartoris II, who always called her "Granny Millard." She lived at the Sartoris home during the Civil War. With the help of Ab Snopes she engaged in tricking the Union Army out of horses and mules, resold them back to the Army, and then used the money to help the needy of Yoknapatawpha County. She was shot and killed by a raider named Grumby when she went to see him about a deal they were working on. Appears in *The Unvanquished* and "My Grandmother Millard." Is referred to in *The Hamlet*.

Miller, Mr. A men's class Sunday School teacher in Jefferson ("Uncle Willy").

Miller, Mrs. A dressmaker in Charlestown, Georgia, who gave Emmy a job after she had left home and before she went to Dr. Mahon's (*Soldiers' Pay*).

Millingham. Mentioned by Gavin Stevens in *Intruder in the Dust* as a family name in the Frenchman's Bend region.

Mills City. A place two hundred miles from Jefferson where Elly's uncle lived ("Elly").

Mink. The driver from the livery stable whom Jason Compson got to drive the team when he took young Quentin to let Caddy see her (*The Sound and the Fury*).

Mink. Book I of *The Mansion*.

Mink Snopes. The title given to Chapters I and II of *The Mansion* when they were preprinted in *Esquire,* Dec. 1959.

Minnie. Reba Rivers' colored maid (*Sanctuary, The Mansion,* and *The Reivers*).

Minton County. The county where Colonel Devries' sister lived ("By the People"). In the revised version (in *The Mansion*) the name was changed to Cumberland County.

Mirror of Youth. The title given to *A Green Bough,* XVI, when it was reprinted in *Mississippi Verse,* edited by Alice James.

Mirrors of Chartres Street. A sketch in the New Orleans *Times-Picayune* Sunday section, Feb. 8, 1925, pp. 1 and 6. Reprinted in *New Orleans Sketches* (ed. Collins).

Mirrors of Chartres Street. A book of eleven of the sixteen sketches from the New Orleans *Times-Picayune* Sunday section published by Faulkner Studies, Minneapolis, 1953, with an introduction by William Van O'Connor. Those omitted are "Jealousy," "The Liar," "Episode," "Country Mice," and "Yo Ho and Two Bottles of Rum."

Mississippi. An article in *Holiday*, XV (Apr. 1954), 35-46. Part was revised for the third interlude of *Big Woods*.

Miss Zilphia Gant. A short story published by The Book Club of Texas, 1932, in a limited edition of 300 copies, with a preface by Henry Smith. Not published elsewhere.

Mistairy. Mr. Harry (or 'Arry), the only name by which the English groom was known to the Rev. Tobe Sutterfield. The name, to carry through the symbolism of the novel, may have been chosen to suggest "mystery" (*A Fable*).

Mist' Bob. The employer of the Negro who took a Mississippi River boat which he thought would take him to Africa ("Sunset").

Mister Ernest. The widower farmer who took care of the twelve-year-old boy after his mother ran away and his father disappeared ("Race at Morning").

Mistral. A short story in *Collected Stories*. First published in *These 13*. A non-Yoknapatawpha story about two Americans travelling in Italy and their encounter with a strange intrigue among a priest, the girl he has raised, and a young soldier who had been courting her. A mistral is a cold and dry north wind which blows over the Mediterranean coast.

Mitchell. The owner of the store in the small settlement where Lonnie Grinnup lived ("Hand Upon the Waters" in *Knight's Gambit*). Also a man (and apparently a settlement given his name) through which a railroad ran ("The Liar").

Mitchell, Belle. The daughter of Harry Mitchell and his wife Belle. She was called Little Belle by her mother and sometimes Titania by her stepfather, Horace Benbow (*Sartoris*).

Mitchell, Few. Known as "Unc" Few Mitchell, and referred to by Louvinia as a man "born loony" ("Retreat" in *The Unvanquished*).

Mitchell, Harry.   A friend of the Sartorises and Benbows in Jefferson. His wife Belle divorced him and married Horace Benbow (*Sartoris*).

Mitchell, Hugh.   A farmer from Beat Four (*The Hamlet*).

Mitchell, Mrs.   A lady referred to by Mrs. Burney as a local gossip (*Soldiers' Pay*).

Mohataha.   The sister of Issetibbeha and mother of Ikkemotubbe. Referred to in *Requiem for a Nun* and *The Mansion*.

Moketubbe.   The son of Issetibbeha. He succeeded his father as Chief of the Chickasaws. When his cousin Ikkemotubbe returned from New Orleans and poisoned his eight-year-old son, Moketubbe abdicated and Ikkemotubbe became chief. The suffix "tubbe" is a Chickasaw word meaning "chief." Appears in "Red Leaves" and "A Courtship." Is referred to in "The Old People" (*Go Down, Moses*) and *The Reivers*.

Monghan, Buck.   A flyer in World War I and a friend of the Sartoris boys. Bayard met him later in Chicago. He became a stunt flyer and worked with a man named Howard Rogers. Later he became a car demonstrator. Appears in "Ad Astra," *Sartoris,* and "Honor." There is also an American flyer named Monaghan in the squadron to which Gerald David Levine was assigned (*A Fable*).

Monckton.   A philosophizing sailor ("Divorce in Naples").

Monk.   The nickname of Stonewall Jackson Odlethrop ("Monk" in *Knight's Gambit*). Also one of the airport crew at the Feinman Airport (*Pylon*).

Monk.   The second story in *Knight's Gambit*. First published in *Scribner's Magazine,* May 1937. About the feeble-minded Monk (Stonewall Jackson Odlethrop) who was sent to prison for a killing he did not do and then executed for another which he was not responsible for.

Montgomery, Jake.   A lumberman who worked with Vinson Gowrie. His body was found in Vinson's grave when Chick Mallison and Miss Habersham and Aleck Sander opened it (*Intruder in the Dust*).

✳Montigny, de. The interne from whom Harry Wilbourne borrowed a suit to go to the party at which he met Charlotte (*The Wild Palms*).

✳Montigny, Captain de. The aide to General Martel. The relatives of the Corporal came to his office to seek information about the Corporal (*A Fable*).

✳Montigny, Paul de. A part-Negro man from Louisiana whom Elly wanted to marry ("Elly").

Moony. The foreman in the sawmill in Jefferson where Byron Bunch, Joe Christmas, and Joe Brown worked (*Light in August*).

Moore, Brother. One of the deputation from the Second Baptist Church who came to see Simon Strother about the money he had embezzled from the church funds (*Sartoris*).

Morache. One of the French soldiers who sold the body of an anonymous soldier (which they had been sent out to get for the Tomb of the Unknown Soldier) to an old farm woman for a hundred francs so they could buy brandy. The old woman thought the body was that of her dead son Theodule (*A Fable*).

✳Moreover. The name given by McCord to the imaginary dog Charlotte was looking for after Harry lost his job (*The Wild Palms*).

Mosby, Hogeye. An epileptic who lived in the poorhouse (*Intruder in the Dust*).

Moseley. The owner of a drugstore in Mottson (Mottstown) where Dewey Dell Bundren went to get something for an abortion (*As I Lay Dying*).

✳Moses. A dog belonging to the McCaslins ("Was" in *Go Down, Moses*).

Mosquitoes. A novel published by Boni and Liveright, New York, 1927. Dedicated to "Helen." A non-Yoknapatawpha novel about wealthy and artistic people in New Orleans.

✳Mossop. The family name of the wife of Hence Cayley ("Knight's Gambit").

Mother and Child. The title given to *A Green Bough*, XIV, when it was reprinted in *Mississippi Verse*, edited by Alice James.

Mothershed. An agnostic friend of Judge Allison, whom the judge met in "heaven" ("Beyond").

Mott County. A neighboring county to Yoknapatawpha County.

Mottson. See **Mottstown.**

Mottstown. The county seat of Okataba County, called Mottson in *The Sound and the Fury* and *As I Lay Dying,* but called Mottstown elsewhere.

Mountain Victory. A short story in *Collected Stories.* First published in *The Saturday Evening Post,* Dec. 3, 1932, as "A Mountain Victory." Reprinted in *Doctor Martino and Other Stories.* It is included in *Selected Short Stories.* About the death of Major Saucier Weddel at the hands of East Tennessee Union sympathizers.

Mount Vernon. A small settlement six miles from the McCallum place (*Sartoris* and *As I Lay Dying*).

Muir. A family name of the east central Yoknapatawpha County region (*The Town*).

Mulberry. See **Gombault, Pete.**

Mule in the Yard. A short story in *Collected Stories.* First published in *Scribner's Magazine,* Aug. 1934. It was rewritten as pages 231-256 of *The Town.*

Murray. Mentioned in *The Hamlet* as one of the old family names of the Frenchman's Bend region.

My Epitaph. A poem in *Contempo,* I (Feb. 1, 1932), 2. Reprinted as *This Earth* and then as *A Green Bough,* XLIV.

My Grandmother Millard and General Bedford Forrest and the Battle of Harrykin Creek. A short story in *Collected Stories.* First published in *Story,* Mar.-Apr. 1943. A fugitive story in *The Unvanquished* series.

Myrtle. Doctor Alford's assistant (*Sartoris*). Also the sheriff's daughter (*The Sound and the Fury*).

Myrtle, Miss. A guest of Reba Rivers' after Red's funeral (*Sanctuary*).

N

Naiads' Song. A poem in *The Mississippian*, IX (Feb. 4, 1920), 3. Reprinted in *William Faulkner: Early Prose and Poetry*, ed. Carvel Collins, pp. 55-56.

Name for the City, A. A short story in *Harper's Magazine*, Oct. 1950. Rewritten for pages 3-48 of *Requiem for a Nun*.

Nancy. An animal, probably a dog, shot by Roskus and left in the ditch. The buzzards ate it, and the Compson children hoped they would not "undress" Damuddy as they had Nancy (*The Sound and the Fury*). See also **Mannigoe, Nancy.**

Natalie. A local girl whom Quentin Compson kissed, and about whom Caddy taunted him (*The Sound and the Fury*).

Nausikaa. The name of Mrs. Maurier's yacht (*Mosquitoes*).

Nelson, Caroline (Aunt Callie). The old Negro woman who had taken care of Donald Mahon when he was a baby (*Soldiers' Pay*).

Nelson, Loosh. A young Negro, the grandson of Aunt Callie Nelson. He had been a corporal in the army during World War I (*Soldiers' Pay*).

Never Be Afraid. See *Address to the graduating class of University High School, Oxford, Mississippi* under **Addresses by Faulkner.**

Newberry, Colonel G. W. A Yankee officer from an Illinois regiment, and one of the officers whose name Rosa Millard used on her forged papers to get horses and mules from the federal troops ("Riposte in Tertio" in *The Unvanquished*).

New Hope. A small settlement three miles from the Bundren home, where Anse Bundren's people were buried (*As I Lay Dying*).

New Market. A small settlement somewhere in Yoknapatawpha County (*The Town*).

New Orleans. A descriptive sketch published in *The Double*

Dealer, VII (Jan.-Feb. 1925), 102-107. Reprinted in *Salmagundi* and in *New Orleans Sketches* (ed. Collins). Contains eleven poeticized monologues: (1) Wealthy Jew, (2) The Priest, (3) Frankie and Johnny, (4) The Sailor, (5) The Cobbler, (6) The Longshoreman, (7) The Cop, (8) The Beggar, (9) The Artist, (10) Magdalen, and (11) The Tourist.

New Orleans Sketches.   A book published by Rutgers University Press, New Brunswick, 1958, with an introduction by Carvel Collins. It contains "New Orleans," from *The Double Dealer,* Jan.-Feb. 1925, and the sixteen sketches from the New Orleans *Times-Picayune* Sunday section, published there between Feb. 8 and Sept. 27, 1925. The sketches are: "Mirrors of Chartres Street," "Damon and Pythias Unlimited," "Home," "Jealousy," "Cheest," "Out of Nazareth," "The Kingdom of God," "The Rosary," "The Cobbler," "Chance," "Sunset," "The Kid Learns," "The Liar," "Episode," "Country Mice," and "Yo Ho and Two Bottles of Rum." Also a book published by the Hokuseido Press, Tokyo, 1955, edited by Ichiro Nishizaki. It contains thirteen of the sixteen sketches from the *Times-Picayune* Sunday section. Those omitted are: "The Liar," "Country Mice," and "Yo Ho and Two Bottles of Rum."

New Valois.   A city in Franciana, the setting of *Pylon.*

Nigger Hollow.   The Negro section of Jefferson, sometimes called "The Hollow."

Nightingale, Tug.   The son of the widowed cobbler of Jefferson. He joined the regiment formed by McLendon in 1917, for which his father kicked him out because he had joined the "Yankee" army. He was made a cook and sent to Europe, and did not return to Jefferson until 1919 (*The Mansion*).

Night in the Vieux Carré.   Section III of *Pylon.*

Night Piece.   A poem in *The New Republic,* LXXIV (Apr. 12, 1933), 253. Reprinted as *A Green Bough,* VII.

Nine Mile Branch Bridge.   A bridge on the road between Beat Four and Jefferson (*Intruder in the Dust*).

Nocturne.   A poem in *Ole Miss,* xxv, pp. 214-215. Reproduced in facsimile in James B. Meriwether, *The Literary Career of William Faulkner,* Princeton University Library, 1961, Pl. 2, and in

William Faulkner: Early Prose and Poetry, ed. Carvel Collins, pp. 82-83. This poem has a special interest because it covers a full double-face spread with borders and text designed by Faulkner. It begins on page 215 and is completed on page 214. Besides that, all the letters "s" are backward and the capital "N" has the diagonal running from bottom to top.

[Note] to *The Mansion*. An unnumbered page following the Contents of *The Mansion* contains a brief note on the Snopes trilogy, of which *The Mansion* is the final volume.

[Note] to *Requiem for a Nun, a Play*. An unnumbered page facing the copyright page of the play version of *Requiem for a Nun* by Ruth Ford contains a brief note about that version.

Notes on a Horsethief. A fragment published by the Levee Press, Greenville, Mississippi, 1950, in a limited signed edition of 975 copies. In a revised form it became pages 151-189 of *A Fable*. The revised form was printed as "Notes on a Horsethief" in *Vogue,* July 1954.

Notice [to hunters]. In the Oxford *Eagle,* Oct. 22, 1959, p. 7. The brief text is reprinted in *Time,* LXXIV (Nov. 2, 1959), 29. A humorous exhortation to hunters on his farm not to shoot his horses, his cow, or other hunters.

Noyades Street. A street in New Valois (*Pylon*).

Nunnery, Cedric. A five-year-old boy who was lost and whose disappearance caused the death of Eck Snopes when Eck carried a lighted lantern into an oil storage tank in search of the boy (*The Town*).

[margin handwritten note: Nunnery, Mrs. —]

O

[margin handwritten note: Odlethrop, Mrs. —]

Odlethrop, Stonewall Jackson. The real name of Monk, a twenty-five-year-old moron who came from the hill country in eastern Yoknapatawpha County. He was sent to prison for a murder he did not commit and then was executed for a murder he was not responsible for ("Monk" in *Knight's Gambit*).

Odor of Verbena, An.   The seventh and last story in *The Unvanquished*. Not before published. It is reprinted in *The Faulkner Reader* and *The Portable Faulkner*.

Odum, Cliff.   A farmer in the Frenchman's Bend region (*The Hamlet*).

Okataba County.   The county directly south of Yoknapatawpha County. Its county seat is Mottstown.

✗ **Old Ben.**   The name of the bear which had been hunted for years. He was killed by Boon Hogganbeck in 1883 ("The Bear" in *Go Down, Moses*).

Old Frenchman's Place, The.   The name given to the plantation originally settled by Louis Grenier in southeastern Yoknapatawpha County. The place was acquired by Will Varner sometime in the late nineteenth century. He gave it to Flem Snopes as a wedding gift, and Flem sold it to Odum Bookwright, Henry Armstid, and V. K. Ratliff, after salting the garden with silver dollars. In 1930 Lee Goodwin was living there making bootleg whiskey. The place is the setting for part of *The Hamlet* and *Sanctuary* and is referred to frequently elsewhere.

✗ **Old Het.**   See **Het.**

✗ **Old Hundred.**   One of the mules belonging to the Sartoris' which was taken by the federal troops and taken back to Granny Millard ("Retreat" in *The Unvanquished*).

Old Man.   The title given to the novelette which constitutes chapters 2, 4, 6, 8, and 10 of *The Wild Palms*. It is reprinted in *The Faulkner Reader, The Portable Faulkner,* and *Three Famous Short Novels*. The story was adapted for television by Horton Foote and presented on Playhouse 90 November 20, 1958, with Geraldine Page and Sterling Hayden. The text of the television production is published in Foote's *Three Plays,* New York: Harcourt, Brace & World, 1962, pp. 3-47. A selection from the story is read by Faulkner on Caedmon long playing record number TC-1035.

Old People, The. The fourth story in *Go Down, Moses*. First published in *Harper's Magazine*, Sept. 1940. It is reprinted in *Big Woods*. About Sam Fathers teaching Isaac McCaslin the lore of the woods and initiating him into the rites of hunting.

Old Wyottsport. A small settlement north of Jefferson on the river where Luther Biglin lived (*The Mansion*). This may be another name for Wyott's Crossing.

Oliver. The hired man on Faulkner's farm ("Afternoon of a Cow").

Once Aboard the Lugger. A short story in *Contempo*, I (Feb. 1, 1932), 1 and 4. Uncollected. A non-Yoknapatawpha story about the "I" of the story and a nineteen-year-old youth named Pete, a boat captain, and a Negro, who go out from New Orleans to an island reef to dig for buried treasure.

On Criticism. An article in *The Double Dealer*, VII (Jan.-Feb., 1925), 83-84. Reprinted in *Salmagundi* and in *William Faulkner: Early Prose and Poetry*, ed. Carvel Collins, pp. 109-112.

On Fear: The South in Labor. An article in *Harper's Magazine*, CCXII (June 1956), 29-34.

On Privacy. The American Dream: What Happened to It. See *Address at the University of Oregon* under **Addresses by Faulkner.**

Ord, Matt. A former flyer, holder of the world's land plane *Ord, Mrs.* — speed record. Now in the Ord-Atkinson Aircraft plant (*Pylon*).

Oscar. One of Roth Edmonds's lotmen ("The Fire and the Hearth" in *Go Down, Moses*).

Osgood. A member of the flight squadron commanded by Major Bridesman (*A Fable*).

Otis. The fourteen-year-old juvenile delinquent nephew of Everbe Corinthia (*The Reivers*).

Ott, Jimmy. A stunt flyer at the dedication airshow at the Feinman Airport (*Pylon*).

Otto. A friend of Johnny Gray ("The Kid Learns").

Out of Nazareth. A sketch in the New Orleans *Times-Picayune* Sunday section, Apr. 12, 1925, p. 4. Illustrated by William Spratling. Reprinted in *New Orleans Sketches* (ed. Collins).

Over the World's Rim. A poem in *The New Republic*, LXXIV (Apr. 12, 1933), 253. Reprinted as *A Green Bough*, XXVIII.

Owl-by-Night. One of the young Indians who sought Herman Basket's sister's hand until he discovered that Ikkemotubbe wanted her ("A Courtship").

P

Painter. A rancher living near Blizzard, Arizona ("Idyll in the Desert").

Pantaloon in Black. The third story in *Go Down, Moses*. First published in *Harper's Magazine*, Oct. 1940. This is the only story in the collection not about the McCaslin-Edmonds-Beauchamp families, and is related because Rider, the central character, lives on Roth Edmonds's land.

Paoli. The Italian fencing master who taught Max Harriss to fence ("Knight's Gambit").

Pap. A blind and deaf old man living with Lee Goodwin on the Old Frenchman's Place (*Sanctuary*).

Paralee. The mother of Aleck Sander (according to *Intruder in the Dust*). In *The Town* she is called Guster.

Parsham. The small Tennessee town where Colonel Linscomb lived and where the race was held. The Negroes called it Possum (*The Reivers*).

Pate, Lucy. The childhood sweetheart of Jack Houston, whom he married after his return from Texas. She was killed by a stallion (*The Hamlet*). In *The Town*, however, Jack's wife was the former Letty Bookwright.

Patterson, Mr. and Mrs. Neighbors of the Compsons who once sent Benjy some candy. Mrs. Patterson was carrying on an affair with Uncle Maury Bascomb (*The Sound and the Fury*).

Paul. A Breton; one of the twelve followers of the Corporal (*A Fable*).

Peabody, Doctor Lucius Quintus. As the name Whitfield is associated with Yoknapatawpha County churches, the name Peabody is associated with the practice of medicine in the county. A Doctor Peabody succeeds Doctor Habersham at the Chickasaw Agency before 1799, and is an important figure in the founding of Jefferson (*Requiem for a Nun*). Ab Snopes sends for a bottle of whiskey from Doc Peabody (*The Hamlet*). Quentin Compson recalls the fat Doc Peabody when he (Quentin) was a child (*The Sound and the Fury*). He is eighty-seven years old, weighs three hundred and ten pounds, was reported once to have proposed to Aunt Jenny Du Pre, and has a thirty-year-old son who is a surgeon in New York (*Sartoris*). He took care of the sick Addie Bundren (*As I Lay Dying*). He cared for Judge Allison before the judge died ("Beyond"). He warned Bayard Sartoris about his weak heart (*The Town*). His office was above Christian's drugstore (*The Reivers*).

Pearson, Mr. A federal investigator from Jackson, sent to the McCallum farm to arrest the twin sons of Buddy McCallum for not registering for the draft ("The Tall Men").

Peasants, The. Book IV of *The Hamlet*. It contains the expanded version of "Spotted Horses."

Peddlers Field Old Town. A section of Jefferson (*Intruder in the Dust*).

Peebles, E. E. A Negro lawyer in Memphis who took care of Joanna Burden's affairs (*Light in August*).

Pennsylvania Station. A short story in *Collected Stories*. First published in *The American Mercury*, Feb. 1934. A non-Yoknapatawpha story about an old man and a young man sitting in the station to keep warm and the story which the old man tells about his sister and her son.

✳Penny Wise. A race horse on which the beggar put five dollars and won two thousand, only to have it lost through a series of bad luck accidents ("Chance").

Percy Grimm. The title given to a selection from *Light in*

August which was reprinted in *The Faulkner Reader* and *The Portable Faulkner*.

~~Perry.~~   Bayard Sartoris III's pony (*Sartoris*).

Pete.   The younger brother (about twenty-five) of Red, the man whom Popeye had brought to the Memphis brothel to have affairs with Temple Drake. He had some letters Temple had written, and tried at first to blackmail her, but she fell in love with him and they planned to run away together (*Requiem for a Nun*). Also the nineteen-year-old brother of Joe, the man who hired a boat to seek the buried treasure. Pete got seasick on the trip and could not help dig ("Once Aboard the Lugger"). Also the Mexican servant in the San Antonio brothel where Harry went to get help about Charlotte's pregnancy (*The Wild Palms*). Also one of the companions of Jean-Baptiste ("Home").

Pettibone.   The wealthy Virginian to whose plantation Sutpen's father brought his family in 1817 (*Absalom, Absalom!*).

Pettigrew.   Judge Allison's lawyer who took care of the Judge's will ("Beyond").

Pettigrew, Thomas Jefferson.   The mail rider after whom the city of Jefferson was named (*Requiem for a Nun*).

Peyton, George.   A kennel owner who raised bird dogs (*The Reivers*).

Philadelphia.   "Philadelphy," the wife of Loosh (Lucius), a slave on the Sartoris plantation. Appears in *The Unvanquished* and "My Grandmother Millard."

Philip.   The assistant cashier in a Jefferson bank. Elly was engaged to him ("Elly").

Phoebe (Fibby).   The wife of Rocius (Roskus), and the mother of Thucydides. She was brought from Carolina by L. Q. L. McCaslin. When he died she was freed but she refused to leave. She died August 1, 1849 ("The Bear" in *Go Down, Moses*).

Picklock.   The nickname of one of the French soldiers who sold the body of an anonymous soldier to an old farm woman for a hundred francs so they could buy brandy. The name "Picklock" was derived from the soldier's "profession" before entering the army (*A Fable*).

Pinckski, Mr.   The man who sold Mrs. Gihon her casket on the installment plan ("Pennsylvania Station").

Pinkie.   The Negro cook at the Roger Howes home ("Artist at Home").

Pittman County.   A Mississippi county from which Deputy Warden Buckworth came ("Old Man" in *The Wild Palms*).   *Plockner*

Plex, Plexiglass.   See **Baddrington, Harold.**

Plump Convict, The.   The descriptive title given the second unnamed convict in "Old Man." He went on the rescue mission with the tall convict, but was soon lost from the boat and returned to the prison alone (*The Wild Palms*).

Point of Law, A.   A short story in *Collier's Magazine*, June 22, 1940. It was later incorporated into "The Fire and the Hearth" in *Go Down, Moses.*

Polcheck.   One of the twelve followers of the Corporal. He was the betrayer of the Corporal (*A Fable*).

Polemus, Mr.   The constable in Parsham (*The Reivers*).

Pomp.   A slave who belonged to Hightower's grandfather (*Light in August*).

Popeye.   A gangster who sold bootleg whiskey in Memphis. His real name was Vitelli. He was impotent, and raped Temple Drake with a corncob, after which he took her to a house of prostitution in Memphis. He was later hanged in Alabama for a crime he did not commit. Appears (only as Popeye) in *Sanctuary*. Is referred to (where the name Vitelli is given) in *Requiem for a Nun.*

Poplar, A.   A poem in *The Mississippian,* IX (Mar. 17, 1920), 7. Reprinted in Martha Mayes's "Faulkner Juvenilia," *New Campus Writing No. 2,* ed. Nolan Miller, pp, 137-138, and in *William Faulkner: Early Prose and Poetry,* ed. Carvel Collins, p. 60.

Portable Faulkner, The.   A collection published by the Viking Press, New York, 1946. Edited and with an Introduction by Malcolm Cowley. Contains the first publication of the "Appendix" to *The Sound and the Fury* and a map of Yoknapatawpha County newly drawn for the book. The book is divided into seven sections: 1. The Old People, containing "A Justice," "Wedding in the Rain" (Chapter II of *Absalom, Absalom!*), "Red

Leaves," and "Was" (from *Go Down, Moses*). 2. The Unvanquished, containing "Raid" (from *The Unvanquished*), "Wash," and "An Odor of Verbena" (from *The Unvanquished*). 3. The Last Wilderness, containing "The Bear" (from *Go Down, Moses*). 4. The Peasants, containing "Spotted Horses" (from *The Hamlet*). 5. The End of an Order, containing "That Evening Sun," "Ad Astra," "A Rose for Emily," and "Dilsey" (from *The Sound and the Fury*). 6. Mississippi Flood, containing "Old Man" (from *The Wild Palms*). 7. Modern Times, containing "Death Drag," "Uncle Bud and the Three Madams" (from *Sanctuary*), "Percy Grimm" (from *Light in August*), and "Delta Autumn" (from *Go Down, Moses*).

[handwritten: Porter on the Train]

Porterfield.   The town where Henry Stribling (Hakshaw) worked before he went to Jefferson ("Hair").

Portrait.   A poem in *The Double Dealer*, III (June 1922), 337. Reprinted in *Salmagundi* and in *William Faulkner: Early Prose and Poetry*, ed. Carvel Collins, pp. 99-100.

Pose.   One of the four men who claimed Lonnie Grinnup's body after he had been discovered drowned ("Hand Upon the Waters" in *Knight's Gambit*).

Possum.   The way the Negroes pronounced "Parsham" (*The Reivers*).

Potter, Jack.   A jockey; the narrator of "Cheest!"

Powell, John.   A Negro, the head hostler of the Priest livery stable (*The Reivers*).

Powers, Margaret.   The widow of a lieutenant killed in World War I. She helped take care of Donald Mahon, married him, and stayed with him until he died (*Soldiers' Pay*).

[handwritten: President of the U.S.]

Powers, Richard.   A young lieutenant, the husband of Margaret Powers. Three days after their marriage he went overseas, and was killed there by his own soldiers (*Soldiers' Pay*).

[handwritten: Price]
[handwritten: Priest Roman Catholic (1) (2)]

Priest, Alexander.   The baby brother of Lucius Priest (*The Reivers*).

Priest, Alison Lessep.   The wife of Maury Priest I and mother of Lucius (*The Reivers*).

Priest, Lessep.   A younger brother of Lucius Priest (*The Reivers*).

Priest, Lucius Quintus Carothers (Boss). A distant relative of the McCaslins, he came to Jefferson in 1865 from Carolina looking for his cousins. He married a granddaughter of old Lucius Quintus Carothers McCaslin named Sarah Edmonds in 1869. He was the father of Maury Priest I and was president of the Bank of Jefferson (*The Reivers*).

Priest, Lucius Quintus Carothers II. The son of Maury Priest I and grandson of old Lucius Quintus Carothers (Boss) Priest and great-great grandson of old McCaslin. He was eleven years old in 1905 and went on the escapade to Memphis with Boon Hogganbeck and Ned McCaslin and was the jockey in the race at Parsham. He narrates *The Reivers*.

Priest, Lucius Quintus Carothers III. While his last name may not be Priest, he is the grandson of Lucius Quintus Carothers Priest II, and the "you" to whom the story of *The Reivers* is related. He speaks the first two words of the novel.

Priest, Maurice. The husband of the former Sally Hampton, who used to go out with Grenier Weddel. When Weddel sent her a corsage, Priest got in a fight with him and then gave his wife a black eye (*The Town*).

Priest, Maury I. The son of Boss Priest and father of the narrator of *The Reivers*. He ran a livery stable in Jefferson.

Priest, Maury II. A younger brother of Lucius Priest (*The Reivers*).

Priest, Sarah Edmonds. The wife of Boss Priest and grandmother of young Lucius. She was born in 1854 and was a granddaughter of old Lucius Quintus Carothers McCaslin (*The Reivers*).

Prince. One of the Compsons' horses (*The Sound and the Fury*).

Pritchel, Wesley. An irascible farmer, the father of Joel Flint's wife. Flint killed him and then impersonated him ("An Error in Chemistry" in *Knight's Gambit*).

Provine, Lucius. A man about forty, known as "Luke" or "Butch," formerly the leader of a gang which used to terrorize the neighborhood. His family was supported by Major de Spain. He was cured of hiccups by Ratliff and Uncle Ash by having him frightened by the Indians. This is the person in "A Bear Hunt" as it is in the *Collected Stories*. In the version in *Big Woods* he is Lucius Hogganbeck.

Provine, Wilbur.   A moonshiner who was arrested and tried before Judge Long (*The Town*).

Pruitt, Mr.   The president of the Compress Association in Mottstown where Uncle Rodney worked, and from which he stole some bonds ("That Will Be Fine").

Pruitt, Rufus.   A neighbor of the Fentrys ("Tomorrow" in *Knight's Gambit*).

Punkin Creek.   A settlement near Frenchman's Bend (*The Mansion*).

Pylon.   A novel published by Harrison Smith and Robert Haas, New York, 1935. A non-Yoknapatawpha novel about stunt flyers. Contains the following sections: "Dedication of an Airport," "An Evening in New Valois," "Nights in the Vieux Carré," "Tomorrow," "And Tomorrow," "Lovesong of J. A. Prufrock," and "The Scavengers." A "pylon" is a structure which guides aviators and often marks the course in an air race. In 1957 the novel was made into a motion picture by Universal Pictures, directed by Douglas Sirk, and starring Rock Hudson, Robert Stack, Dorothy Malone, Jack Carson, and Robert Middleton. The motion picture title was "The Tarnished Angels."

Q

Queenie.   One of the Compson horses (*The Sound and the Fury*).

Quick, Ben.   A resident of the Frenchman's Bend region. In one account he is a farmer who raised goats (*The Hamlet*). In another account he is the owner of a sawmill ("Tomorrow" in

Knight's Gambit). In the former account the sawmill owner is called Lon Quick.

Quick, Isham. The son of Ben Quick. He discovered the body of Buck Thorpe ("Tomorrow" in *Knight's Gambit*).

Quick, Lon (Solon) I. The owner of the sawmill in French-man's Bend (*The Hamlet*), and the man who sold Jewel Bundren a horse descended from one of Flem Snopes' spotted horses (*As I Lay Dying*).

Quick, Lon (Solon) II. The son of Lon Quick I. He attended Addie Bundren's funeral (*As I Lay Dying*).

Quick, Solon. The constable in Frenchman's Bend in 1908 (*The Mansion*). Also a farmer in the Frenchman's Bend region around 1940. He drove the school bus. During the 1930s he tried to get in on WPA work until he discovered that he would have to get rid of his farm in order to do so ("Shingles for the Lord" and "Shall Not Perish").

Quick, Theron. One of the young men who courted Eula Varner. He was struck on the head with a buggy whip when he and some of the other young men tried to interfere with Eula and Hoake McCarron. As soon as Eula's engagement to Flem Snopes was announced, Theron and Herman Bookwright left town (*The Mansion*).

Quinn, Doctor. Reba Rivers' doctor, who took care of her and examined her girls (*Sanctuary*).

Quistenberry, Dink. A relative by marriage of the Snopeses who ran the Jefferson Hotel (formerly the Snopes Hotel) after I. O. Snopes had left town (*The Town*).

R

Race at Morning. A short story in *Big Woods*. First published in *The Saturday Evening Post*, Mar. 5, 1955. It is included in

Selected Short Stories. A hunting story, related to "Delta Autumn," in that Ike McCaslin, Roth Edmonds, Will Legate, and Walter Ewell appear in it, although the story centers not around them but around an orphan boy and Mister Ernest, his guardian.

Race's Splendor, The. A poem in *The New Republic,* LXXIV (Apr. 12, 1933), 253. Reprinted as *A Green Bough,* XXXVII.

Rachel. "Aunt Rachel," the mother (or foster mother) of Jesus ("That Evening Sun"). Also "Sister Rachel," the cook at the Harry Mitchell home (*Sartoris*).

Raid. The third story in *The Unvanquished.* First published in *The Saturday Evening Post,* Nov. 3, 1934. It is reprinted in *The Portable Faulkner.*

Ralph. Referred to as an uncle of the Rittenmeyer children (*The Wild Palms*).

Rambaud. The lake, part of which was filled in to make the Feinman Airport (*Pylon*).

Ratcliffe. The post trader at the Chickasaw Agency in 1833, at which time they decided on the name Jefferson. The name later became Ratliff (*Requiem for a Nun*).

Ratcliffe, Nelly. The great (or great great) grandmother of V. K. Ratliff (*The Mansion*).

Ratliff, V(ladimir) K(yrilytch). A sewing machine (and sometime parlor organ, radio, and television) salesman from Jefferson. Ratliff grew up on a farm his father rented from Anse Holland, and was a neighbor of the Snopes family. He had a partnership with a cousin, Grover Cleveland Winbush, in a sidestreet restaurant in Jefferson, which he lost to Flem Snopes. He lived with his sister and her family in Jefferson. He was descended from a Russian mercenary in the British Army during the Revolution, who was sent to Virginia when Burgoyne surrendered at Saratoga, escaped, and was kept hidden by a girl named Nelly Ratcliffe, on whom he fathered a child. No one knew his last name, but his first and second were Vladimir Kyrilytch, and a son in each generation bore those two names. The child was the Ratcliffe who went to Mississippi at the time Habersham, Holston, and Grenier did, and was the ancestor of the sewing machine salesman, V. K. Ratliff. Ratliff appears in "A Bear Hunt," *The Hamlet, The Town,* and *The Mansion* under that name. In *Sartoris, As I Lay Dying,* and two short stories ("Lizards in Jamshyd's Courtyard" and "Centaur in Brass"), both later rewritten, he is called V. K. Suratt. The name was changed to Ratliff because there was an actual person by the other name.

Reba, Miss. See **Rivers, Reba.**

Recordings. Faulkner made two long playing records reading from his own works. Caedmon record number TC-1035 contains the Nobel Prize Address and selections from "Old Man," *As I Lay Dying,* and *A Fable.* MGM record number E3617 ARC contains selections from *Light in August* and *The Sound and the Fury.*

Red. The young man Popeye brought to Temple Drake's room. He was later killed because he tried to help Temple escape (*Sanctuary*). In *Requiem for a Nun* he is referred to as Alabama Red.

Redlaw. See **Redmond, Ben J.**

Red Leaves. A short story in *Collected Stories.* First published in *The Saturday Evening Post,* Oct. 25, 1930. Reprinted in *These 13.* It is included in *The Portable Faulkner* and *Selected Short Stories.* Part was revised for the first interlude of *Big Woods.* An anachronistic story about the death of Issetibbeha.

Redmond, Ben J. A lawyer, a carpetbagger from Missouri who stayed in Jefferson and later became associated with Colonel Sartoris in building the railroad through Jefferson. He ran for the legislature against the Colonel, and when he was defeated he shot and killed the Colonel. He was later faced by the Colonel's son Bayard, at whom he shot and missed, and then left town and was not heard of again. In *Sartoris* he is referred to as Redlaw. In "An Odor of Verbena" (*The Unvanquished*) and *Requiem for a Nun* he appears as Redmond.

Reed, Susan. An orphan girl raised by the Burchett family in Jefferson. She grew up to become a young flirt and later a promiscuous young lady. She finally married Henry Stribling (Hawkshaw), the barber in Maxey's barbershop ("Hair").

Reeves. An able seaman on the vessel manned by Claude Hope and Ronnie Smith ("Turnabout").

Reichman, Mr. A New Orleans businessman to whom Major Ayers hoped to sell a line of laxatives (*Mosquitoes*).

Rinehardt. An automobile dealer for whom Buck Monaghan worked ("Honor").

Reivers, The. A novel published by Random House, New York, 1962. Subtitled "A Reminiscence." Dedicated to Victoria, Mark, Paul, William, Burks. About an escapade to Memphis by Boon Hogganbeck, Ned McCaslin, and the eleven-year-old Lucius Priest. The time of the action is 1905, although the story is being related in 1961. The story is related by the approximately sixty-seven-year-old Lucius to his young grandson of the same name. Pages 75-91 were preprinted in *The Saturday Evening Post*, Mar. 31, 1962, under the title "Hell Creek Crossing." Material between pages 95 and 161 was preprinted in *Esquire*, May 1962, under the title "The Education of Lucius Priest." "Reiver" is the Scottish variant of "reaver," an archaic word meaning raider—or robber, or plunderer—and refers to the three who stole (or "borrowed") first, the boy's grandfather's car, and then (through Bobo Beauchamp), Mr. van Tosch's horse. The word is pronounced "reever."

Remish. A tiny settlement near Frenchman's Bend. It was named for the Remish Musical Company of South Bend, Indiana, which manufactured parlor organs sold by Ratliff ("By the People"). In the revised version (in *The Mansion*) Remish does not appear.

Renaud's. A restaurant in New Valois (*Pylon*).

Renfro. A city not far from Jefferson where Hoke Christian was going to learn to fly his plane ("Uncle Willy").

Reno. One of the Negro musicians Bayard Sartoris, Hub, and Mitch took with them on their drinking spree (*Sartoris*).

Reporter, The. An unnamed newspaper reporter in New Valois who interested himself in Roger and Laverne Shumann and Jack Holmes, and through whose consciousness a great deal of their story is interpreted (*Pylon*). In connection with the Reporter Faulkner said: "There was one in *Pylon,* for instance, he was the central character in the book, he never did tell me who he was. I don't know until now what his name was. That was the reporter, he was a protagonist."

Requiem for a Nun. A novel published by Random House, New York, 1951. Cast in the form of a three-act play with a prose introduction to each act. The opening section—"The Courthouse"—is reprinted in *The Faulkner Reader.* Part of the second prose section—"The Golden Dome"—was revised for the prelude of *Big Woods.* The first and third prose sections sketch in some of the background history of Jefferson and Yoknapatawpha County. The second prose section is about Jackson, Mississippi's state capital. The play sections are a kind of sequel to *Sanctuary.* The title refers to Nancy Mannigoe, and, as Faulkner said, "it was paradoxical, the use of the word *Nun* for her, but I—but to me that added something to her tragedy." The novel was adapted for the stage by Ruth Ford.

Requiem for a Nun, a Play. A play published by Random House, New York, 1959. Adapted for the stage by Ruth Ford. The book has a short "note" by Faulkner. The play was first produced at the John Golden Theatre, New York, on January 28, 1959, with Bertice Reading, Ruth Ford, Scott McKay, Zachary Scott, House Jameson, Christian Flanders, and John Dorman.

Res. A cashier at the Sartoris bank (*Sartoris*).

Retreat. The second story in *The Unvanquished.* First published in *The Saturday Evening Post,* Oct. 13, 1934.

Reviews. See **Book Reviews.**

Rhodes, Miss. Young Lucius Priest's schoolteacher (*The Reivers*).

Richard. A Negro boy living at the MacCallum place (*Sartoris*)

Richardson, Doctor. The doctor at the hospital where Charlotte was taken after Harry had performed an unsuccessful operation on her (*The Wild Palms*).

Riddell. The family name of a highway engineer in Jefferson whose little boy got polio and as a result the school was closed (*The Town*).

Riddup. Mentioned in *The Hamlet* as one of the old family names in the Frenchman's Bend region.

Rideout, —

Rideout, Aaron. A cousin of V. K. Ratliff. He owned half of the sidestreet restaurant in Jefferson of which Ratliff owned the other half (*The Hamlet*). In *The Town* and *The Mansion* he becomes Grover Cleveland Winbush.

Rideout, Doctor. The doctor who took care of Mollie Beauchamp when she was sick ("The Fire and the Hearth" in *Go Down, Moses*).

Rider. A twenty-four-year-old Negro renter from Roth Edmonds and head of a timber gang at a local sawmill. When his six-months' bride Mannie died he became crazed with grief, killed a white man and was lynched ("Pantaloon in Black" in *Go Down, Moses*).

Ringo. The son of Simon, Colonel Sartoris' body servant while he was away at war, and the grandson of Joby and Louvinia. He was the constant companion of the young Bayard Sartoris, both being the same age. His real name was Marengo. Appears in *The Unvanquished* and "My Grandmother Millard."

Riposte in Tertio. The fourth story in *The Unvanquished*. First published in *The Saturday Evening Post,* Nov. 14, 1934, under the title "The Unvanquished."

Rittenmeyer, Ann. A daughter of Charlotte and Francis Rittenmeyer (*The Wild Palms*).

Rittenmeyer, Charlotte. The wife of Francis Rittenmeyer of New Orleans. She ran away with Harry Wilbourne, and died after he had performed an unsuccessful abortion on her (*The Wild Palms*).

Rittenmeyer, Charlotte II. A daughter of Charlotte and Francis Rittenmeyer (*The Wild Palms*).

Rittenmeyer, Francis ("Rat"). The husband of Charlotte Rittenmeyer (*The Wild Palms*).

Rivers, Lee. A young man from Charlestown, Georgia, who

went to Princeton. He was too young to have been in the war (*Soldiers' Pay*).

Rivers, Reba. The owner and madam of a house of prostitution in Memphis. It was to her place that Popeye took Temple Drake (*Sanctuary*), and where Virgil Snopes and Fonzo Winbush stayed (*Sanctuary* and *The Mansion*). It was also where Boon Hogganbeck and young Lucius Priest stayed (*The Reivers*). In *Requiem for a Nun* only the place is mentioned. Robert, Uncle

Robinson. MacWyrglinchbeath's fellow officer who flew with him. He was killed in a battle with German planes ("Thrift").

Rob Roy. The horse which Sutpen rode during the war ("Wash").

Robyn, Henry. The father of Patricia and Theodore Robyn. Referred to in *Mosquitoes*.

Robyn, Patricia. The eighteen-year-old niece of Mrs. Maurier and her guest on the yachting party. She eloped with the yacht's steward, David West (*Mosquitoes*).

Robyn, Theodore. The brother of Patricia Robyn, who called him "Josh" (*Mosquitoes*).

Rocius (Roskus). A slave brought by old Carothers McCaslin from Carolina. He had a wife Phoebe (Fibby) and a son Thucydides. When McCaslin died in 1837 he and his wife were freed but they refused to leave. He died on Jan. 12, 1841 ("The Bear" in *Go Down, Moses*). Also the real name of the husband of Dilsey. See **Roskus.**

Rockyford. One of the small settlements where Ratliff sold sewing machines (*The Mansion*).

Rodney. The uncle of the seven-year-old Georgie. He used to carry on affairs with married ladies in Jefferson and Mottstown ("That Will Be Fine").

Roebuck, John Wesley. A boyhood friend of Chick Mallison. He was once shot in the back by Ab Snopes when he was trying to steal watermelons (*The Town*).

Rogers, Deacon. The owner of a store and restaurant, known as Rogers' Café, where Bayard Sartoris and Rafe MacCallum went to drink and where Bayard and Hub returned later to get something to eat (*Sartoris*). Also where Jason Compson and Earl would eat when they were too busy to go home (*The Sound and the Fury*).

Rogers, Howard.   The pilot with whom Buck Monaghan used to do stunt flying ("Honor").

Rogers, Ken.   The sheriff who got Ek to help him ("The Liar").

Rogers, Mildred.   The wife of the pilot Howard Rogers. She carried on an affair with Buck Monaghan ("Honor").

Roosevelt and Taft.   Twin horses belonging to Bayard Sartoris II (*Sartoris*).

[margin handwriting: Ronnie / Rosa Coldfield II / Aunt]

Rosary, The.   A sketch in the New Orleans *Times-Picayune* Sunday section, May 3, 1925, p. 2. Reprinted in *New Orleans Sketches* (ed. Collins).

Rose for Emily, A.   A short story in *Collected Stories*. First published in *The Forum*, Apr. 1930. Reprinted in *These 13*. It is included in *The Faulkner Reader, The Portable Faulkner,* and *Selected Short Stories*. Not including student writing, this is Faulkner's first published short story. About Miss Emily Grierson of Jefferson and her hapless lover, Homer Barron. The title, said Faulkner, is "allegorical . . . the meaning was, here was a woman who had had a tragedy, an irrevocable tragedy and nothing could be done about it, and I pitied her and this was a salute, just as if you were to make a gesture, a salute, to anyone; to a woman you would hand a rose. . . ."

Rose Hill.   The name given to the Backus farm after it was turned into a showplace by the bootlegger Harriss (*The Mansion*).

Rosie.   The colored cook and housemaid at Georgie's home ("That Will Be Fine").

Roskus (Rocius).   The husband of Dilsey and father of Versh, Frony, and T. P. He died sometime in the 1920s. Appears in *The Sound and the Fury* and "A Justice." See also **Rocius.**

Ross, Frank.   The husband of Martha Ross ("The Brooch").

Ross, Martha.   A friend of Amy Boyd, with whom she used to go to dances on Saturday night ("The Brooch").

Rouncewell Boy, The.   A Jefferson high school athlete who used to drink Cokes with Linda Snopes at the Christian drugstore (*The Town* and *The Mansion*).

Rouncewell, Mr. The oil company agent in Jefferson (*The Reivers*).

Rouncewell, Mrs. A boardinghouse landlady in Jefferson to whose place the jury was moved in the trial of Bookwright for the murder of Buck Thorpe ("Tomorrow" in *Knight's Gambit*). The boardinghouse, we discover in *The Town* and *The Reivers*, is the Commercial Hotel, which Flem Snopes took over and renamed the Snopes Hotel, and which later became the Jefferson Hotel. We learn also, in *The Town*, that Mrs. Rouncewell ran a flower shop in Jefferson around 1912.

Rouncewell, Whit. The person who saw the robbers in Uncle Willy Christian's drugstore (*The Town*). He is probably "the Rouncewell boy," although this is not clear.

Rouncewell's. The store in Jefferson which Samuel Worsham Beauchamp robbed ("Go Down, Moses"). Whether this is Mrs. Rouncewell's flower shop is not clear.

✗ **Rover.** See **Grover.**

Roxanne. Aunt Roxanne, a slave of General Compson's during the Civil War ("My Grandmother Millard").

Roy. The boy friend of Jenny's friend Thelma Frances (*Mosquitoes*).

✗ **Ruby.** One of Bayard Sartoris' hunting dogs (*Sartoris*). *Remove, The*

Russell. A deputy sheriff of Okataba County (*Light in August*).

Russell, Ab. A farmer past whose place Jason Compson drove when he was trying to find young Quentin and the man with the red tie who had eloped with her (*The Sound and the Fury*).

Rust, Everbe Corinthia. A young English country girl whom George and Davy used to see when they went punting. Her father, Simon Rust, took care of the locks. She went mad from an apparition and died ("The Leg").

Rust, Jotham. The brother of Everbe Corinthia Rust. He deserted from the army in order to find his sister's betrayer. He attacked Davy, and was captured and punished ("The Leg").

Rust, Simon. The father of Everbe Corinthia Rust. He died not long after she did ("The Leg").

Ryan, Mr. and Mrs. A policeman and his wife in New Orleans whom Johnny Gray knew and at whose place he left the girl who had been attacked by Tony the Wop ("The Kid Learns").

S

Saddie. The daughter of Elnora, the Sartoris cook, and a sister of Isom ("There Was a Queen").

Saint Jules Avenue. A street in New Valois (*Pylon*).

Sales. A federal aviation inspector (*Pylon*).

Salmagundi. A book of three essays and five poems published by the Casanova Press, Milwaukee, 1932. Edited and with a Preface by Paul Romaine. This collection contains all of Faulkner's contributions to *The Double Dealer* and his first published poem. The three essays are "New Orleans," "On Criticism," and "Verse Old and Nascent: A Pilgrimage." The five poems are "The Faun," "Dying Gladiator," "Portrait," and "The Lilacs," all from *The Double Dealer,* and "L'Après-midi d'un Faune," from *The New Republic.* "The Lilacs" was later reprinted as *A Green Bough,* I. "New Orleans" was reprinted in *New Orleans Sketches* (ed. Collins). The other two essays and four poems were reprinted in *William Faulkner: Early Prose and Poetry,* ed. Carvel Collins. The back cover of the book reprints Hemingway's poem "Ultimately."

Salmon. A garageman in Mottstown who rented cars (*Light in August*).

Sam. Will Varner's colored servant (*The Hamlet*).

Samson. The hotel porter in Jefferson (*The Town*).

Samson, Rachel. The wife of the Samson of Samson's Bridge where the Bundrens stayed overnight because the bridge was washed out (*As I Lay Dying*).

Samson's Bridge. One of the bridges that was washed out in the flood when Anse Bundren tried to get to Jefferson with his *Samuel* wife's body (*As I Lay Dying*).

Sanctuary. A novel published by Jonathan Cape and Harrison Smith, New York, 1931. A reprint of the novel in 1932 in the Modern Library edition contains an Introduction by Faulkner. Chapter XXV is reprinted in *The Portable Faulkner* under the title "Uncle Bud and the Three Madams." About Temple Drake, Gowan Stevens, Popeye, and Lee Goodwin, with the setting the Old Frenchman's Place and Memphis. Horace and Narcissa Benbow, Miss Reba Rivers, and Clarence Snopes are also among the characters. The title, said Faulkner, means "that everyone must have some safe secure place to which he can hurry, run, from trouble." In 1932 the novel was made into a motion picture by Paramount, directed by Stephen Roberts and starring Miriam Hopkins and Jack LaRue, under the title, "The Story of Temple Drake." In 1960 it was remade into a motion picture by 20th Century-Fox, directed by Tony Richardson and starring Lee Remick and Yves Montand.

Sanctuary and Requiem for a Nun. In 1954 the two novels were printed together in a paperback edition as a Signet book, *Sande, Earl* published by the New American Library. *Sander, Mark*

Sapphics. A poem in *The Mississippian*, IX (Nov. 26, 1919), 3. Reprinted in *William Faulkner: Early Prose and Poetry,* ed. Carvel Collins, pp. 51-52.

Sarah. The first name of Georgie's mother and the wife of George, a livery stable owner in Jefferson ("That Will Be Fine").

Sartoris. A novel published by Harcourt, Brace and Company, New York, 1929. Dedicated to Sherwood Anderson. About the Sartoris family, especially around 1919-1920. This is Faulkner's first published novel in the Yoknapatawpha series.

Sartoris, Bayard I. The brother of Colonel John Sartoris. He was born around 1838 and was a soldier in the Civil War. He was killed in 1862 by a Union Army cook when he tried to "capture" some anchovies from the army mess. Referred to in "An Odor of Verbena" (*The Unvanquished*) and *Sartoris*. The name "Bayard" means a gentleman of great courage and honor, and derives from the knight the Chevalier Bayard (1473?-1524), who was "sans peur at sans reproche." The name spelled with a small letter, however, also means a stupid or blindly reckless person.

Sartoris, Bayard II.   The son of Colonel John Sartoris. He was born around 1852 at the Sartoris plantation, four miles north of Jefferson. During the Civil War he was engaged in a number of exciting adventures along with his Negro companion Ringo and ran down and killed the man Grumby who had murdered his grandmother. He later studied law at Oxford, Mississippi. He married and had one son, John, who died in 1901. He became mayor of Jefferson around 1894 and a few years later established the Merchants and Farmers Bank in Jefferson. He died of a heart attack in December 1919 while on a wild automobile ride with his grandson Bayard III. Appears in *The Unvanquished*, "My Grandmother Millard" (both of which he relates), and *Sartoris*. Is referred to in "A Rose for Emily," "There Was a Queen," "The Bear," *The Hamlet, Requiem for a Nun, The Town, The Mansion,* and *The Reivers*.

Sartoris, Bayard III.   The son of John Sartoris II, grandson of Bayard Sartoris II, and twin brother of John Sartoris III. He was born on March 16, 1893. He studied at the University of Virginia, and then taught flying at a Memphis school, where he met and married Caroline White. She and a newborn child died on October 27, 1918, while Bayard was overseas as a flyer with the Canadian Air Corps. When he returned home he married Narcissa Benbow. He was killed testing a defective airplane at Akron, Ohio, June 11, 1920, the same day his son was born. Appears in *Sartoris* and "Ad Astra." Is referred to in "There Was a Queen," *Requiem for a Nun, The Town,* and *The Mansion*.

Sartoris, Benbow.   The son of Bayard Sartoris III and Narcissa Benbow. He was born on June 11, 1920, the day his father was killed in a plane crash. In 1942 he became an officer in the United

States Army and was on a secret mission in England. Appears in *Sartoris*, *Sanctuary*, and "There Was a Queen." Is referred to in "Knight's Gambit," *The Town*, and *The Mansion*.

Sartoris, Colonel John. The first of the Sartorises in Yoknapatawpha County. He was born in Carolina in 1823 and reported to have arrived in Jefferson around 1837, where he built a large plantation home four miles north of the city. He married a Millard girl and had, according to one report (*Sartoris*), two daughters and a son, but according to another (*The Unvanquished*), only a son. During the Civil War he recruited a regiment in Yoknapatawpha County and became a colonel. A year later he was demoted and his place was taken by Thomas Sutpen. He remarried in 1865, a cousin of his first wife, a girl named Drusilla Hawk. He killed two carpetbaggers who were trying to take over the county, and became a leader in the county during the Reconstruction period. He built a railroad in the county, and when it was finished (in 1876) he ran for Congress. He was shot and killed by his partner in the railroad enterprise, Ben J. Redmond, on September 4, 1876. Appears in *The Unvanquished* and *Requiem for a Nun*. Is referred to in "My Grandmother Millard," *Light in August, Sartoris, The Sound and the Fury, The Hamlet, Absalom, Absalom!*, "Barn Burning," "Shall Not Perish," "There Was a Queen," *The Town*, and *The Reivers*.

Sartoris, John II. The son of Bayard Sartoris II, and the father of the twins Bayard III and John III. He married a girl named Lucy Cranston. He had been wounded in the Spanish-American War and died of yellow fever in 1901. Is referred to in *Sartoris*, "There Was a Queen," and (merely as Bayard Sartoris' son) in "The Bear" (*Go Down, Moses*).

Sartoris, John III. The son of John Sartoris II and a twin brother of Bayard Sartoris III. He was born on March 16, 1893. He went to Princeton and then joined the Canadian Air Corps and was killed in action on July 5, 1918. Appears in "All the Dead Pilots." Is referred to in *Sartoris*, "There Was a Queen," *The Town*, and *The Mansion*.

Sartoris, Narcissa Benbow. The sister of Horace Benbow. She married Bayard Sartoris III in 1919 when she was twenty-six. They had one son, Benbow Sartoris, who was born on June 11, 1920. She was involved in a situation concerning some love letters sent to her anonymously by Byron Snopes and later stolen back by him, and in 1930 she had to give herself to a federal investigator in order to get the letters back. After the Sartorises had all died she remained on the old plantation with her son. Appears in *Sartoris, Sanctuary,* and "There Was a Queen." Is referred to in *The Town.*

✻ **Sartoris, Mrs. Virginia.**   The name Aunt Jennie Du Pre was called in "All the Dead Pilots."

Sartoris Bank, The.   See **Merchants and Farmers Bank.**

Sartoris Rifles.   A company organized by Captain McLendon in 1917 (*The Mansion*).

Satyricon in Starlight.   The title of a book of poems read by Dawson Fairchild (*Mosquitoes*).

Saunders, Cecily.   A young lady of Charlestown, Georgia, engaged to Donald Mahon. She lost her virginity to a fellow named George Farr and then married him (*Soldiers' Pay*).

Saunders, Minnie.   The mother of Cecily Saunders (*Soldiers' Pay*).

Saunders, Robert I.   The father of Cecily Saunders (*Soldiers' Pay*).

Saunders, Robert II.   The young brother of Cecily Saunders. He used to spy on Joe Gilligan and Margaret Powers (*Soldiers' Pay*).

Savoy Hotel, The.   A sidestreet hotel in Jefferson where Mrs. Mink Snopes worked while her husband was in jail awaiting trial for murdering Jack Houston (*The Hamlet*).

Scavengers, The.   The seventh and last section of *Pylon.*

Schluss.   A travelling salesman for women's garments on the same train with Joe Gilligan and Donald Mahon. The conductor got him to watch the drunken soldiers, and he proceeded to get himself drunk on the whiskey they proffered him (*Soldiers' Pay*).

Schofield, Doctor.   A Jefferson doctor who came out to see about Buddy McCallum's injured leg ("The Tall Men").

Schultz, Reverend. The minister who tried to cure Uncle Willy Christian of taking dope ("Uncle Willy").

Secretary. A colored boy Hoke Christian got to drive for him ("Uncle Willy").

Selected Short Stories of William Faulkner. Published by The Modern Library, New York, 1962. Contains 13 stories: "Barn Burning," "Two Soldiers," "A Rose for Emily," "Dry September," "That Evening Sun," "Red Leaves," "Lo!," "Turnabout," "Honor," "There Was a Queen," "Mountain Victory," and "Beyond," all reprinted from the *Collected Stories*, and "Race at Morning," reprinted from *Big Woods*.

Seminary, The. Apparently another name for the Academy. In *The Town* we are told that Linda Snopes went to the Academy after she finished high school. When referring to it in *The Mansion* Ratliff calls it the Seminary.

Seminary Hill. A small settlement near Jefferson where a man named Garraway had a store (*The Town*).

Semiramis. A nickname that Quentin Compson and Shreve applied to Mrs. Bland (*The Sound and the Fury*). Semiramis was a legendary Assyrian queen of great wisdom and beauty, and reputedly the founder of Babylon.

Semmes, Mr. A dealer in Memphis to whose place Boon Hogganbeck and Ike McCaslin went to get whiskey ("The Bear" in *Go Down, Moses*).

Sepulture South: Gaslight. An article in *Harper's Bazaar*, LXXXVIII (Dec. 1954), 84, 140 and 141. A reminiscent piece about the death and funeral of Faulkner's grandfather.

Shall Not Perish. A short story in *Collected Stories*. First published in *Story*, XXIII (July-Aug. 1943), 40-47. About the Grier family, a sequel to "Two Soldiers." The story was adapted for television by Faulkner and performed on the "Video Theatre," CBS, February 11, 1954, with Fay Bainter and Raymond Burr.

Sharp, Sam. The travelling photographer who had intentions not the most honorable toward Laura Jerico ("The Graduation Dress").

Shegog, Reverend. A preacher from St. Louis who preached in the Negro church in Jefferson on Easter Sunday, April 8, 1928 (*The Sound and the Fury*).

Sherwood Anderson. A critical essay in the Dallas *Morning News,* Apr. 26, 1925, Part III, p. 7. Reprinted in the *Princeton University Library Chronicle,* XVIII (Spring 1957), 89-94.

Sherwood Anderson: An Appreciation. An article in *The Atlantic Monthly,* CXCI (June 1953), 27-29.

Sherwood Anderson & Other Famous Creoles: A Gallery of Contemporary New Orleans. A book of drawings by William Spratling, arranged and with a Foreword by Faulkner. The brief Foreword is a parody of Anderson's style. Published by the Pelican Bookshop Press, New Orleans, 1926. The text of the Foreword is reprinted in *The Tangled Fire of William Faulkner,* by William Van O'Connor, Minneapolis: The University of Minnesota Press, 1954, pp. 22-23.

Shingles for the Lord. A short story in *Collected Stories.* First published in *The Saturday Evening Post,* Feb. 13, 1943. It is reprinted in *The Faulkner Reader.* About the farmers of French-man's Bend around 1940, and especially the Res Grier family. Related to "Two Soldiers" and "Shall Not Perish."

Ship of Night, The. A poem in *The New Republic,* LXXIV (Apr. 19, 1933), 272. Reprinted as *A Green Bough,* XXXIV.

Short, Herman. A farmer from Beat Four who got a horse from Pat Stamper and sold it to Beasley Kemp, who in turn traded it to Ab Snopes (*The Hamlet*).

Shumann, Dr. Carl. The father of Roger Shumann. He lived in Myron, Ohio (*Pylon*).

Shumann, Jack. The son of Laverne Shumann. His father was either Roger Shumann or Jack Holmes; no one knew which, since both men shared Laverne (*Pylon*).

Shumann, Laverne. The wife of Roger Shumann and the mother of Jack (*Pylon*).

Shumann, Roger. A stunt flyer, the husband of Laverne. He was killed flying a defective plane at the Feinman Airport (*Pylon*).

Sibleigh. One of the flight commanders in Major Bridesman's command (*A Fable*).

Sickymo. An ex-slave of a Jefferson doctor. He became a United States marshal in Jefferson during Reconstruction days, attaining his high office because his half-white sister was the mistress of the Federal A.P.M. ("The Bear" in *Go Down, Moses*).

Simmons. The caretaker of the old opera house in Jefferson where were stored the papers of the old Merchants' and Farmers' Bank, and where Jason Compson got out-of-town check blanks which he used to fool his mother about the money Caddy sent for the support of young Quentin (*The Sound and the Fury*).

Simms. The owner of the sawmill in Jefferson where Byron Bunch, Joe Christmas, and Joe Brown worked (*Light in August*).

Simon. The son of Joby and the father of Ringo. He went with Colonel Sartoris during the war (*The Unvanquished*). Also the camp cook ("Race at Morning"). See also **Strother, Simon.**

Simpson. The family name of some people who made whiskey ("The Liar").

Sivgut. A rude camp built forty miles from Blizzard, Arizona, by the Blizzard Chamber of Commerce for tubercular patients ("Idyll in the Desert").

Skipworth. The constable in Beat Four. Lucas Beauchamp was held at his home before being taken to the jail in Jefferson (*Intruder in the Dust*).

Skirmish at Sartoris. The sixth story in *The Unvanquished*. First published in *Scribner's Magazine*, April 1935.

Smith, Lieutenant. A British guard whom the runner knocked out with the flat side of his pistol when the runner and the Rev. Tobe Sutterfield went to get the sentry out of the guardhouse (*A Fable*).

Smith, McKinley. An ex-Marine corporal from east Texas. He married Essie Meadowfill (*The Mansion*).

Smith, Mrs. The switchboard operator at the clinic in Memphis where Bayard Sartoris II went to have the blemish removed from his face (*Sartoris*).

Smith, R. Boyce (Ronnie). A midshipman in the British Navy who piloted the boat on which Claude Hope manned the torpedoes ("Turnabout").

Smitty.   A feature editor on Hagood's paper (*Pylon*).

Smoke.   The first story in *Knight's Gambit*. First published in *Harper's Magazine*, April 1932. Reprinted in *Doctor Martino and Other Stories*. About the deaths of Anse Holland and Judge Dukinfield. The story was adapted for television by Gore Vidal and performed on CBS "Suspense" May 4, 1954, with E. G. Marshall, Pat Hingle, Bart Burns, George Mitchell, G. Albert Smith, and Kenny Delmar. The text of the television production is printed in Vidal's *Visit to a Small Planet and Other Television Plays,* Boston: Little, Brown and Co., 1956, pp. 219-233.

Snopes.   The title of the trilogy consisting of *The Hamlet, The Town,* and *The Mansion.*

Snopes.   There was a Snopes with no given first name, known as a nephew of Flem, who ran a farm in the Frenchman's Bend region around 1930. He appears in *As I Lay Dying.* Another Snopes, also a farmer with no given first name (and perhaps the same one), was living there around 1940. He appears in "Shingles for the Lord." Since the only known brother of Flem was Colonel Sartoris Snopes, who ran away as a child and was not heard of again, the farmer was not likely a nephew of Flem's.

Snopes, Abner (Ab).   The first of the Snopeses. As a young man he stayed around the Sartoris plantation, helping out while the Colonel was away at war. He took the horses and mules which Granny Millard got away from the federal troops to Memphis, to resell back to the Union Army. Colonel Sartoris was reported to have shot him in the foot for trying to steal his horse. Ab hid out in Beat Four until the Colonel was killed, and then rented from a Mr. Harris in Grenier County, and burned his barn. Later, while renting from Major de Spain, he ruined a valuable rug belonging to the Major, and when the Major attempted to exact payment he burned the Major's barn. Next he rented from the McCaslins, and around 1902 he appeared in Frenchman's Bend to rent from Will Varner. He was twice married, first to a Jefferson girl named Vynie, and then to a

woman he called Lennie, who bore him four children, Flem,
Colonel Sartoris (Sarty), and twin girls. Around 1910 he moved
to a small garden farm outside Jefferson, where he raised watermelons and kept off the boys with a shotgun until around 1925
when he shot a boy in the back and was ordered by the sheriff
not to use his gun again. Appears in *The Unvanquished,* "My
Grandmother Millard," "Barn Burning," *The Hamlet, The
Town,* and *The Mansion.*

Snopes, Admiral Dewey. The younger son of Eck Snopes.
Appears in *The Town.* Is referred to in *The Mansion* and (not
by name) in *The Hamlet.*

Snopes, Bilbo. A twin (with Vardaman) son of I. O. Snopes
by his second wife. When Ab and his old maid daughter moved
to near Jefferson in 1910 the twins went with them. Appears in
The Town and *The Mansion.*

Snopes, Byron. The son of Wesley Snopes and a brother of
Virgil. He was sent to business school in Memphis by Bayard
Sartoris and then became a bookkeeper in the Sartoris bank. He
used to write anonymous love letters to Narcissa Benbow, and
when she married Bayard Sartoris III he stole the letters back,
embezzled some money from the bank, and disappeared. He
fled to Mexico, and nothing was heard of him for ten years,
when Flem received by express four of his halfbreed children.
Appears in *Sartoris* and *The Town.* Is referred to in *The
Mansion* and (not by name) in "There Was a Queen."

Snopes, Clarence (Egglestone). A son of I. O. Snopes by his
second wife. He became a state senator from Yoknapatawpha
County after having been a constable in Beat Two, and later
ran for United States representative, but was withdrawn from
the race by Will Varner after an incident involving the neighborhood dogs. Appears in *Sanctuary, The Town,* and *The Mansion.*

Snopes, Colonel Sartoris (Sarty). The younger son of Ab
Snopes. When his father burned Mr. Harris' barn he was so
upset that when his father set out to burn Major de Spain's
barn he tried to warn the Major, and then ran away. He was

not heard of again. Appears in "Barn Burning." Is referred to (not by name) in *The Hamlet.*

Snopes, Doris. Purportedly the youngest brother of Clarence Snopes. He is referred to only once, in *The Mansion,* and then in connection with an episode that in *The Town* involved Clarence himself—that of being tied to a tree and having a fire set around him by Byron Snopes's halfbreed children.

Snopes, Eckrum (Eck). A cousin of Flem Snopes and a nephew of I. O. Snopes. He had married when he was sixteen and had a son which he did not name for about ten years. That was Wallstreet Panic Snopes. He married a second time and was supposed to have had three more children, but only one of them, Admiral Dewey, is mentioned later. After Flem Snopes became superintendent of the Jefferson power plant, Eck moved in from Frenchman's Bend (where he had been blacksmith and then manager of the sawmill) and took over the restaurant. He was too honest for the job, though, so Flem got rid of him. He next became the night watchman of some oil storage tanks, and in 1917 was killed in an explosion when he carried a lighted lantern into one of the tanks in search of a lost little boy. Appears in *The Hamlet* and *The Town.* Is referred to in *The Mansion.*

Snopes, Eula Varner. See **Varner, Eula.**

Snopes, Flem. The eldest son of Ab Snopes. He arrived in Frenchman's Bend in 1902 and got a job in the Varner store. Soon he had all his relatives working in and around Frenchman's Bend. Through various financial operations—lending money, buying and selling, etc.—he made money. He married the pregnant daughter of Will Varner (Flem himself was impotent) and got the Old Frenchman's Place as a wedding gift from his father-in-law. He sold it by trickery and moved to Jefferson where he began as a part-owner of a restaurant. Soon he was superintendent of the municipal water works, and in 1919 became vice-president of the Merchants and Farmers Bank of Jefferson. He succeeded to the presidency of the bank in 1927, after his wife committed suicide and his predecessor (and his wife's lover) left town. In 1946 he was killed by Mink Snopes, who for some thirty-eight years had nursed a grudge against him. Appears in *Sartoris, The Hamlet, The Town* and *The Mansion.* Is referred to in *As I Lay Dying* and *The Reivers* and (not by name) in "Barn Burning."

Snopes, I. O. Another Snopes of undetermined relationship. He appeared in Frenchman's Bend shortly after Flem did and took over the blacksmith shop when Eck became manager of the sawmill. He was no blacksmith, so when the young teacher Labove left he took over the teaching position in Frenchman's Bend. He married a relative of Mrs. Vernon Tull and had three children, Clarence and the twins Bilbo and Vardaman. But meanwhile a first wife and a five-year-old son appeared on the scene. The son was named Montgomery Ward Snopes. I. O. succeeded Eck Snopes in the restaurant in Jefferson and later was engaged in buying and selling mules until he conceived the idea of having the mules tied to the railroad at a blind curve so the freight trains would strike and kill them and the railroad would have to compensate him. This lasted until the man working for him was also killed, after which Flem made I. O. leave Jefferson. Appears in *The Sound and the Fury, The Hamlet,* and *The Town.* Is referred to in *The Mansion.*

Snopes, Isaac (Ike). A cousin of the Snopes clan, a twenty-one-year-old idiot. He used to help Mrs. Littlejohn at her hotel in Frenchman's Bend. He fell in love with a cow belonging to Jack Houston, and Houston gave him the cow, which he kept in a barn back of the Littlejohn Hotel. When Ratliff discovered that people were watching him make love to the cow, he made the other Snopeses get rid of it. Eck Snopes then bought Ike a toy cow to play with (*The Hamlet*).

Snopes, Launcelot (Lump). A Snopes cousin. He took Flem's place in the Varner store when Flem's operations got too extensive for such limiting activities. Appears in *The Hamlet.* Is referred to in *The Mansion.*

Snopes, Lennie. Ab Snopes's second wife, the mother of his children. Appears in "Barn Burning" and (not by name) in *The Hamlet.*

Snopes, Linda. No Snopes at all, but the illegitimate daughter of Eula Varner Snopes and Hoake McCarron. She grew up in Jefferson, attended high school there, and after a short while at the Academy she went to the University of Mississippi. After her mother committed suicide she went to Greenwich Village in New York, where she met a Jewish sculptor named Barton Kohl and lived with him. When the Civil War broke out in Spain they got married and went there to help the Loyalists. Barton was killed and Linda was in an accident which made her deaf. She returned to Jefferson and lived with her stepfather except for a period during World War II when she worked in a defense plant in Pascagoula. She was instrumental in getting Mink Snopes released from the penitentiary in 1946 and after he killed Flem she left Jefferson. Appears in *The Town* and *The Mansion.*

Snopes, Mink. Another Snopes cousin. He was a farmer in Frenchman's Bend. In 1908 he killed Jack Houston for impounding one of his stray cows and was sent to the penitentiary. Because Flem did not show up at the trial to help him he vowed revenge, and in 1923, when he was eligible for release Flem manipulated affairs to have Montgomery Ward Snopes sent to the penitentiary to talk Mink into attempting to escape, which he did, and which got him another twenty-five years. He finally was released in 1946, whereupon he proceeded to carry out his revenge by shooting Flem. He was given money by Linda Snopes Kohl, which was delivered to him by Gavin Stevens and Ratliff, after which he left the county. Appears in *The Hamlet* and *The Mansion.* Is referred to in *The Town.*

Snopes, Montgomery Ward. The eldest son of I. O. Snopes, a child of the first wife. During World War I he went to France with Gavin Stevens to work for the Y. M. C. A. He turned the canteen in which he was working into a brothel for soldiers, and when a stop was put to that he went to Paris and opened another one. He returned to Jefferson after the war and opened a photography shop. It was not long before all of his business seemed to be nighttime business, and it was discovered that he was doing a profitable traffic by reproducing French postcards. He was arrested on a charge of possessing pornography, but before the trial Flem Snopes substituted illegal whiskey for the developing fluid in his shop so that he would be tried on a state offense instead of a federal offense and thereby be sent to the state penitentiary where he could get Mink Snopes to attempt to escape. For this, of course, Flem paid him, and the sentence was for only two years. When he left prison he went to Los Angeles, where he was reported to be doing well in the motion picture industry. Appears in *The Town* and *The Mansion* (part of the latter he relates). Is referred to in *Sartoris*.

Snopes, Net.   One of the twin daughters of Ab Snopes. Appears in "Barn Burning" and (not by name) in *The Hamlet*. Whether she is the daughter who moved with Ab in 1910 to a farm outside Jefferson is not known.

Snopes, Orestes (Res).   A Snopes imported to Jefferson by Flem in the 1940s to "manage" the old Compson place, which Flem was turning into a housing subdivision (*The Mansion*).

Snopes, St. Elmo.   An unidentified son of I. O. Snopes. Is referred to only in *The Hamlet*.

Snopes, Vardaman.   A twin (with Bilbo) son of I. O. Snopes by his second wife. When Ab and his old maid daughter moved to near Jefferson in 1910 the twins went with them. Appears in *The Town* and *The Mansion*.

Snopes, Virgil.   The son of Wesley Snopes and a younger brother of Byron. He went to Memphis to barber school with Fonzo Winbush and they stayed at Miss Reba Rivers' place, which they took for a boarding house. Virgil became famous in Memphis brothel circles for his sexual prowess. Appears in *Sanctuary* and *The Mansion*. Is referred to in *The Town*.

Snopes, Vynie.   Ab Snopes's first wife, a girl from Jefferson. They had no children (*The Hamlet*).

Snopes, Wallstreet Panic (Wall).   The son of Eck Snopes by his first marriage. He was not named until he was about ten years old, and then so named by I. O. Snopes in the hope that he might become rich like those people who ran the Wallstreet panic. The charm evidently worked, for Wallstreet took the insurance money from his father's fatal accident, bought part interest in a grocery in Jefferson, soon bought out his partner, and opened the first supermarket in the town. From there he went on into the wholesale business, and by the 1940s he was situated in Memphis, the head of a large wholesale grocery chain. Appears in *The Hamlet, The Town,* and *The Mansion.*

Snopes, Watkins Products (Wat). Another of Flem Snopes's imports to Jefferson. Wat was a carpenter and he was in charge of remodelling the old de Spain house for Flem. Later he was in charge of the building of the subdivision out of the old Compson place (*The Mansion*).

Snopes, Wesley. The father of Byron and Virgil Snopes. He took I. O. Snopes's place as schoolteacher in Frenchman's Bend. He used to sing at revival meetings until he was caught with a fourteen-year-old girl in an empty cotton house, after which he was tarred and feathered and run out of town. He appears (but not by name) in *The Town.* He is referred to (where his name is given) in *The Mansion.*

Snopes, Yettie. Mrs. Mink Snopes. She appears (as Mrs. Snopes) in *The Hamlet.* She is referred to as Yettie in *The Mansion.*

Snopes Hotel, The. When Flem Snopes took over the Commercial Hotel in Jefferson around 1910 or so, he renamed it the Snopes Hotel. When he sold it in the 1920s it was renamed the Jefferson Hotel (*The Town* and *The Reivers*).

Sol. The porter at the depot in Jefferson who carried Horace Benbow's bags (*Sartoris*).

Soldiers' Pay. A novel published by Boni and Liveright, New York, 1926. A non-Yoknapatawpha novel set in Charlestown, Georgia, concerning the return home of the wounded veteran Donald Mahon. This is Faulkner's first published novel.

Sometimes-Wakeup. The brother of Issetibbeha, next in line for the chieftainship of the Chickasaws after Issetibbeha and his

son Moketubbe died. He refused the chieftainship, so Ikkemotubbe became chief ("A Justice").

Sothey. A dog belonging to the McCaslins ("Was" in *Go
Down, Moses*).

Sound and the Fury, The. A novel published by Jonathan
Cape and Harrison Smith, New York, 1929. About the Compson
family, especially the children of Jason Richmond Compson.
The time covered is only four different days, June 2, 1910, and
April 6, 7, and 8, 1928, but in retrospect the period from about
1898 to 1928 is covered. The complete novel (with Appendix) is
reprinted in *The Faulkner Reader*. Part of section four was
reprinted in *The Portable Faulkner* under the title "Dilsey."
Two selections from the novel are read by Faulkner on MGM
long playing record number E3617 ARC. The title is from Act
V of *Macbeth:* "It is a tale/Told by an idiot, full of sound and
fury,/Signifying nothing." The definite articles were added, said
Faulkner, for emphasis and rhythm. The novel was adapted
for television by William F. Durkee, Jr. and presented on NBC
"Playwrights '56," Dec. 6, 1955, with Franchot Tone, Lillian
Gish, Ethel Waters, and Valerie Bettis. In 1959 the novel was
made into a motion picture by 20th Century-Fox, directed by
Martin Ritt, and starring Yul Brunner and Joanne Woodward.

Sound and the Fury, The, & As I Lay Dying. In 1946 the
two novels were published in one volume by Random House in
the Modern Library series. *The Sound and the Fury* contains
the Appendix "as a Foreword." When asked if there was "any
particular reason" for the two novels being published in one
volume, Faulkner replied that "together [they] made exactly
enough pages to make a proper-sized book that the publisher
could charge the regulation price on."

Speeches. See **Addressess by Faulkner.**

Spilmer. A farmer, a neighbor of Mrs. Hait (*The Town*).

Spintrius. See **Brownlee, Percival.** (A *spintria* was a male
prostitute, so called from the group of sexual perverts known as
the *Spintriae,* which Tiberius kept for his entertainment.)

Spoade. A senior at Harvard from South Carolina whom

Quentin Compson knew (*The Sound and the Fury*). Also presumably, his son, a student from Charleston, South Carolina, at Harvard in 1937, and a friend of Chick Mallison. His father, said Chick, had been at Harvard in 1909 with Gavin Stevens (*The Mansion*).

Spoomer. A Guards' Captain in the R.A.F. He and John Sartoris used to fight over British and French girls ("All the Dead Pilots").

Spoot. The childhood nickname of Rider ("Pantaloon in Black" in *Go Down, Moses*).

Spotted Horses. A short story in *Scribner's Magazine*, LXXXIX (June 1931), 585-597. Rewritten for *The Hamlet*. The rewritten version is reprinted in *The Faulkner Reader*, *The Portable Faulkner*, and *Three Famous Short Novels*.

Spring. A poem in *Contempo*, I (Feb. 1, 1932), 2. Reprinted as *A Green Bough*, XXXVI.

Stamper, Pat. A fabulous horse trader known all over the South. He once got the best of Ab Snopes in a horsetrading deal. Later Tug Nightingale worked for him (*The Hamlet* and *The Mansion*).

Starnes, Joe. A hill country farmer on whose farm the murder in Ek's story took place ("The Liar").

Starnes, Sophia. The daughter of Will Starnes. She was engaged to Henry Stribling, the barber. She died on April 16, 1905, after making Stribling promise to take care of the Starnes place and pay off the mortgage ("Hair").

Starnes, Will. The father of Sophia Starnes. He owned the house in Division on which Henry Stribling paid off the mortgage ("Hair").

Stefan. The first name of the Corporal who led the mutiny. After he was shot his body was given to his sisters and he was buried on his sister's farm. It was later disinterred, taken to Paris, and buried in the Tomb of the Unknown Soldier. Whether he was known by the last name of Brzonyi, or whether Brzonyi was the French corporal whom Major Blum saw killed earlier, is not clear in context (*A Fable*).

Steinbauer, Genevieve (Jenny). A young lady of New Orleans who was invited on Mrs. Maurier's yachting party by Patricia Robyn. Jenny was the girl friend of Pete Ginotta (*Mosquitoes*).

Stevens, Bucky. The four-year-old son of Gowan and Temple Stevens (*Requiem for a Nun*).

Stevens, Captain. See **Stevens, Lemuel.**

Stevens, Gavin. A Jefferson lawyer, educated at Harvard and Heidelberg, a Phi Beta Kappa member, and later a classmate of Roth Edmonds at the University of Mississippi, where he took a law degree. He was the son of Judge Lemuel Stevens and a Margaret Dandridge, the twin brother of Mrs. Charles Mallison, Sr., a first cousin once removed of Gowan Stevens, and an uncle of Charles Mallison, Jr. As a lawyer he aided those in trouble, oftentimes without pay. When not engaged in law practice he spent his time translating the Old Testament into classical Greek. He was born, according to the best conjecture, around 1890. In 1942 he married the widowed Mrs. Harriss, a childhood sweetheart. He was variously county attorney (*Knight's Gambit*, *Requiem for a Nun*, *The Town*, and *The Mansion*) and district attorney (*Light in August* and "Hair"). Has a major role in *Knight's Gambit*. *Intruder in the Dust*, *Requiem for a Nun*. *The Town*, and *The Mansion* (part of the last two he relates). Appears more briefly in *Light in August*, "Go Down, Moses," "The Tall Men," and "Hair."

Stevens, Gowan. A first cousin once removed of Gavin Stevens. His father worked for the State Department, and when he was sent to Asia when Gowan was a child, Gowan stayed with the Judge Stevens family in Jefferson. He studied at the University of Virginia, and during vacations used to come back to Jefferson to see Narcissa Benbow Sartoris. Through his drunkenness he was instrumental in getting Temple Drake stranded at the Old Frenchman's Place, where she was left to the mercy of Poyeye. A year or so later he married Temple in Paris. They had two children. Appears in *Sanctuary* and *Requiem for a Nun* and, vicariously, in *The Town*.

Stevens, Judge.   The mayor of Jefferson around 1900, a man eighty years old at that time ("A Rose for Emily"). His relationship with the Stevens family is not clear, but his age and profession could conceivably make him a grandfather of Gavin.

Stevens, Lemuel.   The father of Gavin Stevens and Mrs. Charles Mallison. He was a judge in Jefferson around 1912. He died in 1919. Appears in *The Town*. Is referred to in *The Mansion*. He is referred to also in "Tomorrow" (*Knight's Gambit*), but as Captain Stevens. He is probably the Judge Stevens of the *Reivers*.

Stevens, Maggie.   See **Mallison, Mrs. Margaret Stevens.**

Stevens, Mrs. Melisandre Backus Harriss.   The wife of Gavin Stevens, whom he married in 1942. She was the daughter of a farmer near Jefferson and married a bootlegger from New Orleans who turned the Backus farm into a showplace. They had two children, Max and a girl who married an Argentine named Sebastian Gualdres. Harriss was shot to death, after which Mrs. Harriss spent several years travelling with the children. She then returned home and was courted and married by Gavin Stevens, who had known her as a child. Appears in "Knight's Gambit," *The Town*, and *The Mansion*. During the Civil War there was a cousin of the Sartoris family known as "Cousin Melisandre" who married another Sartoris cousin named Philip St.-Just Backus. Although it is not stated, Mrs. Gavin Stevens may be a descendant of theirs. They appear in "My Grandmother Millard."

Stevens, Mrs. Temple Drake.   The daughter of a Jackson judge and a student at the University of Mississippi around 1930. She was marooned one day at the Old Frenchman's Place following an accident in a car driven by Gowan Stevens. There she was raped with a corncob by the impotent Popeye and then taken to Memphis to a house of prostitution to be healed and then to participate in sexual activity with a man named Red under the watchful eye of Popeye. After she escaped she was sent to Paris by her father. There, a year or so later, she married Gowan Stevens. They had two children, the youngest, a six-months-old daughter, being murdered in 1938 by its Negro nurse, Nancy Mannigoe. Appears in *Sanctuary* and *Requiem for a Nun*.

Stillwell, Shuford H. A gambler, in the state penitentiary for cutting the throat of a Vicksburg prostitute. An attempt to escape was foiled by Mink Snopes, and when he did escape he wrote back a letter threatening Mink's life. Some four years later he was killed in San Diego, California, when a building he was in collapsed (*The Mansion*).

Stoke, Mr. The manager of the Compson plantation ("A Justice").

Stone. An Oxford lawyer who drew up Linda Snopes's will (*The Town*). He is probably Phil Stone, to whom the Snopes trilogy is dedicated.

Stonewall. A large and vicious horse that ran away from the grass fire ("Afternoon of a Cow").

Story of Temple Drake, The. The title given the motion picture made in 1932 of *Sanctuary*.

Stovall, Mr. The cashier in a Jefferson bank and a deacon in the Baptist church. He had been having an affair with Nancy, and when she asked him for money he knocked her down and kicked her teeth in. Is referred to in "That Evening Sun" and (not by name) in *Requiem for a Nun*.

Straud, Dr. The partner of young Dr. Lucius Peabody in New York (*Sartoris*).

Streets. A poem in *The Mississippian*, IX (Mar. 17, 1920), 2. Subtitled "From Paul Verlaine." Reprinted in *William Faulkner: Early Prose and Poetry*, ed. Carvel Collins, p. 59.

Stribling, Henry. A man who was engaged to a Sophia Starnes of Division. Before she died in 1905 she made him promise to take care of her home, so he learned barbering and used his earnings to pay off the mortgage. Every spring he would take a vacation to go to Division to clean up the place. In Jefferson, where he worked at Maxey's barbershop, he was known as "Hawkshaw." Finally, in 1930 the mortgage was all paid off, and he returned to Jefferson and married the girl Susan Reed, whom he had loved since she was a little girl. Appears in "Hair" and "Dry September."

Strother, Simon. The colored driver for Bayard Sartoris II. He was grandson of old Joby, and the father of Elnora and Caspey. His wife was named Euphronia. Simon took the money left in his trust as treasurer of the Baptist church to give to the Harry Mitchell maid Meloney Harris, so she could open a beauty parlor. He was killed at her place. Appears in *Sartoris*. Is referred to in "There Was a Queen."

Strutterbuck, Captain. An ex-soldier of the Spanish-American War and World War I, a customer in Miss Reba Rivers' place of business in Memphis (*The Mansion*).

Strutterbuck, Q'Milla. The wife, presumably, of Captain Strutterbuck. He used a two-dollar money order she sent him to pay for the woman at the house of prostitution (*The Mansion*).

Stuart, Gen. J.E.B.

Studenmire, Captain. The owner of the steamboat on which David Hogganbeck worked ("A Courtship").

Study. A poem in *The Mississippian*, IX (Apr. 24, 1920), 4. Reprinted in Martha Mayes's "Faulkner Juvenilia, *New Campus Writing No. 2*, ed. Nolan Miller, p. 139 and in *William Faulkner: Early Prose and Poetry*, ed. Carvel Collins, pp. 62-63.

Subadar, The / Subaltern, The

Sue. The sister of the country boy, Hub, to whose place Hub took Suratt and Bayard Sartoris to drink (*Sartoris*).

Sunset. A sketch in the New Orleans *Times-Picayune* Sunday section, May 24, 1925, p. 4. Reprinted in *New Orleans Sketches* (ed. Collins).

Suratt, V. K. See **Ratliff, V. K.**

Sutpen, Clytemnestra (Clytie). The daughter of Thomas Sutpen and a Negro whom he had brought with him from Haiti. She was born in 1834. She remained on the land and later took care of Jim Bond and Henry Sutpen. In December 1909 she set fire to the house and she and Henry were burned to death (*Absalom, Absalom!*)

Sutpen, Ellen Coldfield (see C n)

Sutpen, Henry. The son of Thomas Sutpen and Ellen Coldfield. He was born in 1839. He went to the University of Mississippi, where he met Charles Bon. When his father refused to let his sister Judith marry Charles, he went away with Charles. He joined the army and served in General Compson's regiment. In 1865, when he found out that Charles Bon was his own and Judith's half-brother, he killed Charles and then disappeared. He returned to Sutpen's Hundred around 1906 and died there in 1909 in a fire set by his half-sister Clytie. Appears in *Absalom, Absalom!* Is referred to in "Wash," where it is said that he was killed during the war.

Sutpen, Judith. The daughter of Thomas Sutpen and Ellen Coldfield. She was born October 3, 1841. She became engaged to Charles Bon, but after he was killed she remained at Sutpen's Hundred and never married. She died there on February 12, 1884, of either yellow fever or smallpox. Appears in *Absalom, Absalom!* and "Wash."

Sutpen, Thomas. The founder of the Sutpen family in Yoknapatawpha County. He was born in the mountain country of western Virginia in 1807, and around 1820 went to Haiti, where he married a Eulalia Bon, the daughter of a French planter there. The had one son, Charles Bon. When Sutpen discovered that his wife had Negro blood he divorced her. He arrived in Jefferson in 1833, and built himself a large plantation in the northwestern part of Yoknapatawpha County on a hundred acres of land gotten from the Chickasaws. He married Eleen Coldfield of Jefferson in 1838. They had two children, Henry and Judith. His whole life was dedicated to establishing a family, and when his son disappeared he tried other means of getting a male heir. When he spurned Milly Jones because her child by him was a girl, he was killed by Wash Jones, Milly's grandfather. This was in 1869. Appears in *Absalom, Absalom!*, "Wash," and *Requiem for a Nun*. Is referred to in *The Unvanquished*, "The Old People" (*Go Down, Moses*), *The Town*, and *The Reivers*.

Sutpen's Hundred. The name which Thomas Sutpen gave the hundred acres he bought from Ikkemotubbe and on which he built a plantation. It was in northwestern Yoknapatawpha County, twelve miles from Jefferson. After Sutpen's death part of the land was bought by Major de Spain as a hunting ground (*Absalom, Absalom!*).

Sutterfield, Reverend Tobe. The Negro, who with his grandson and the English groom (Mister 'Arry) took care of the three-legged horse and ran it in races throughout the southeastern part of the United States. While in France he became head of *Les Amis Myriades et Anonymes à la France de Tout le Monde*, and became known as Monsieur Tooleyman (*A Fable*).

Sylvester's John. One of the young Indians who wanted Herman Basket's sister, but who gave up when Ikkemotubbe started courting her ("A Courtship").

T

(as c-n) ✳ **Tall Convict, The.** The descriptive title given the unnamed convict hero of "Old Man." He was twenty-six years old in 1927, and had been in prison since he was nineteen years old (*The Wild Palms*).

Talliaferro, Ernest. A thirty-eight-year-old widower and dilettante, a guest of Mrs. Maurier's on her yachting party (*Mosquitoes*).

Tall Men, The. A short story in *Collected Stories*. First published in *The Saturday Evening Post*, May 31, 1941. About the McCallum twins and the draft law. The story was adapted for television and performed on CBS, *Camera Three*, September 14, 1958, with Richard Shepard.

Tarnished Angels, The. The title given to a motion picture made in 1957 of *Pylon*.

Teaberry Hotel, The. A Memphis hotel where Clarence and Montgomery Ward Snopes stayed when they visited the red light district (*The Mansion*).

Telegraph Operator / *Telegraph Operator at the Depot*

Tennie. A slave girl belonging to the Beauchamps. She

married Tomey's Turl and they started the (Negro) Beauchamp family. Appears in "Was." Is referred to in "The Bear" and *Tennie's Jim* "Delta Autumn." (*Go Down, Moses*), and *The Reivers.*

Ten Sleep. A place where Lucas Crump went from Blizzard to carry mail ("Idyll in the Desert").

Terrebone. A hotel in New Valois (*Pylon*).

Terrel, Bill. A convict at the state prison who was in effect the real killer of the warden Gambrell ("Monk" in *Knight's Gambit*).

That Evening Sun. A short story in *Collected Stories.* First published in *The American Mercury,* Mar. 1941, under the title "That Evening Sun Go Down." It was reprinted in *These 13.* It is included in *The Faulkner Reader, The Portable Faulkner,* and *Selected Short Stories.* A story related by Quentin Compson about Nancy and her great fear of her husband's jealousy. Related to *The Sound and the Fury* through its connection with the Compson family. Related to *Requiem for a Nun* through its connection with Nancy. The title is from W. C. Handy's "St. Louis Blues": "I hate to see that evening sun go down. . . ."

That Will Be Fine. A short story in *Collected Stories.* First published in *The American Mercury,* July 1935. A story narrated by a seven-year-old boy named Georgie about the amorous pursuits of his Uncle Rodney. Most of the setting is in Motts- *T Law, Harry* town.

Thelma. A new girl at Miss Reba Rivers' place of business when Montgomery Ward Snopes was visiting there (*The Mansion*).

Thelma Frances. A girl friend of Jenny Steinbauer's (*Mosquitoes*).

Theodule. A French soldier who had been killed in 1916. When a detachment of soldiers went to Verdun after the war to take back to Paris the body of an unidentified soldier for the Tomb of the Unknown Soldier, Theodule's mother wanted to go with them to search for his body. When the soldiers returned to St. Mihiel, where she was waiting, she gave them a hundred francs for the cadaver, which she said, without even looking at it, was Theodule's body (*A Fable*).

There Was a Queen.   A short story in *Collected Stories*. First published in *Scribner's Magazine*, Jan. 1933. It was reprinted in *Doctor Martino and Other Stories*. It is included in *Selected Short Stories*. About the death of Aunt Jenny Du Pre, and about Narcissa Sartoris' solution to the problem of the anonymous letters sent her.

These 13.   A collection of thirteen stories published by Jonathan Cape and Harrison Smith, New York, 1931. Contains "Victory," "Ad Astra," "All the Dead Pilots," "Crevasse," "Red Leaves," "A Rose for Emily," "A Justice," "Hair," "That Evening Sun," "Dry September," "Mistral," "Divorce in Naples," and "Carcassonne." All were reprinted in *Collected Stories*.

✳ **Theule.**   The name of the fat one of three Cajans who came to watch another Cajan and the tall convict catch alligators ("Old Man" in *The Wild Palms*).

Thisbe.   Aunt Thisbe, the Negro cook and housekeeper for Zack Edmonds at the time Roth was born ("The Fire and the Hearth" in *Go Down, Moses*).

This Earth.   A limited edition (1000 copies) of a short poem published by Equinox Cooperative Press, New York, 1932, with drawings by Albert Hackman. First published in *Contempo*, I (Feb. 1, 1932), 2, under the title "My Epitaph." Reprinted as *A Green Bough*, XLIV.

Thomas, Son.   The youngest driver for the Priest livery stable (*The Reivers*).

Thomasina.   The daughter of Carothers McCaslin and a slave called Eunice. She was born in 1810. Was called Tomey by the family. In 1833 she became the mother of the boy Terrel, whose father was McCaslin ("The Bear" in *Go Down, Moses*).

✳ **Thompson, Cadet.**   A flying cadet and the central character of "Landing in Luck."

Thompson, Pappy.   An old Negro whom Joe Christmas knocked down when he ran into a country church while services were being held (*Light in August*).

Thompson, Roz. The grandson of Pappy Thompson. His skull was fractured by Joe Christmas when he went after Joe for knocking his grandfather down (*Light in August*).

Thompson's. An eating place in Cambridge where Quentin Compson went for breakfast on the day he committed suicide (*The Sound and the Fury*).

Thorndyke, Rev. The Episcopal minister in Jefferson who went to the Mallison home with the Methodist, Baptist, and Presbyterian ministers to discuss who was going to preach Eula Varner's funeral service (*The Town*).

Thorpe. A member of flight squadron commanded by Major Bridesman (*A Fable*).

Thorpe, Buck. A fighter, gambler, moonshiner, and thief who eloped with Bookwright's seventeen-year-old daughter. He was shot, and Bookwright confessed to the murder. As a child he was called Jackson and Longstreet Fentry ("Tomorrow" in *Knight's Gambit*).

Three Famous Short Novels. Published by Random House, New York, 1958. Contains "Spotted Horses" from *The Hamlet*, "Old Man" from *The Wild Palms*, and "The Bear" from *Go Down, Moses*.

Three Mile Bridge. A bridge in the Beat Four region (*The Hamlet*).

Thrift. A short story in *The Saturday Evening Post*, CCIII (Sept. 6, 1930), 16-17ff. Uncollected, but reprinted in *O. Henry Memorial Award Prize Stories of 1931*, ed. Blanche Colton Williams, Garden City: Doubleday, Doran & Co., 1931, pp. 153-169. A non-Yoknapatawpha story about a man named MacWyrglinchbeath, a deserter from two different British outfits during World War I. He joined the Air Corps and was given a commission which he refused, because he had figured out that he could make more money as a non-commissioned officer. He refused to take leaves and saved all his money, which he took back to his farm when he returned home after the war.

Thucydides. The son of Roskus and Fibby, and a slave of Carothers McCaslin. He was born in Carolina in 1779. In 1809 he was married to Eunice, another slave who was about to give birth to a child fathered by McCaslin. In 1841 Thucydides took two hundred dollars he had earned and opened a blacksmith shop in Jefferson. He died on February 17, 1854 ("The Bear" in *Go Down, Moses*).

✻ **Tim.** A man with Sheriff Rogers, probably a deputy ("The Liar").

✻**Tine.** The name of one of the three Cajans who came to watch another Cajan and the tall convict catch alligators ("Old Man" in *The Wild Palms*).

✻**Tinney.** One of the mules belonging to the Sartoris family which was taken by the federal troops and got back by Granny Millard ("Retreat" in *The Unvanquished*).

✻**Titania.** The nickname given Belle Mitchell by her stepfather Horace Benbow (*Sartoris*).

To a Co-ed. A poem in *Ole Miss, 1919-1920*, XXIV, p. 174. Reprinted in the Memphis *Commercial-Appeal*, Nov. 6, 1932, Magazine section, p. 4, in James B. Meriwether, *The Literary Career of William Faulkner*, Princeton University Library, 1961, p. 9, and in *William Faulkner: Early Prose and Poetry*, ed. Carvel Collins, p. 70.

To a Virgin. A poem in *Contempo*, I (Feb. 1, 1932), 2. Reprinted as *A Green Bough*, XXXIX.

Tobe. Miss Emily Grierson's Negro house man ("A Rose for Emily"). Also the Negro hostler at the livery stable where Bayard Sartoris and Rafe MacCallum went to look at a stallion (*Sartoris*). Also the Negro servant at the Robert Saunders home (*Soldiers' Pay*).

To Claim Freedom Is Not Enough. See *Address to the annual meeting of the Southern Historical Association*, under **Addresses by Faulkner.**

Today We Live. The title given to a motion picture made in 1933 of the story "Turnabout."

'Toinette. The French girl whom John Sartoris and Spoomer fought over ("All the Dead Pilots").

Tomey. See **Thomasina.**

Tomey's Turl. See **Beauchamp, Terrel.**

Tommy (Tawmmy). A slow-witted man living with Lee Goodwin on the Old Frenchman's Place. He was killed by Popeye when he tried to protect Temple Drake (*Sanctuary*).

Tomorrow. The fourth story in *Knight's Gambit*. First published in *The Saturday Evening Post,* Nov. 23, 1940. About the trial of Bookwright, accused of killing Buck Thorpe. The story was adapted for television by Horton Foote, and was presented on "Playhouse 90," CBS, May 7, 1960, with Richard Boone, Kim Stanley, Charles Bickford, Chill Wills, Elizabeth Patterson, Beulah Bondi, and Andrew Prine. The text of the television production is published in Foote's *Three Plays,* New York: Harcourt, Brace & World, 1962, pp. 51-93. "Tomorrow" is also the title of Section IV of *Pylon*.

Tom-Tom. A big, sixty-year-old Negro, a day fireman at the municipal power plant in Jefferson ("Centaur in Brass"). In the revised version (in *The Town*) he is known as Tom-Tom Bird.

Tony the Wop. One of the acquaintances of Jean-Baptiste, with whom he was going to rob a bank ("Home").

Tooleyman, M. The name—"Tout le Monde"—assumed by the Rev. Tobe Sutterfield in Paris (*A Fable*).

Top. The husband of Guster and the father of Little Top and, Aleck Sander. Little Top was so called to distinguish him from his father (*The Town*).

To the Voters of Oxford. A broadside distributed locally in 1950. It concerned the question of the legalization of beer. Reprinted in Hodding Carter's "Faulkner and His Folk," the *Princeton University Library Chronicle,* xviii (Spring 1957), 98-99.

To the Youth of Japan. A pamphlet distributed by the U. S. Information Service in Tokyo, 1955, with the text in Japanese and English. The English text is reprinted in *Faulkner at Nagono.*

Toto. The name of one of the three Cajans who came to

watch another Cajan and the tall convict catch alligators ("Old Man" in *The Wild Palms*).

Toulouse Street. A street in New Valois (*Pylon*).

Town, The. A novel published by Random House, New York, 1957. Dedicated to Phil Stone. Subtitled *Snopes*, Vol. II. The second (with *The Hamlet* and *The Mansion*) volume of the trilogy devoted to the Snopes family. It covers action between 1909 and 1929. Pages 3-29 were rewritten from "Centaur in Brass." Pages 231-261 were rewritten from "Mule in the Yard." Pages 359-371 were preprinted in *The Saturday Evening Post*, May 4, 1957, under the title "The Waifs." The "town," of course, is Jefferson.

T. P. The younger son of Roskus and Dilsey. He was born around 1895. After leaving the Compsons' he moved to Memphis and wore flashy clothes along Beale Street. Appears in *The Sound and the Fury* and Appendix and "That Evening Sun."

Triplett, Earl. The man who took over Ike McCaslin's place in McCaslin's hardware store, and whose place, in turn, was taken over by Jason Compson (*The Mansion*). In *The Sound and the Fury* he is known only as Earl.

Trueblood, Ernest V. Known as "William Faulkner's Ghostwriter," the "author" of "Afternoon of a Cow." He was called Ernest be Toogood by the Faulkner boys.

Trumbull. The man who had been running Will Varner's blacksmith shop for twenty years or more before Eck Snopes took it over (*The Hamlet* and *The Town*).

Tubbs, Euphus. The jailor at the county jail in Jefferson. He had charge of Lucas Beauchamp, Nancy Mannigoe, and Montgomery Ward Snopes. Appears in *Intruder in the Dust* and *Requiem for a Nun* only as Tubbs. Appears in *The Mansion* as Euphus Tubbs.

Tucker. The husband of a woman in Jefferson with whom Georgie's Uncle Rodney had been having an affair ("That Will Be Fine").

Tull, Cora. The wife of Vernon Tull. She used to bake

cakes which she sold in Jefferson (*As I Lay Dying*). Mrs. Tull is referred to in *The Town*.

Tull, Odum. A farmer in the Frenchman's Bend region ("Fool About a Horse"). In the revised version (in *The Hamlet*) he becomes Cliff Odum.

Tull, Vernon. A farmer in the Frenchman's Bend region. His wife's name was Cora, and they had four daughters. The Tulls were neighbors of the Bundrens and the Griers, and were reported to have had the place closest to the Old Frenchman's Place. Tull was hurt by one of the spotted horses brought back from Texas by Flem Snopes. Appears in *The Hamlet, The Town, The Mansion, As I Lay Dying*, and "Shingles for the Lord." Is referred to in *Sanctuary*. A young man named Tull was one of the five local boys who tried to court Eula Varner (*The Mansion*), and young Pete Grier used to go "sparking" the Tull girls ("Two Soldiers"). Just how these Tulls are related to the Vernon Tull family is not clear.

Turl. A thirty-year-old night fireman at the municipal power plant in Jefferson who played around with Tom-Tom's wife when Tom-Tom was at work ("Centaur in Brass"). In the revised version (in *The Town*) he becomes Tomey's Turl Beauchamp.

Turnabout. A short story in *Collected Stories*. First published in *The Saturday Evening Post,* Mar. 5, 1932, under the title "Turn About." Reprinted in *Doctor Martino and Other Stories*. It is included in *The Faulkner Reader* and *Selected Short Stories*. A non-Yoknapatawpha story about American airmen and British seamen in World War I. In 1932 it was made into a motion picture by Metro-Goldwyn-Mayer under the title "Today We Live," directed by Howard Hawks, and starring Robert Young, Joan Crawford, Roscoe Karns, Franchot Tone, and Gary Cooper.

Turpin. The last name of one of the Frenchman's Bend youths who, along with the Bookwright, Binford, Quick, and Tull boys, tried to court Eula Varner (*The Mansion*). We are told in *The Hamlet* that Turpin is one of the local names in the Frenchman's Bend region.

Turpin, Buck. The man to whom the circus paid ten dollars for the privilege of showing in Jefferson (*The Sound and the Fury.*)

Twilight.   A poem in *Contempo*, I (Feb. 1, 1932), 1. Reprinted as *A Green Bough*, X.

Two Soldiers.   A short story in *Collected Stories*. First published in the *Saturday Evening Post*, Mar. 28, 1942. It is included in *The Selected Short Stories*. About the enlistment of Pete Grier in the army and his nine-year-old brother's attempt to follow him. Related to "Shall Not Perish" and "Shingles for the Lord."

U

Unc Mose.   A Negro stableman for Harrison Blair ("Fox Hunt").

Uncle Bud.   A five-year-old boy from an Arkansas farm, brought to Miss Reba Revers' by Miss Myrtle. He got drunk after breaking into the icebox and finding the beer (*Sanctuary*).

Uncle Bud and the Three Madams.   The title given to Chapter xxv of *Sanctuary* when it was reprinted in *The Portable Faulkner.*

Uncle Robert.   An uncle of the fourteen-year-old narrator of "Uncle Willy."

Uncle Willy.   A short story in *Collected Stories*. First published in *The American Mercury*, Oct. 1935. A story about a druggist in Jefferson, Hoke Christian, a dope addict whom the ladies of the church tried to reform. The druggist, known as "Uncle Willy" Christian, reappears in *The Town*.

Unvanquished, The.   A short story in *The Saturday Evening Post*, Nov. 14, 1934. Reprinted as the fourth story in *The Unvanquished* under the title "Riposte in Tertio."

Unvanquished, The. A collection of seven related stories published by Random House, New York, 1938. About the Sartoris family during the Civil War, told in the first person by Bayard Sartoris II, who was twelve at the opening of the book. Contains "Ambuscade," "Retreat," "Raid," "Riposte in Tertio," "Vendée," "Skirmish at Sartoris," and "An Odor of Verbena."

Urquhart. See **Workitt, Sudley.**

V

Van. One of the men staying at the Old Frenchman's Place with Lee Goodwin. He got drunk and tried to molest Temple Drake, but Goodwin stopped him (*Sanctuary*).

Van Dorn. The name of the locality where Mister Ernest lived ("Race at Morning").

Van Dyming, Carleton. A wealthy New Yorker who was building a house at his country place in Virginia ("Black Music"). He is mentioned as the man who wanted to buy the horse Harrison Blair wanted ("Fox Hunt").

Van Dyming, Mathilda (Mattie). The wife of Carleton Van Dyming ("Black Music").

van Tosch, Mr. A wealthy former Chicagoan who moved to Memphis and began raising race horses. He was the employer of Bobo Beauchamp, who stole his racing horse Coppermine, which Bobo traded to Ned McCaslin for Boss Priest's car (*The Reivers*).

Varner, Eula. The youngest child of Will and Maggie Varner. She was born in 1889. She was fat and lazy and personified sex to nearly every male who saw her. She was desired by the schoolteacher Labove, and by most of the young men in the region. In

1908 she became pregnant by Hoake McCarron, who then ran away. She was married by her father to Flem Snopes, who took her on a honeymoon to Texas, where her daughter Linda was born. When they moved to Jefferson in 1909 she became the mistress of the mayor, Manfred de Spain, and remained so until 1927, when she shot herself to prevent the knowledge of her behavior disgracing her daughter. Appears in *The Hamlet* and *The Town*. Is referred to in *The Mansion*. A Eula with no last name who appears to be interested in men is referred to in *As I Lay Dying*.

Varner, Jody. The bachelor son of Will Varner, the ninth of sixteen children. He ran the store in Frenchman's Bend for his father. Appears in *The Hamlet, The Town, The Mansion,* and *Light in August.* Is referred to in *As I Lay Dying*.

Varner, Maggie. Will Varner's wife, the mother of Jody and Eula and fourteen other children. Appears in *The Hamlet* and *The Town*.

Varner, Will. A countryman who became the leading citizen of Frenchman's Bend around 1900. He owned the Old Frenchman's Place, the local store and blacksmith shop, held mortgages on many of his neighbors' farms, was a justice of the peace, and the election commissioner. He was reported to have been sixty years old in 1902 and the father of sixteen children, only two of which were at home, Jody and Eula. But as late as 1945 he was still around and still very much active. Has a major role in *The Hamlet*. Appears also in *The Town, The Mansion,* "Tomorrow" (*Knight's Gambit*), and "Shingles for the Lord." Is referred to in *As I Lay Dying*.

Vatch. The Tennessee mountain boy who shot and killed Major Saucier Weddel ("Mountain Victory").

Vendée. The fifth story in *The Unvanquished*. First published in *The Saturday Evening Post,* Dec. 5, 1936.

✳**Venturia, Juan.** The next-door neighbor and bitter enemy of Mr. Harris ("The Rosary").

Vera. One of Miss Reba Rivers' girls who was visiting her parents in Paducah (*The Reivers*).

Vernon. The first name of the sheriff's son-in-law (*The Sound and the Fury*). Also the waiter in the restaurant in Jefferson where Jock and Captain Warren went to eat ("Death Drag").

Verse Old and Nascent: A Pilgrimage. An article in *The Double Dealer*, VII (Apr. 1925), 129-131. Reprinted in *Salmagundi* and in *William Faulkner: Early Prose and Poetry*, ed. Carvel Collins, pp. 114-118.

Versh. The oldest child of Roskus and Dilsey. He took care of Benjy Compson when Benjy was a child. The name, said Faulkner, is probably a corruption of Virgil. Appears in *The Sound and the Fury* and "That Evening Sun."

Victory. A short story in *Collected Stories*. First published in *These 13*. A non-Yoknapatawpha story about a Scottish boy, Alec Gray, in World War I and after.

Vidal, François. See **Weddel, Francis.**

Village, The. Section II of *Collected Stories*. Contains "A Rose for Emily," "Hair," "Centaur in Brass," "Dry September," "Death Drag," "Elly," "Uncle Willy," "Mule in the Yard," "That Will Be Fine," and "That Evening Sun."

Vines, Deacon. A deacon in the Negro church into which Joe Christmas burst, disrupting the services (*Light in August*).

Vinson, Mrs. The woman at a country tavern where stock traders stopped. She ran away to Memphis with Jim Gant. They were followed by Mrs. Gant, who shot and killed them ("Miss Zilphia Gant").

Virgil. The first name of the hotel clerk in the hotel at Parsham (*The Reivers*).

Visions of Spring. A poem in *Contempo*, I (Feb. 1, 1932), 1. Uncollected.

Vitelli. See **Popeye.**

Vitry, Chevalier Soeur-Blonde de. The French companion of Ikkemotubbe. He gave Ikkemotubbe the name Du homme (Doom). Appears in "Red Leaves" and "A Courtship." Is referred to in the Appendix to *The Sound and the Fury* and "The Old People" (*Go Down, Moses*).

W

Wagner, Hal. One of the two "code" names used by Byron Snopes so his young amanuensis, Virgil Beard, would not know the purpose of the letters he was writing (*Sartoris*).

Waifs, The. The title given to pages 359-371 of *The Town* when they were preprinted in *The Saturday Evening Post,* May 4, 1957.

Waldrip. A fellow soldier of Buck Monaghan with whom Buck used to do stunt flying ("Honor").

Waldrip, Mrs. Vernon. The married name of the girl who had been the tall convict's sweetheart ("Old Man" in *The Wild Palms*).

Walker, Ed. The jailor at the Jefferson jail (*Sanctuary*).

Walkley. A subaltern in the British army who, after the war's end, went to Canada and became prosperous ("Victory").

Wallace, Captain. The captain of the State National Guard ("Sunset").

Waller, Hamp. The farmer whose wife discovered the fire at Miss Burden's home (*Light in August*).

Walter. A Negro servant at Mrs. Maurier's. Also one of the men who helped to get the Nausikaa ungrounded (*Mosquitoes*).

Walthall, Parson. The minister of the Methodist church in Jefferson (*The Sound and the Fury*).

Wardle, Mrs. A wealthy lady of Charlestown, Georgia (*Soldiers' Pay*).

Warren, Captain. A Yoknapatawpha County farmer who had been in the R.F.C. during World War I and had been wounded ("Death Drag" and "Knight's Gambit").

Warwick. The Hubert Beauchamp plantation ("Was" and "The Bear" in *Go Down, Moses*).

Was. The first story in *Go Down, Moses*. First published there.

It is included in *The Portable Faulkner*. About the runaway slave, Tomey's Turl, his marriage to Tennie, and about Uncle Buck McCaslin's marriage to Sophonsiba Beauchamp.

Wash. A short story in *Collected Stories*. First published in *Harper's Magazine*, Feb. 1934. Reprinted in *Doctor Martino and Other Stories*. It is included in *The Portable Faulkner* and *The Faulkner Reader*. About the killing of Thomas Sutpen by Wash Jones. The story with some variations is retold in *Absalom, Absalom!*

Wasteland, The. Section IV of *Collected Stories*. Contains "Ad Astra," "Victory," "Crevasse," "Turnabout," and "All the *Watchmaker* Dead Pilots."

Wattman, Jakeleg. A purveyor of illegal whiskey who lived at Wyott's Crossing (*The Mansion*).

Watts. The marshall in Jefferson ("That Will Be Fine"). Also a hardware store owner in Jefferson (*Sartoris*). Also the gunner on the airship piloted by Captain Bogard ("Turnabout").

Watts, Birdie. The owner of a house of prostitution across the street from Reba Rivers' (*The Reivers*).

Weddel,—

Weddel, Francis. Known otherwise as François Vidal, he was an Indian leader (referred to as both Choctaw and Chickasaw), the son of an Indian mother and a French father. He went to Washington to see President Jackson about justice for his people. Appears in "Lo!" Is referred to in "Mountain Victory."

Weddel, Grenier. A bachelor in Jefferson who was engaged to Sally Hampton. She sent his ring back and married Maurice Priest (*The Town*).

Weddel, Saucier. The son of Francis Weddel, and a major in the Civil War. On his return home to Mississippi after the war he was killed in the Tennessee mountains by a partisan named Vatch ("Mountain Victory").

Wedding in the Rain. The title given to Chapter II of *Absalom, Absalom!* when it was reprinted in *The Portable Faulkner*.

West, David. The steward on the Nausikaa. He eloped with Patricia Robyn (*Mosquitoes*).

West, Doctor. A druggest in Jefferson ("Smoke" in *Knight's Gambit*).

West, Miss. The secretary to Reinhardt, the automobile dealer for whom Buck Monaghan worked ("Honor").

Wharton. An unidentified officer or cadet who spoke to the C. O. ("Landing in Luck").

White. A fellow soldier of Buck Monaghan, with whom Buck used to play poker. He had a wife in California ("Honor").

White, Caroline. A Memphis girl who married Bayard Sartoris III while he was teaching flying there. She died in childbirth on October 27, 1918 (*Sartoris*).

White, Hank. A drunken soldier with Julian Lowe and Joe Gilligan on the train (*Soldiers' Pay*).

White, Jed. A man from Jefferson who told Aunt Jenny and Drusilla the news of what happened when Bayard met Ben J. Redmond ("An Odor of Verbena" in *The Unvanquished*).

Whiteby. An officer in the British army who killed himself after he returned home because he could not get a job ("Victory").

Whiteleaf Bridge. A bridge in the Frenchman's Bend region (*The Hamlet*).

Whiteleaf Store. A rural store, eight miles from Jefferson in the direction of Frenchman's Bend (*The Hamlet*). In *The Town* it is called Whiteleaf.

Whiteley. An officer in the R.A.F. who gathered the information about MacWyrglinchbeath's status ("Thrift").

Whitfield. The name associated throughout Yoknapatawpha County history with the church. At the time of the founding of Jefferson in 1833 Doctor Peabody said: "We're going to have a town. We already got a church—that's Whitfield's cabin." (*Requiem for a Nun*). A "Brother Whitfield" appeared around 1900 as the minister of the Frenchman's Bend church—a farmer with no divinity degree (*The Hamlet*). A "Preacher Whitfield" married Jackson Fentry and the Thorpe girl, sometime around 1920 ("Tomorrow" in *Knight's Gambit*). Around 1930 a Whitfield officiates at Addie Bundren's funeral, having some eighteen years or so before become the father of her son Jewel (*As I Lay Dying*).

Then around 1940 a "Reverend Whitfield" has his church burned by Res Grier in an accident which occurred when they were shingling the old church ("Shingles for the Lord").

✗Whittington.   Mentioned in *The Hamlet* as one of the old family names of the Frenchman's Bend region.

Widrington.   The oil company manager in Rincon, at whose house Wilfred Midgleston lived ("Black Music"). Mrs. Widdrington [sic], the manager's wife, is referred to in "Carcassonne." Another Mrs. Widrington was the wife of a wealthy contractor who came to Jefferson in 1928 or 1929, and it was her dog that the halfbreed children of Byron Snopes killed (*The Town*).

Wilbourne, Harry (Henry).   A twenty-eight-year-old interne in a New Orleans hospital who ran away with Charlotte Rittenmeyer. He was born in 1910. After he performed an unsuccessful abortion on Charlotte, which killed her, he was arrested and sent to jail (*The Wild Palms*).

Wildermark's.   The big department store in Jefferson. A "senior" Mr. Wildermark is referred to, but not in connection with the store (*The Town*).

Wilderness, The.   Section III of *Collected Stories*. Contains "Red Leaves," "A Justice," "A Courtship," and "Lo!"

Wild Palms, The.   A novel published by Random House, New York, 1939. Consists of ten chapters, of which the odd numbered ones are devoted to the story of Harry Wilbourne and Charlotte Rittenmeyer (called "Wild Palms"), and the even numbered ones are devoted to the story of "the tall convict" and the Mississippi River Flood of May 1927 (called "Old Man"). Neither is a Yoknapatawpha County story, although in 1946 Faulkner noted that the convict came from the Frenchman's Bend region. The reason for the arrangement of chapters, said Faulkner, was that "the story of Charlotte and Harry Wilbourne . . . needed a contrapuntal quality like music. And so I wrote the other story simply to underline the story of Charlotte and Harry." And the reason the characters in "Old Man" do not have names is that "the story was simply for background effect and they didn't need names. . . ."

Wild Palms, The, and The [sic] Old Man.   In 1954 the two parts of the novel were printed in a paperbound edition by the New American Library as a Signet book, and the two parts appear separately, not in alternating chapters.

Wild Stallion.   The title given to the television adaptation of "Knight's Gambit."

Wilkie.   A servant of the Bland family at their home in Kentucky (*The Sound and the Fury*).

Wilkins, George.   A shiftless young Negro who married Lucas Beauchamp's daughter Nathalie. They later moved to Detroit. Appears in "The Fire and the Hearth" in *Go Down, Moses*. Is referred to (not by name) in *Intruder in the Dust*.

Wilkins, Professor.   A professor at the state university in Oxford. Bayard Sartoris II stayed at his place when Bayard was in school studying law ("An Odor of Verbena" in *The Unvanquished*).

William Faulkner: Early Prose and Poetry.   A collection edited with an Introduction by Carvel Collins, Boston: Little, Brown and Company, 1962. Contains all of Faulkner's known contributions to *Ole Miss* and to *The Mississippian*, except for "The Ivory Tower" and a letter (both of which are quoted in part in the Introduction and are to be found reprinted in full in Martha Mayes's "Faulkner Juvenilia"). Also included are his first published poem, "L 'Après-midi d 'un Faune" (from *The New Republic*), and three poems and two articles from *The Double Dealer*, all of which had been earlier reprinted in *Salmagundi*. (A third prose piece, "New Orleans," was reprinted in *New Orleans Sketches*, edited by Collins, and a poem, "The Lilacs," became the first poem of *A Green Bough*.) This book also reproduces the drawings and cartoons which Faulkner contributed to *Ole Miss*, *The Mississippian*, and *The Scream*.

Willow, Colonel.   A colonel in the Civil War who informed Thomas Sutpen where his son Henry was stationed (*Absalom, Absalom!*)

Wilmoth, Mr.   The editor of the local paper in Jefferson. Gavin Stevens got him to help pay for bringing the body of

Samuel Worsham Beauchamp home for burial ("Go Down, Moses").

Winbush, Fonzo. A nephew of Grover Cleveland Winbush. He went with Virgil Snopes to Memphis to barber school. In *Sanctuary* he is known only as Fonzo. In *The Mansion* he is identified as Fonzo Winbush.

Winbush, Grover Cleveland. A relative of V. K. Ratliff who owned half-interest in the sidestreet restaurant taken over by Flem Snopes. After Flem had ousted him he became night marshall, and after he was found out for his connection with the Montgomery Ward Snopes affair he became the night watchman at a brick yard (*The Town* and *The Mansion*). In *The Hamlet* Ratliff's cousin who owned the restaurant with him is called Aaron Rideout.

Winbush, Mack. A seller of whiskey made by Calvin Bookwright (*The Reivers*).

Winterbottom. A neighbor living five miles from Henry Armstid, to whose place Armstid went to buy a cultivator (*Light in August*).

Winterbottom, Mrs. A boardinghouse lady in Jefferson at the time of the Civil War. The two Burdens stayed at her place. Referred to in *Sartoris*.

Winterbottom's. A boardinghouse in Frenchman's Bend where Lump Snopes stayed (*The Hamlet*).

Winter Is Gone. A poem in *Contempo*, I (Feb. 1, 1932), 2. Uncollected.

Wiseman, Mrs. Eva. The sister of Julius, the "Semitic man," and a guest of Mrs. Maurier's on her yachting party (*Mosquitoes*).

Witt. One of the flight commanders in Major Bridesman's command (*A Fable*).

Word to Virginians, A. See *Address to the Raven, Jefferson, and ODK Societies* under **Addresses by Faulkner.**

Word to Young Writers, A. See *Address to the English Club of the University of Virginia* under **Addresses by Faulkner.**

Wordwin, Mr. A bachelor, the cashier in Boss Priest's bank (*The Reivers*).

(as c–r) ✳ **Workitt, Amanda.** The maiden name of Nub Gowrie's wife (*Intruder in the Dust*).

Workitt, Sudley. An uncle of Nub Gowrie's wife. He was a lumberman in Beat Four and his great nephew Vinson Gowrie worked with him. The name was originally Urquhart (*Intruder in the Dust*).

Workman, Mr. An insurance adjustor who came to investigate the death of Mrs. Joel Flint ("An Error in Chemistry" in *Knight's Gambit*).

Worsham, Belle. The last surviving member of the family Mollie Beauchamp's people belonged to. Appears in "Go Down, Moses." She is probably the same person as Eunice Habersham.

Worsham, Doctor. The Episcopal minister in Jefferson at the of the Civil War ("Riposte in Tertio" in *The Unvanquished*).

Worsham, Samuel **Worsham, Hamp.** Mollie Beauchamp's brother, according to the account in "Go Down, Moses." In *Intruder in the Dust* the name is Habersham.

Worthington, Mrs. A very wealthy widow living in Charlestown, Georgia (*Soldiers' Pay*).

Wright, Doc. One of the men who used to hang around the telegraph office to wait for stock reports on cotton (*The Sound and the Fury*).

Wutherspoon, Jamie. A midshipman in the British Navy, a friend of Claude Hope ("Turnabout").

Wyatt. The family name of a great aunt of Emily Grierson. She had gone insane ("A Rose for Emily").

Wyatt, George. A member of Colonel Sartoris' regiment who was later involved in Bayard Sartoris' meeting with Redmond ("Skirmish at Sartoris" and "An Odor of Verbena" in *The Unvanquished*).

Wyatt, Henry. A man who used to go hunting with Roth Edmonds, Ike McCaslin, and Will Legate ("Delta Autumn" in *Go Down, Moses*).

Wyatt, Sally. An elderly spinster, a neighbor of the Benbows, who lived with Narcissa while Horace was away at war (*Sartoris*).

Wyatt, Sophia. The older sister of Sally Wyatt (*Sartoris*).

Wylie, Ashby (Ash). Major de Spain's cook on their hunting trips. His wife's name was Daisy. Appears (only as Uncle Ash) in "The Old People" and "The Bear" (*Go Down, Moses*), and is referred to in "A Bear Hunt," where his son, also Ashby Wylie, is a camp cook, and where the last name is given.

Wylie, Job. An aged Negro who helped out Hoke Christian in his drugstore ("Uncle Willy"). In *The Town* the Negro who helped Uucle Willy was called Walter Christian.

Wyott, Doctor. The president emeritus of the Academy. His grandfather had founded it (*The Town*).

Wyott, Mr. A friend of the Priest family who lived eight miles from Jefferson (*The Reivers*).

Wyott, Vaiden. The second grade teacher in the Jefferson school. She was Wallstreet Panic Snopes's teacher. After he finished high school he proposed to her (*The Town*).

Wyott's Crossing. A small settlement north of Jefferson on the Tallahatchie River. Jakeleg Wattman's place, where he sold illegal whiskey, was located there (*The Town* and *The Mansion*). Whether this is the same place as Old Woyttsport is not clear. According to *The Reivers* the name was changed to Ballenbaugh's Ferry.

Y

Yaphank. The nickname of Joe Gilligan (*Soldiers' Pay*).

Yo Ho. The messboy on the *Diana* whom Freddie Ayers inadvertently killed ("Yo Ho and Two Bottles of Rum").

Yo Ho and Two Bottles of Rum. A sketch in the New Orleans *Times-Picayune* Sunday section, Sept. 27, 1925, pp. 1-2. Reprinted in *New Orleans Sketches* (ed. Collins).

Yoknapatwpha Clarion. The weekly newspaper published in Jefferson ("Knight's Gambit").

Yoknapatawpha County. A county in northwestern Mississippi. Its county seat is Jefferson. It is bounded on the north by the Tallahatchie River (an actual river in Mississippi), and on the south by the Yoknapatawpha River. It consists of 2,400 square miles. It was originally Chickasaw country. Most of the eastern half is pine hill country, and there is a small section of pine hill country in the southwest corner also. The county was settled by whites around 1800. In 1936 the population was 15,611, of which 6,298 were whites and 9,313 were Negroes. Before the Civil War the county consisted of several large plantations: Grenier's in the southeast, McCaslin's in the northeast, Sutpen's in the northwest, and Compson's and Sartoris' in the immediate vicinity of Jefferson. Later the county became mostly small farms. The name Yoknapatawpha is derived from two Chickasaw words—*Yocona* and *petopha,* meaning "split land." That was the original name for the actual Yocona River, which runs through the southern part of Lafayette County, of which Oxford is the county seat. The compound word, however, according to Faulkner, means "water flowing slow through the flatland." The word is pronounced Yok'na pa *TAW* pha.

Z

Zilich, Mrs. Sophie. The next-door neighbor of Mrs. Gihon ("Pennsylvania Station").

Zsettlani. A name variously applied to Pierre Bouc (Piotr) and Polchek (*A Fable*).

APPENDIXES

Appendix I

A BIOGRAPHICAL SKETCH

WILLIAM FAULKNER was born on September 25, 1897, in New Albany, Mississippi, the eldest of four sons of Murray Charles and Maude Butler Falkner.[1] He was named for his great-grandfather, Colonel William Cuthbert Falkner, soldier of the Mexican and Civil Wars, railroad builder, politician, and author of *The White Rose of Memphis,* a Scott-like novel which his great-grandson and namesake was later to characterize as pure escapism.

About 1900 the family moved to Oxford, Mississippi, where Faulkner's father owned a livery stable and where he later became business manager of the University of Mississippi. Faulkner entered public school there and went easily through the first five grades. After that his schooling was erratic. He left high school before graduating to work in his grandfather's bank. When he was sixteen he enrolled at the University as a special student, at which time he discovered Swinburne, who, he said, "completely satisfied" him. He read Keats and Shelley also, but at the time they left him unmoved.

The outbreak of the war sent him to Canada, where he joined the Canadian Flying Corps. At a training field near Toronto he learned flying, and after the Armistice he left the service

[1] The addition of the "u" to the name came around 1919 or 1920. Faulkner's first published work, a poem in *The New Republic,* is attributed to "William Faulkner," but as late as May 1921 a poem in *The Mississippian,* the University literary magazine, is listed as by "William Falkner." Most (but not all) of the locally published piececs, when signed at all or with more than the initials "W. F.," use the family spelling. Those published elsewhere invariably use the now recognized and accepted spelling. In the 1960 Oxford telephone directory he was listed as "Falkner, William."

with a lieutenancy in the Royal Air Corps. Returning to Oxford, he wrote and saw printed his first published work—a poem in *The New Republic* for August 6, 1919, called "L'Après-midi d'un Faune." On September 19 he enrolled once more at the University. It is reported that he did well in French and Spanish but poorly in English. Even so, the University yearbook published his poem "To a Co-ed" that year, and another "Nocturne" the following year. Meanwhile, *The Mississippian*, the student weekly, reprinted "L'Après-midi d'un Faune" in the October 29 issue, and between then and December 15, 1922, twenty-three other pieces appeared in that publication, among them poems, stories, articles, sketches, and reviews. In November 1920 he left the university and went to New York, where the summer before Stark Young had urged him to go. Young persuaded Elizabeth Prall, who was then head of Lord and Taylor's book section, to give Faulkner a job as clerk, but after only a few months he returned to Oxford and worked for a short while at such odd jobs as roof-painting, paper-hanging, and carpentry. He still had time for writing, however, and besides contributing regularly to *The Mississippian*, he had a poem called "Portrait" published in the June 1922 *The Double Dealer*, a New Orleans literary magazine.

From 1922 to 1924 Faulkner was the United States postmaster at the University. During that time he read a great deal—"undirected and uncorrelated reading"—so much so that he was fired for neglecting his work while on duty. The firing, in keeping with governmental procedure, came in the form of a request for his resignation, which Faulkner complied with forthrightly:

> As long as I live under the capitalistic system, I expect to have my life influenced by the demands of moneyed people. But I will be damned if I propose to be at the beck and call of every itinerant scoundrel[2] who has two cents to invest in a postage stamp. This, sir, is my resignation.

[2] It has been reported that "itinerant scoundrel" is a euphemism for what was originally "son of a bitch."

During Faulkner's stint as a government employee a friend in Oxford, Phil Stone—to whom he later dedicated the Snopes trilogy—put up enough money for the publication of a volume of his poems "in order to get Faulkner before the public." The volume, called *The Marble Faun,* appeared in 1924 with a preface by Stone. But so indifferent was public interest that most of the copies were sold at a bookstore for ten cents each.

Although Faulkner's foremost interest as a youth was to become a writer, he dabbled in other art forms and at one time had contemplated going to New York to study graphic arts. In the 1920-1921 issue of *Ole Miss* he was listed, in addition to being a contributing editor to *The Mississippian,* as a property man of the Marionettes (the school dramatic club) and a member of the art staff of the yearbook. He had a cartoon published in the yearbook as early as the 1916-1917 issue, and the 1917-1918, 1919-1920, 1920-1921, and 1921-1922 issues all contained one or more of his cartoons. The poem, "Nocturne," in the 1920-1921 issue was a reproduction of his own design with borders and text drawn by himself, and it had the unique distinction of beginning on page 215 and continuing on page 214 (in a double-face spread) and of having all the letters "s" backward. *The Scream,* the short-lived campus humor magazine, was established in the fall of 1924, and by February of 1925 Faulkner was listed on the masthead as a member of the art staff. The May 1925 issue contained three of his cartoons, but presumably by that time the artist himself had already left for New Orleans. (For the next two years of the magazine's life his brother John Faulkner was listed as an art editor and apparently the cartoons in those issues signed "Falkner" were by John.) Faulkner's interests in drawing, in writing, and in the theater had all combined in 1920 when he wrote a one-act play, *Marionettes,* which he illustrated, set up, and bound himself.

But with two poems already in national magazines and a book of verse published, the young writer was probably seeking horizons beyond student publications, and with the loss of a steady income as postmaster he set out for New Orleans where he hoped to find work on a freighter that would take him to Europe. When no such work was forthcoming he took on another sea-faring job, in which, in his own words, he "worked for a bootlegger," running "a launch from New Orleans across Ponchartrain down the Industrial Canal out into the Gulf," there to unload and bring back raw alcohol from a schooner operating out of Cuba. While in New Orleans he looked up Miss Prall, who had recently married Sherwood Anderson. Faulkner and Anderson became friends, and for the Dallas *Morning News* for April 26, 1925, Faulkner wrote an article on Anderson. During the same period he wrote sixteen descriptive sketches for the *Times-Picayune* and contributed, again to *The Double Dealer,* three articles and three poems. He also wrote a Foreword to a book of drawings by William Spratling called *Sherwood Anderson and Other Famous Creoles: A Gallery of Contemporary New Orleans,* which was published in 1926. Faulkner became, through his connections with *The Double Dealer,* acquainted with the literary set of New Orleans, which he was later supposed to have satirized in *Mosquitoes.*

Faulkner wrote his first novel, he said, because he liked the way of life led by the one novelist he knew, Sherwood Anderson. "If this is what it takes to be a novelist, then that's the life for me." He completed the novel in six weeks, and Anderson said he would send it to his publisher provided he did not have to read it first. The novel was *Soldiers' Pay,* but before it was published Faulkner at last got the job he had been looking for, and in the summer of 1925 he shipped as a deckhand on a freighter bound for the Mediterranean and Genoa. He spent from six to eight weeks tramping about Europe, mostly in Italy and France.

He returned to Oxford, and with *Soldiers' Pay* in print he settled down to write fiction. "When I found poetry was not suited to what I had to say," he once said, "I changed my medium." *Mosquitoes* appeared in 1927. The next novel—*The Sound and the Fury,* into which Faulkner said he had written his guts—was written but not published until after the fourth,

Sartoris, although both appeared in the same year, 1929. Boni and Liveright, Anderson's publishers, had published the first two novels, and the third to be published, *Sartoris*—dedicated to Anderson—appeared under the Harcourt, Brace imprint. Jonathan Cape and Harrison Smith became the publishers of *The Sound of the Fury*, and they remained Faulkner's publishers (later as Harrison Smith and Robert Haas) until 1936, when Random House took over his work. None of these books had made any money for Faulkner, so he decided to write the most sensational novel of which his imagination was capable. He was about to be married and needed the money. The book he wrote was *Sanctuary*, but when he sent it off to Harrison Smith, Smith wrote back that if he published it both he and Faulkner would go to jail. It was published in 1931, but only after Faulkner had torn up the galley proofs and completely rewritten it.

On June 20, 1929, Faulkner married Mrs. Estelle Oldham Franklin, the mother of two children by a former marriage. That same summer he got a job on the night shift of the Oxford power plant, shoveling coal from six in the evening to six in the morning. Toward midnight, when there was little electricity being used and therefore less work to do, Faulkner would turn a wheelbarrow upside down to use as a table; on it he wrote *As I Lay Dying*, working nights from twelve to four for six weeks. He sent it, "without changing a word," to Harrison Smith —to whom it was dedicated—and the novel was published in 1930.

That same year his first short story, "A Rose for Emily," was published in the April *Forum*. Three more stories, "Honor," "Thrift," and "Red Leaves," appeared the same year, the first in *The American Mercury* and the last two in *The Saturday Evening Post*. From then on, every year from 1930 to 1943— with the exception of 1938—one or more of his stories appeared in periodicals, sometimes as many as eight or nine a year.

When *As I Lay Dying* was finished Faulkner recalled *Sanctuary*, which was already in galleys. He reread it and decided it was too bad to publish in its present form, so he rewrote it.

When it appeared in 1931 it was an immediate success, giving Faulkner, for the first time, both public acclaim and money. The motion picture industry then got interested in him and invited him to Hollywood to write. In 1932 he went there and adapted his short story "Turn About" for Metro-Goldwyn-Mayer. It was produced in April of that year as "Today We Live," starring Joan Crawford and Gary Cooper—this despite the fact that no female appears in the original story. In June of the same year Paramount turned *Sanctuary* into a picture called "The Story of Temple Drake," with Miriam Hopkins and Jack Larue in the leading roles. Faulkner did not write the dialogue for this picture. He did, however, work off and on in Hollywood, helping with the scripts for "The Road to Glory" (1936), "Slave Ship" (1937), "To Have and Have Not" (1944), and "The Big Sleep" (1946). And as late as 1954 he journeyed to Egypt with Howard Hawks to work on a Cinemascope extravaganza entitled "Land of the Pharaohs," which was duly advertized as "written by William Faulkner." Faulkner called himself not a script writer but a "motion picture doctor," one who rewrote a dialogue until it was satisfactory to the director.

Meanwhile Faulkner continued writing short stories and novels. His first collection of stories, *These 13*, appeared in 1931, the same year as *Sanctuary*. Of the thirteen stories, seven made their first appearance here. He also reviewed for the May 20 *The New Republic* Erich Maria Remarque's *The Road Back*. During the same year Random House published a limited edition of a short story, *Idyll in the Desert*, which had not before and has not since been published elsewhere. Whether due to the vogue of *Sanctuary* or to the printing of this limited edition or both, three more pieces of Faulkner esoterica appeared the following year. One was a book called *Salmagundi*, published with a preface by Paul Romaine. It consisted of Faulkner's contributions to *The Double Dealer*, the one poem of 1922 and the three poems and articles of 1925, plus his first published poem—the one in the August 6, 1919, *The New Republic*. To add to its exotic nature (it was limited to 525 copies), the back cover contained a poem by Ernest M. Hemingway, printed, according to Romaine, as a "whim," because it had appeared on the same page of *The Double Dealer* as Faulkner's "Portrait." The second limited edition book to appear in 1932 was another short story, "Miss Zilphia Gant," published by the Book Club of Texas for distribution to its members, with a preface by Henry Smith, in which he remarked that such publication was "appropriate" because "Faulkner's work is so closely identified with the South that it seems almost out of place on an Eastern publisher's list." The third was a pamphlet consisting of a single eight-line poem which had appeared in February of the same year in *Contempo*, a newspaper-like magazine of which the entire issue had been devoted to Faulkner's work. Called "My Epitaph" in its first printing, the poem was revised and rechristened *This Earth* for its solo publication. More important to the year 1932 was the appearance of *Light in August*.

In 1933 Faulkner's daughter and only surviving child, Jill, was born. For publication, that year saw only *A Green Bough*, Faulkner's last book of poems, which contained most of the poems previously published in magazines plus quite a few more published here for the first time. Because the book had been announced as early as 1925, the assumption is that most of the poems in it were early work, although many of those which had previously appeared were revised for the book publication. In 1947 Faulkner said that at the age of twenty-three he quite writing poetry, which, if accurate, would mean that all his poems were written before 1920.

The tremendous spurt of creative activity between 1929 and 1932 had quieted down, and Faulkner's books from that time on were to appear more generously spaced. Only one book appeared in 1934—*Doctor Martino and Other Stories*—fourteen stories, all but two reprinted from earlier magazine publication. In 1935 came his novel about stunt flyers, *Pylon*, and a review of another book on flying, *Test Pilot*, by Jimmy Collins, published in the November *American Mercury*. Faulkner had bought a small plane with some of his Hollywood money, and had helped finance one of his brothers who was a stunt flyer. When the brother was killed in a crash in 1935, Faulkner gave up flying. In 1936 appeared *Absalom, Absalom!* and in 1938 *The Unvanquished,* which consisted of seven related short stories, all but one of them having had earlier magazine publication. In January 1939 Faulkner was elected to membership in the National Institute of Arts and Letters, and later the same year *The Wild Palms* was published.

Faulkner's output during the 1940s was far less than that of the 1930s. (Meanwhile his brother John had started publishing novels.) In 1940 appeared *The Hamlet* and in 1942 *Go Down, Moses and Other Stories,* parts of both having been made up of earlier published short stories. Even his contribution of short stories to magazines dwindled. 1940 saw five, 1941 two, 1942 three, and 1943 three.[3] Between 1943 and 1948 only one short story of Faulkner's was published, that in *Ellery Queen's Mystery Magazine* in 1946. And by that time all of his novels (and other books) with the single exception of *Sanctuary* were out of print. The vogue of Faulkner—if there had been a vogue—was over. Then in 1946 Malcom Cowley edited for the Viking Press in its "Portable" series a *Portable Faulkner,* which included an introduction that routed a lot of the misconceptions which had been built up around Faulkner by earlier critics, and which presented a revaluation of him in terms of the whole fabric of the Yoknapatawpha County novels and stories. This helped to spark a revival of Faulkner, which moved rapidly to its climax in November 1950, when the announcement was made that he had been awarded the 1949 Nobel Prize for literature.

Meanwhile in 1948 Faulkner had published one novel, *Intruder in the Dust,* and one short story, "A Courtship," and in 1949 a collection of six related stories, *Knight's Gambit,* four of them having been published in magazines between 1932 and 1940, and a fifth in 1946. Also in 1949 *Intruder in the Dust*

---

[3] There were four stories published in 1943 if one counts Maurice Edgar Coindreau's translation of "Afternoon of a Cow" in a French periodical. The original was not published until 1947.

was made into a motion picture by Merto-Goldywn-Mayer, starring David Brian, Claude Jarman, Jr., and Juano Hernandez, with Oxford, Mississippi as the location. In 1950 the *Collected Stories* appeared, as well as a limited signed edition of *Notes on a Horsethief*, which was a seventy-one page narrative that later became part of *A Fable*, and "A Name for the City," a short story which became part of *Requiem for a Nun*.

Honors for William Faulkner began to come rapidly about this time. The Summer, 1949 and Autumn, 1950 issues of *Perspective* were devoted entirely to Faulkner studies. In 1950 he received the Howells Medal of the American Academy of Arts and Letters —and the Nobel Prize. In 1951 he received the National Book award "for distinguished literary achievement" and the Legion of Honor of France. The November 1951 issue of the *Harvard Advocate* was an all-Faulkner number. In 1951, also, appeared two full-length books on Faulkner, and in 1952 two more. Within a decade there were sixteen books about Faulkner in print and several more "all-Faulkner" issues of magazines had appeared. In 1952 in Denver was started a small newsletter type of magazine called *Faulkner Studies* (it was moved to Minneapolis in 1953 and lasted until 1955). In 1951 Faulkner published another novel, *Requiem for a Nun*, a kind of sequel to *Sanctuary*. No fiction of his appeared in 1952 or 1953. In April 1953 he adapted his story "The Brooch" for television, and in 1954 *A Fable* was published, which received both the National Book Award and the Pulitzer Prize. Earlier that year *The Faulkner Reader*, containing a representative selection but nothing new except the Foreword, had appeared. In 1955 there were two new short stories, "Race at Morning" in the March 5 *Saturday Evening Post*, and "By the People" in the October *Mademoiselle*. The former was revised for inclusion in *Big Woods*, a 1955 collection of four hunting stories, all the rest of the book being made up of earlier published material. "By the People" was rewritten for inclusion in *The Mansion*. In 1957 came *The Town* and in 1959 *The Mansion*, which, along with *The Hamlet*, made up the trilogy devoted to the Snopes family. In 1962 appeared *The*

Reivers, which introduced a new family, the Priests, of Yoknap-
atwapha County.

Up until 1950 and the award of the Nobel Prize, Faulkner
the man was a person more legendary than real. Except for a
few brief jaunts into the alien world he remained in Oxford, a
farmer who preferred to talk with his neighbors and go hunting
than to be interviewed and meet celebrities. "Because I write
doesn't make what I eat for breakfast or think of the international situation a matter of news or public concern," he once
remarked. And except for a rare lettter to the Oxford *Eagle* or
to the Memphis *Commercial-Appeal*, he did not express his
personal views in print.

It was something of a shock, then, when people read in *Intruder
in the Dust* (in the words of the lawyer Gavin Stevens) what
seemed like the Mississippi gentleman farmer speaking directly on
current racial issues, and using the tarnished argument that the
South must work out its own problems without interference from
ignorant outsiders. Jefferson and Yoknapatawpha County seemed
suddenly to merge with Oxford and Lafayette County, to come
out of the geography of William Faulkner's imagination and into
the geography of actual American social and political history.
Critics argued, but since the book *was* a novel, the controversy
it stirred up was transitory. There were statements in print about
Faulkner the citizen made by others (some of whom were his
close friends), but there was precious little information about him
to be got from Faulkner himself. The 1925 essay "Verse Old and
Nascent: A Pilgrimage," a facetiously worded note to the editor
of *The Forum* published in the April 1930 issue, and the 1932
Introduction to the Modern Library edition of *Sanctuary* were
the only autobiographical and personal opinion remarks to be
had from him.[4]

But during the 1950's all this changed. Faulkner had not wanted
to go to Stockholm to receive the Nobel Prize in person but he

---

[4] Faulkner had allowed students in writing classes at the University of
Mississippi in 1947 to ask him questions, but no report of the interviews was
published until 1951.

was finally persuaded to go. The highly publicized trip and the interest aroused by the now famous acceptance speech seemed to awaken a public consciousness in Faulkner, and it was not long before he was making all kinds of public appearances, from talking before his daughter's high school graduating class to addressing the national conference of the U. S. National Commission for UNESCO. At the behest of the State Department he travelled to Europe and Japan as a cultural representative of this country. He attended the International Congress of Writers in Brazil. In each place he let himself be interviewed freely on various topics. He gave interviews to American reporters. He wrote letters to the *New York Times* expressing his opinion on current events. He permitted two commercially produced long-playing records of him reading from his works to be released. He wrote an appreciation of Sherwood Anderson for the *Atlantic Monthly,* an article on his home state for *Holiday,* a nostalgic piece on his grandfather's funeral for *Harper's Bazaar,* and an approval of the New England character for *Ford Times.* He even turned to reportage for Henry Luce's *Sports Illustrated,* writing on a hockey game and the Kentucky Derby. In 1957 and 1958 he was "Writer-in-Residence" at the University of Virginia.

All this was perhaps not to be expected from a man who deemed privacy a first freedom, but it was not especially unusual. What was unusual was the letters, speeches, and articles he wrote and delivered concerning the desegregation issues following the Supreme Court decision of 1954. They started early in 1955 in a series of letters to the Memphis *Commercial-Appeal* in which he came out strongly in favor of school integration. The letters were followed by a speech before a meeting of the Southern Historical Association, an interview in *The Reporter,* and articles in *Life, Harper's,* and *Ebony.* Whatever the total aim, the combination succeeded in alienating most Southern conservatives and many Northern liberals, for along with his arguments for school integration went warnings to the North to keep hands off. To the South, of course, he was a renegade, and he was not only insulted but threatened as well. He spoke with a voice of reason at a time when emotion dominated both camps. But it was a voice consistent with the views he had expressed throughout the 1950's, from the Nobel Prize speech of November 1950 to the UNESCO speech of October 1959, in which he repeatedly emphasized his belief in the individual dignity of man (and which many of his earlier novels and stories had profusely illustrated among both Negro and white characters).

Faulkner enjoyed his stint as Writer-in-Residence at the University of Virginia in 1957 and 1958, and in 1959 he bought a house in Charlottesville. He lived there during the school year, continuing intermittently as Writer-in-Residence, but returned to Oxford for the summers. The university was only part of the reason for the partial abandonment of Oxford, for Faulkner's daughter was married and living in Charlottesville, and it was there that his grandchildren were. At the end of the school year in the spring of 1962 Faulkner and his wife went back to Oxford, and on July 6 of that year he died of a heart attack, just one month and two days after the publication of *The Reivers*.

As a man Faulkner was a Southerner and a Mississippian, spiritually as well as environmentally. (He once said that he would fight in the streets for Mississippi against the United States if need be.) But although the vast majority of his novels and stories have a Mississippi setting, as a writer Faulkner was not a Southerner spiritually. Many have been the attempts to make a regionalist out of him, but his themes are too universally human to be confined to a single locality. When Faulkner was once asked why he used his own locality for the settings of most of his stories he replied: "I have seen no other." That Oxford and Lafayette County provide the tangible supports for the more levitated Jefferson and Yoknapatawpha County has never been doubted nor denied, and the similarities between the two towns and counties are striking. Both are situated in the pine hill country of northwestern Mississippi. Both were originally Chickasaw country. Both have the Tallahatchie River for a northern boundary. (Yoknapatawpha County has the Yoknapatawpha River for a southern boundary, while Lafayette County has the Yocona—

formerly Yocanapatafa—River running through its southwestern corner.) Both Oxford and Jefferson are seventy-five miles southeast of Memphis (Oxford and Jefferson, however, are forty miles apart). The general layout of Jefferson corresponds to that of Oxford. Names which are a part of Oxford history appear in Yoknapatawpha County stories. Oxford was founded by a Thomas Dudley Isom from Maury County, Tennessee, and both Isom and Maury are names to be found in the stories. Probably Oxford's most distinquished citizen (before William Faulkner) was Lucius Quintus Cincinnatus Lamar, the Secretary of the Interior in Cleveland's cabinet. The same initials and the same first two names are given to the characters Peabody, McCaslin, and Priest, while Lamar is the name given to Lee Goodwin's (common-law) wife. A man named Howard W. Odum studied at the University of Mississippi, and Odum becomes both a first and a last name. A Judge Stevens was at one time mayor of Oxford and of Jefferson. Senator Vardaman has given (perhaps) his name to the youngest Bundren son, and the Gowrie and Snopes twins are named Vardaman and Bilbo. And so on. The external details of Colonel Sartoris' life correspond generally with those of Faulkner's great-grandfather, Colonel William C. Falkner. It has been said that Gavin Stevens was patterned after Phil Stone, Faulkner's lawyer friend. Rumor tells us that many more Yoknapatawpha County inhabitants have their counterparts in real people of the region, past and present, and that many of the incidents in the stories are based upon local history and lore. But to read the stories and novels as literal regionalism is to make a vast mistake. They so far transcend any merely local significance that it becomes a travesty to set the county of Yoknapatawpha solely in one single geographical location. "The area," said Faulkner, "is incidental."

According to Faulkner himself, what he tried to do in his writings was "to tell the truth of man." He said that he made use of imagination when he "had to," and presented pictures of cruelty "as a last resort," and that his purpose was "to create out of the materials of the human spirit something which did not exist before." "One writes," he said, "to help people." Of his books he mentioned *As I Lay Dying, The Sound and the Fury,* and *Go Down, Moses,* among his favorites, and said that *Sanctuary* is "not a very good book." He believed that form is important to the novel, and that an author should be daring in his handling of vocabulary. He ranked (with certain qualifications) among his contemporaries Wolfe, Dos Passos, Hemingway, Steinbeck, and Willa Cather as the best.

Appendix II

THE POETRY

FAULKNER'S KNOWN published poetry consists of seventy different pieces, all of them published between 1919 and 1933. Only six of them remain uncollected, those six having all been published in *Contempo*. Of the remaining sixty-four, thirty-one first appeared in periodicals and the other thirty-three had their first appearance in book form. There are two books of Faulkner's verse, *The Marble Faun* (1924) and *A Green Bough* (1933), a pamphlet, *This Earth* (1932), and parts of two other volumes, *Salmagundi* (1932), and *William Faulkner: Early Prose and Poetry* (1962).

Faulkner's first published poem and first published piece of any kind was "l'Après-midi d'un Faune," which appeared in *The New Republic* for August 6, 1919. Next came his contributions to *Ole Miss*, the yearbook of the University of Mississippi, one poem in the 1919-1920 issue and another in the 1920-1921 issue, and to the student weekly, *The Mississippian,* thirteen poems which appeared between November 12, 1919, and May 4, 1921. His next poem, "Portrait," was published in *The Double Dealer* in 1922. This was followed by *The Marble Faun* in 1924 and by three more poems in *The Double Dealer* in 1925. Aside from one poem and several fragments which appeared in *Soldier's Pay* and *Mosquitoes,* no more verse was published until 1932, when ten poems were published in *Contempo* for February 1 and one for May 25. In 1933, the same year as the publication of *A Green Bough,* seven more poems were published, one in the June 25 issue of *Contempo,* and four in the April 12, one in the April 19, and one in the May 3 *The New Republic.*

The verse in *The Marble Faun*—a single cyclic poem of 806

lines—appears only there. The verse in *Salmagundi* contains the four contributions to *The Double Dealer* and Faulkner's first published poem. *William Faulkner: Early Prose and Poetry* contains the two poems from *Ole Miss,* the thirteen from *The Mississippian,* "L'Après-midi d'un Faune," and three of the four *Double Dealer* poems. *A Green Bough,* consisting of forty-four poems, contains thirty-one not published elsewhere, although among them are the completed forms of the fragments of three which had been published in his first two novels. *A Green Bough,* Faulkner's last book of verse, besides presenting much new material, gathers up a number of earlier published poems and fragments, nearly all of them in revised form. One of the *Double Dealer* poems (already in *Salmagundi*), five of the *Contempo* poems, six of the *New Republic* poems, and one from *Mosquitoes* are there. In addition, the four-line epigraph on the half-title page of *Soldiers' Pay* and stanzas and fragmentary lines from *Mosquitoes* are incorporated into three other poems in the volume. The pamphlet, *This Earth,* which originally appeared somewhat differently in *Contempo,* becomes the final poem in *A Green Bough.*

William Faulkner was twenty-two when his first poem appeared. He was thirty-six when the last of his poems was published. He once said that the best age for writing poetry is from seventeen to twenty-six, and that he quit writing at the age of twenty-three. There is no question that his poetry is all youthful work. The text of *The Marble Faun* is dated April, May, June, 1919. As early as 1925 *A Green Bough* (then called *The Greening Bough*) was announced. Its eight-year delay was perhaps due to the poor reception of *The Marble Faun* the year previous, and its appearance in 1933 due to the hope that the resulting popularity of *Sanctuary* would help with its sales. But because there were poems published in magazines as late as 1932 and 1933, there is no reason to believe that they were newly written, even though those which appeared in 1932 and included in *A Green Bough* were included there in revised form. One writes poetry, said Faulkner, when he is "seventeen, eighteen, nineteen," and "you don't think of printing it until later."

All the volumes of Faulkner's verse have long been out of print. A few poems have been reprinted in anthologies, and even fewer have appeared in various studies or catalogues of material on Faulkner by other hands. The following bibliography lists the poems in chronological order of their original publication and tries to list as completely as possible the appearance of individual poems in later and generally more accessible places.[1]

BIBLIOGRAPHY:

Following are the volumes containing Faulkner's poetry:

The Marble Faun. Boston: The Four Seas Company, 1924. With a preface by Phil Stone. [A single poem of 806 lines including a prologue and epilogue. Not published elsewhere.]

Salmagundi. Milwaukee: The Casanova Press, 1932. Edited with an introduction by Paul Romaine. [Contains "L'Après-midi d'un Faune," "Portrait," "Dying Gladiator," "The Faun," and "Lilacs," all reprinted from elsewhere.]

This Earth. New York: The Equinox Cooperative Press, 1932. [This is "My Epitaph" (see below); it became the final poem in *A Green Bough.*]

A Green Bough. New York: Harrison Smith and Robert Haas, 1933. [Contains forty-four poems, thirteen from previous publication and thirty-one new.]

William Faulkner: Early Prose and Poetry. Boston: Little, Brown and Co., 1962. Edited with an introduction and notes by Carvel Collins. [Contains nineteen poems, all reprinted from elsewhere.]

The appearance of individual poems follows:
"L'Après-midi d'un Faune." *The New Republic,* XX (Aug. 6,

---

[1] In 1955 Gallimard of Paris published a bilingual (English-French) edition of *A Green Bough,* the French translation by R. N. Raimbault, under the title *Le Rameau Vert.* It is probably more readily available than the original 1933 volume of the poems.

1919), 24 [reprinted in *The Mississippian,* IX (Oct. 29, 1919), 4, *Salmagundi,* pp. 52-53, and *William Faulkner: Early Prose and Poetry,* pp. 39-40].

"Cathay." *The Mississippian,* IX (Nov. 12, 1919), 8 [reprinted in *William Faulkner: Early Prose and Poetry,* p. 41].

"Sapphics." *The Mississippian,* IX (Nov. 26, 1919), 3 [reprinted in *William Faulkner: Early Prose and Poetry,* pp. 51-52].

"After Fifty Years." *The Mississippian,* IX (Dec. 10, 1919), 4 [reprinted in Martha Mayes's "Faulkner Juvenilia," *New Campus Writing No. 2,* ed. Nolan Miller (New York: Bantam Books, 1957), p. 138, and in *William Faulkner: Early Prose and Poetry,* p. 53].

"Une Ballade des Femmes Perdues." *The Mississippian,* IX (Jan. 28, 1920), 3 [reprinted in Martha Mayes's "Faulkner Juvenilia," pp. 139-140, and in *William Faulkner: Early Prose and Poetry,* p. 54].

"Naiad's Song." *The Mississippian,* IX (Feb. 4, 1920), 3 [reprinted in *William Faulkner: Early Prose and Poetry,* pp. 55-56].

"Fantouches." *The Mississippian,* IX (Feb. 25, 1920), 3 [reprinted in Martha Mayes's "Faulkner Juvenilia," p. 141, and (as "Fantoches") in *William Faulkner: Early Prose and Poetry,* p. 57].

"Clair de Lune." *The Mississippian,* IX (Mar. 3, 1920), 6 [reprinted in *William Faulkner: Early Prose and Poetry,* p. 58].

"Streets." *The Mississippian,* IX (Mar. 17, 1920, 2 [reprinted in *William Faulkner: Early Prose and Poetry,* p. 59].

"A Poplar." *The Mississippian,* IX (Mar. 17, 1920), 7 [reprinted in Martha Mayes's "Faulkner Juvenilia," pp. 137-138, and in *William Faulkner: Early Prose and Poetry,* p. 60].

"A Clymene." *The Mississippian,* IX (Apr. 14, 1920), 3 [reprinted in *William Faulkner: Early Prose and Poetry,* p. 61].

"Study." *The Mississippian,* IX (Apr. 24, 1920), 4 [reprinted in Martha Mayes's "Faulkner Juvenilia," p. 139, and in *William Faulkner: Early Prose and Poetry,* pp. 62-63].

"Alma Mater." *The Mississippian,* IX (May 12, 1920), 3 [reprinted in *William Faulkner: Early Prose and Poetry,* p. 64].

"To a Co-ed." *Ole Miss, the Yearbook of the University of*

Mississippi, XXIV (1919-1920), p. 174 [reprinted in the Memphis *Commercial-Appeal*, Nov. 6, 1932, Magazine section, p. 4, in James B. Meriwether, *The Literary Career of William Faulkner*, Princeton University Library, 1961, p. 9, and in *William Faulkner: Early Prose and Poetry*, p. 70].

"Co-Education at Ole Miss." *The Mississippian*, X (May 4, 1921), 5 [reprinted in *William Faulkner: Early Prose and Poetry*, p. 77].

"Nocturne." *Ole Miss, the Yearbook of the University of Mississippi*, XXV (1920-1921), pp. 214-215 [reproduced in facsimile in James B. Meriwether, *The Literary Career of William Faulkner*, Princeton University Library, 1961, Pl. 2, and in *William Faulkner: Early Prose and Poetry*, pp. 82-83 (see note on this in Glossary)].

"Portrait." *The Double Dealer*, II (June 1922), 337 [reprinted in *Salmagundi*, pp. 45-46, and in *William Faulkner: Early Prose and Poetry*, pp. 99-100].

"Dying Gladiator." *The Double Dealer*, VII (Jan.-Feb. 1925), 85 [reprinted in *Salmagundi*, pp. 43-44, and in *William Faulkner: Early Prose and Poetry*, p. 113].

"The Faun." *The Double Dealer*, VII (Apr. 1925), 148 [reprinted in *Salmagundi*, p. 42, and in *William Faulkner: Early Prose and Poetry*, p. 119].

"The Lilacs." *The Double Dealer*, VII (June 1925), 185-187 [reprinted in *Salmagundi*, pp. 47-51, and (revised) as *A Green Bough*, I; also in *Anthology of Magazine Verse for 1925*, ed. William Stanley Braithwaite, Boston, B. J. Brimmer Co., 1925, pp. 115-118].

"Hermaphroditus." In *Mosquitoes*, p. 252 [reprinted (revised) as *A Green Bough*, XXX].

"I Will Not Weep for Youth." *Contempo*, I (Feb. 1, 1932), 1 [uncollected, but reprinted in *An Anthology of the Younger Poets*, ed. Oliver Wells, Philadelphia: The Centaur Press, 1932, p. 122].

"Knew I Love Once." *Contempo*, I (Feb. 1, 1932), 1 [reprinted, revised, as *A Green Bough*, XXXIII; also in *An Anthology of the Younger Poets*, p. 125].

"Twilight." *Contempo*, I (Feb. 1, 1932), 1 [reprinted, revised, as *A Green Bough*, X; also in *An Anthology of the Younger Poets*, p. 126].

"Visions in Spring." *Contempo*, I (Feb. 1, 1932), 1 [uncollected].

"Spring." *Contempo*, I (Feb. 1, 1932), 2 [reprinted, revised, as *A Green Bough*, XXXVI].

"April." *Contempo*, I (Feb. 1, 1932), 2 [uncollected].

"To a Virgin." *Contempo*, I (Feb. 1, 1932), 2 [reprinted, revised, as *A Green Bough*, XXXIX; also in *An Anthology of the Younger Poets*, p .123].

"Winter Is Gone." *Contempo*, I (Feb. 1, 1932), 2 [uncollected, but reprinted in *An Anthology of the Younger Poets*, p. 124].

"My Epitaph." *Contempo*, I (Feb. 1, 1932), 2 [reprinted, revised, as *This Earth*, and, again revised, as *A Green Bough*, XLIV; also as "My Epitaph" in *An Anthology of the Younger Poets*, p. 123, in *Mississippi Verse*, ed. Alice James, Chapel Hill: University of North Carolina Press, 1934, p. 33, under the title "If There Be Grief," and in *Life*, LIII (July 20, 1952), 42].

"A Child Looks from His Window." *Contempo*, II (May 25, 1932), 3 [uncollected].

"The Race's Splendor." *The New Republic*, LXXIV (Apr. 12, 1933), 253 [reprinted as *A Green Bough*, XXXVII; also in *The New Republic*, CXXXI (Nov. 22, 1954), 82].

"Night Piece." *The New Republic*, LXXIV (Apr. 12, 1933), 253 [reprinted as *A Green Bough*, VII].

"Gray the Day." *The New Republic*, LXXIV (Apr. 12, 1933), 253 [reprinted as *A Green Bough*, XXX].

"Over the World's Rim." *The New Republic*, LXXIV (Apr. 12, 1933), 253 [reprinted as *A Green Bough*, XXVIII].

"The Ship of Night." *The New Republic*, LXXIV (Apr. 19, 1933), 272 [reprinted as *A Green Bough*, XXXIV].

"Man Comes, Man Goes." *The New Republic*, LXXIV (May 3, 1933), 338 [reprinted as *A Green Bough*, VI; also in *The New Republic Anthology: 1915-1935*, ed. Groff Conklin, New York:

The Dodge Publishing Company, 1936, p. 451, and in *Fiction Parade*, V (Oct. 1937), 740].

"The Flowers That Died." *Contempo*, III (June 25, 1933), 1 [uncollected].

The following anthologies contain selections from Faulkner's poetry:

Anthology of Magazine Verse for 1925 and Yearbook of American Poetry, ed. William Stanley Braithwaite, Boston: B. J. Brimmer Company, 1925. [Contains "The Lilacs," pp. 115-118.]

An Anthology of the Younger Poets, ed. Oliver Wells with a Preface by Archibald MacLeish, Philadelphia: The Centaur Press, 1932. [Contains "I Will Not Weep for Youth," p. 122; "My Epitaph," p. 123; "To a Virgin," p. 123; "Winter is Gone," p. 124; "Knew I Love Once," p. 125; and "Twilight," p. 126.]

Mississippi Verse, ed. Alice James, Chapel Hill: The University of North Carolina Press, 1934. [Contains, with titles added, the following, all from *A Green Bough*: "Mirror of Youth," p. 31 (*A Green Bough*, XVI); "The Courtesan Is Dead," p. 32 (*A Green Bough*, XXXV); "Green Is the Water," p. 32 (*A Green Bough*, XIX); "If There Be Grief," p. 33 (*A Green Bough*, XLIV); "Here He Stands," p. 33 (*A Green Bough*, XX); "Boy and Eagle," p. 34 (*A Green Bough*, XVIII); and "Mother and Child," pp. 34-35 (*A Green Bough*, XIV).]

Appendix III
THE NONFICTION PROSE

FAULKNER'S NONFICTION prose is scanty, and belongs almost wholly to an early and a late period. Between 1935 and 1950, for instance, there was published (not including letters) just one short piece, and that only locally. The earliest known of Faulkner's non-poetry and nonfiction are his contributions to *The Mississippian,* the student weekly of the university, between 1919 and 1922. There he reviewed books (by W. A. Percy, Edna St. Vincent Millay, Conrad Aiken, and Joseph Hergesheimer), wrote two articles on American drama, and contributed other minor pieces. He moved to New Orleans early in 1925 and at once began contributing to periodicals there. Between January and September he wrote sixteen descriptive sketches for the Sunday section of the *Times-Picayune,* and for the January-February and April issues of *The Double Dealer* he contributed three pieces. He also wrote an article on Sherwood Anderson for the Dallas *Morning News* during the same period. These all appeared before he had published any standard fiction, and shortly after his first book of poems had come out.

Some months after the appearance of his first novel, *Soldiers' Pay,* in 1926, Faulkner once more appeared in print, this time in a Foreword to a book of drawings by William Spratling called *Sherwood Anderson & Other Famous Creoles: A Gallery of Contemporary New Orleans.* The rest of the decade being taken up with fiction (five novels, one collection of short stories, and thirteen individually published short stories between 1927 and 1931), no nonfiction prose appeared until 1931, when he wrote a review of *The Road Back* by Erich Maria Remarque for the May 20

New Republic. Another book review, that of Jimmy Collins' *Test Pilot,* appeared in the *American Mercury* for November 1935, the same year as Faulkner's own novel on flying, *Pylon,* was published. Meanwhile, in 1932 appeared his now famed Introduction to the Modern Library reprint of *Sanctuary,* the earliest and one of the few comments on his own writing.

After the review of *Test Pilot,* almost seventeen years were to pass before Faulkner published any more expository prose for the general public. His only piece of nonfiction prose published during the 1940s appeared in the Oxford *Eagle* in 1946 in a bitter statement when a hit-and-run driver killed his daughter's dog. In 1950 he distributed a broadside addressed "To the Voters of Oxford," a reply and a "Correction" to statements made by three local clergymen concerning the evils of beer, and signed, "William Faulkner, Private Citizen."

During the 1950's Faulkner produced a larger body of nonfiction prose, which was further enlarged by the publication of twelve speeches given during the decade and by a number of letters—not to mention the appearance in print of several interviews. In 1952 he reviewed Hemingway's *The Old Man and the Sea* for *Shenandoah.* In 1953 he contributed three "local color" pieces to three different magazines, one on "Mississippi" to *Holiday,* one on his grandfather's funeral to *Harper's Bazaar,* and one on the people of New England to *Ford Times.* In 1955 came a stint as a reporter, with a piece on a hockey game and another on the Kentucky Derby for *Sports Illustrated.* His "Impressions of Japan" also appeared in 1955. Three articles on the racial problem appeared in 1956, one in *Life,* one in *Harper's,* and one in *Ebony.* These, along with a number of letters, the speeches, and a Foreword and a couple of "Notes" to editions of his works, make up the output of nonfiction prose during the 1950s.

Excluding the interviews, the bibliography of the nonfiction prose of Faulkner consists of ninety-five items. One, the sketch (actually a short story) "Landing in Luck," appeared in 1919. Of the other ninety-three, thirty were published during the 1920's, ten during the 1930's and 1940's, forty-nine during the 1950's, and five during the 1960's. The distribution speaks for itself.

BIBLIOGRAPHY:

ARTICLES

"The Ivory Tower." *The Mississippian,* IX (Mar. 17, 1920), 4. Reprinted slightly changed in Martha Mayes's "Faulkner Juvenilia," *New Campus Writing No. 2,* ed. Nolan Miller, New York: Bantam Books, 1957, pp. 142-143. [This is a humorously sarcastic criticism of a writer who had parodied Faulkner's poems "Une Ballade des Femmes Perdues" and "Fantouches."]

"American Drama: Eugene O'Neill." *The Mississippian,* XI (Feb. 3, 1922), 5. Reprinted in *William Faulkner: Early Prose and Poetry,* pp. 86-89.

"American Drama: Inhibitions." *The Mississippian,* XI (Mar. 17, 1822), 5 and (Mar. 24, 1922), 5. Reprinted in *William Faulkner: Early Prose and Poetry,* pp. 93-97.

"On Criticism." *The Double Dealer,* VII (Jan.-Feb. 1925), 83-84. Reprinted in *Salmagundi,* pp. 29-33, and in *William Faulkner: Early Prose and Poetry,* pp. 109-112,

"Verse Old and Nascent: A Pilgrimage." *The Double Dealer,* VII (Apr. 1925), 129-131. Reprinted in *Salmagundi,* pp. 34-39, and in *William Faulkner: Early Prose and Poetry,* pp. 114-118.

"Sherwood Anderson." The Dallas *Morning News,* Apr. 26, 1925, Pt. III, p. 7. Reprinted in the *Princeton University Library Chronicle,* XVIII (Spring 1957), 89-94.

"His Name Was Pete." The Oxford *Eagle,* Aug. 15, 1946, p. 1. Reprinted in same (with slight changes), Dec. 21, 1950, p. 25; in *Magazine Digest,* XXVI (Jan. 1953), 93-94; and in the Milwaukee *Journal,* Jan. 28, 1953, p. 24.

"Sherwood Anderson: An Appreciation." *The Atlantic Monthly,* CXCI (June 1953), 27-29.

"Mississippi." *Holiday,* XV (Apr. 1954), 33-47. Part of this appeared in a different form in *Big Woods,* pp. 165-171 (unnumbered).

"Sepulture South: Gaslight." *Harper's Bazaar,* LXXXVIII (Dec. 1954), 84, 140, and 141.

"A Guest's Impression of New England." *New England Journeys No. 2* (*Ford Times* Special Edition), 1954, 6-8.

"An Innocent at Rinkside." *Sports Illustrated*, II (Jan. 24, 1955), 15.

"Kentucky: May: Saturday." *Sports Illustrated*, II (May 16, 1955), 22-24 and 26. Reprinted in *Essays Today 2*, ed. Richard M. Ludwig, New York: Harcourt, Brace & Co., 1956, pp. 41-45.

"Impressions of Japan." A release by the United States Embassy in Tokyo. The Memphis *Commercial-Appeal*, Sept. 26, 1955, Sec. V, p. 14, and Oct. 2, 1955, Sec. V, p. 10. Reprinted in *Esquire*, L (Dec. 1958), 140, and in *Faulkner at Nagano*, pp. 178-184.

"Message Given at Nagano." *Faulkner at Nagano*, pp. 175-177.

"To the Youth of Japan." U. S. information Service, Tokyo, 1955. A pamphlet, with text in both Japanese and English. English version reprinted in *Faulkner at Nagano*, pp. 185-188.

"A Letter to the North." *Life*, XL (Mar. 5, 1956), 51-52. A condensed version appeared in *Readers' Digest*, LXVIII (May 1956), 75-78. On the school integration question.

"On Fear: The South in Labor." *Harper's Magazine*, CCXII (June 1956), 29-34. On the school integration question.

"If I Were a Negro." *Ebony*, XI (Sept. 1956), 70-73. On the school integration question.

"Albert Camus." *The Transatlantic Review No. 6* (Spring 1961), 5. An appreciation of Camus after his death.

BOOK REVIEWS

Review of *In April Once* by W. A. Percy. *The Mississippian*, IX (Nov. 10, 1920), 5. Reprinted in *William Faulkner: Early Prose and Poetry*, pp. 71-73.

Review of *Turns and Movies* by Conrad Aiken. *The Mississippian*, X (Feb. 16, 1921), 5. Reprinted in *William Faulkner: Early Prose and Poetry*, pp. 74-76.

Review of *Aria da Capo* by Edna St. Vincent Millay. *The Mississipian*, XI (Jan. 13, 1922), 5. Reprinted in *William Faulkner: Early Prose and Poetry*, pp. 84-85.

Review of *Linda Condon, Cytherea,* and *The Bright Shawl* by Joseph Hergesheimer. *The Mississippian,* XII (Dec. 15, 1922), 5. Reprinted in *William Faulkner: Early Prose and Poetry,* pp. 101-103.

"Beyond the Talking." (Review of *The Road Back* by Erich Maria Remarque.) *The New Republic,* LXVII (May 20, 1931), 23-24.

"Folklore of the Air." (Review of *Test Pilot* by Jimmy Collins.) *The American Mercury,* XXXVI (Nov. 1935), 370-372.

Review of *The Old Man and the Sea* by Ernest Hemingway. *Shenandoah,* III (Autumn 1952), 55.

INTRODUCTIONS

"Foreword" to *Sherwood Anderson & Other Famous Creoles: A Gallery of Contemporary New Orleans* by William Spratling, New Orleans: The Pelican Bookshop Press, 1926, pp. 7-8 (unnumbered). The full text is reprinted in William Van O'Connor's *The Tangled Fire of William Faulkner,* Minneapolis: The University of Minnesota Press, 1954, pp. 22-23.

"Introduction" to *Sanctuary,* New York: The Modern Library, Inc., 1932, pp. v-viii.

"Foreword" to *The Faulkner Reader,* New York: Random House, 1954, pp. ix-xi.

[Note] to *The Mansion,* New York: Random House, 1959, p. unnumbered following Contents.

[Note] to *Requiem for a Nun: a Play,* adapted to the stage by Ruth Ford, New York: Random House, 1959, p. unnumbered facing copyright page.

ADDRESSES

Address upon award of the Nobel Prize for Literature. Delivered in Stockholm, Sweden, Dec. 10, 1950. Published in *Les Prix Nobel en 1950,* Stockholm, 1951, pp. 71-72. A slightly different version was published in pamphlet form by the Spiral Press, New York, 1951, and in several newspapers and magazines. It is available in *The Faulkner Reader,* pp. 3-4, and in *Faulkner at Nagano,* pp. 204-206. It can be heard, read by Faulkner, on Caedmon long playing record number TC-1035.

Address to the graduating class of University High School, Oxford, Mississippi. Delivered May 28, 1951. Printed in the Oxford *Eagle,* May 31, 1951, p. 1; reprinted (with slight changes) in *The Harvard Advocate,* CXXXV (Nov. 1951), 7, under the title "Never Be Afraid."

Address upon being made an Officer of the Legion of Honor. Delivered in New Orleans, Louisiana, Oct. 26, 1951. The manuscript (in French) is reproduced in facsimile in the *Princeton University Library Chronicle,* XVIII (Spring 1957), Pl. 1.

Address to the annual meeting of the Delta Council. Delivered in Cleveland, Mississippi, May 15, 1952. Printed in the Greenville, Mississippi, *Delta Democrat-Times,* May 18, 1952, p. 9; published as a pamphlet under the title *An Address Delivered by William Faulkner* by the Delta Council, 1952; reprinted in *Vital Speeches of the Day,* XVIII (Sept. 15, 1952), 728-730, under the title "Man's Responsibility to Fellow Man."

Address to the graduating class of Pine Manor Junior College, Wellesley, Massachusetts. Delivered June 8, 1953. Printed in *The Atlantic Monthly,* CXCII (Aug. 1953), 53-55, under the title "Faith or Fear."

Address upon receiving the National Book Award for Fiction. Delivered in New York, Jan. 25, 1955. Printed in the *New York Times Book Review,* Feb. 6, 1955, pp. 2 and 4.

Address at the University of Oregon. Delivered in Eugene, Oregon, April 13, 1955. Printed in *Harper's Magazine,* CCXI (July 1955), 33-38, under the title "On Privacy. The American Dream: What Happened to It." [Faulkner had planned to include this in a collection of essays he was to have entitled *The American Dream.*]

Address to the annual meeting of the Southern Historical Association. Delivered in Memphis, Tennessee, Nov. 10, 1955. Printed in the Memphis *Commercial-Appeal,* Nov. 11, 1955, p. 8. This version was reprinted in *The Christian Century,* LXXII (Nov.

30, 1955), 1395-1396, under the title "To Claim Freedom Is Not Enough." A somewhat different version, including three added paragraphs, appeared in the pamphlet, *Three Views of the Segregation Decisions,* Atlanta, Georgia: The Southern Regional Council, 1956, pp. 9-12, under the title "American Segregation and the World Crisis."

Address upon receiving the Silver Medal of the Athens Academy, 1957. Delivered in Athens, Greece, Mar. 28, 1957. Printed in James B. Meriwether, *The Literary Career of William Faulkner,* Princeton University Library, 1961, p. 51.

Address to the Raven, Jefferson, and ODK Societies. Delivered in Charlottesville, Virginia, Feb. 20, 1958. Printed in *The University of Virginia Magazine,* II (Spring 1958), 11-14, under the title "A Word to Virginians." Reprinted in *Faulkner in the University,* ed. Gwynn and Blotner, Charlottesville: The University of Virginia Press, 1959, pp. 209-212.

Address to the English Club of the University of Virginia. Delivered April 24, 1958. Printed in *Faulkner in the University,* pp. 241-245, under the title "A Word to Young Writers."

Address to the seventh national conference of the U. S. National Commission for UNESCO. Delivered in Denver, Colorado, Oct. 2, 1959. Printed in *Saturday Review,* XLII (Nov. 14, 1959), 21, under the title "From Yoknapatawpha to UNESCO, the Dream."

Address upon receiving the Gold Medal for Fiction of the National Institute of Arts and Letters. Delivered in New York, May 24, 1962. Printed in *Proceedings of the American Academy of Arts and Letters and the National Institute of Arts and Letters,* Second Series, No. 13, New York, 1963, pp. 226-227.

SKETCHES

[It is undoubtedly a critical misdemeanor to list Faulkner's nonpoetry and noncritical prose which appeared in *The Mississippian, The Double Dealer,* and the New Orleans *Times-Picayune* under the "nonfiction prose" heading. One of the two pieces in

The Mississippian and several of the *Times-Picayune* sketches are actually short stories. But in order to avoid creating a separate category, and to keep them apart from the better known short stories, they are included here.]

"Landing in Luck." *The Mississippian*, IX (Nov. 26, 1919), 2 and 7. Reprinted in *William Faulkner: Early Prose and Poetry*, pp. 42-50. [This is a short story and is so designated at the heading. It, then, and not "A Rose for Emily," can claim the honor for being Faulkner's first published short story. It concerns a young flying cadet with the Royal Flying Corps and his first solo flight.]

"The Hill." *The Mississippian*, XI (Mar. 10, 1922), 1-2. Reprinted in *William Faulkner: Early Prose and Poetry*, pp. 90-92.

"New Orleans." *The Double Dealer*, VII (Jan.-Feb. 1925), 102-107. Reprinted in *Salmagundi*, pp. 13-28, and in *New Orleans Sketches*, ed. Carvel Collins, New Brunswick: Rutgers University Press, 1958, pp. 37-50.

"Mirrors of Chartres Street." The New Orleans *Times-Picayune*, Feb. 8, 1925, pp. 1 and 6. Reprinted in *Mirrors of Chartres Street*, Minneapolis: Faulkner Studies, 1953, pp. 1-5; in *New Orleans Sketches*, ed. Ichiro Nishizaki, Tokyo: The Hokuseido Press, 1955, pp. 48-52; and in *New Orleans Sketches*, ed. Carvel Collins, pp. 53-57. [The texts of this (and most of the *Times-Picayune* sketches) vary slightly from one another. The text edited by Collins is the most reliable.]

"Damon and Pythias Unlimited." The New Orleans *Times-Picayune*, Feb. 15, 1925, p. 7. Reprinted in *Mirrors of Chartres Street*, pp. 7-16; in *New Orleans Sketches* (ed. Nishizaki), pp. 100-111; and in *New Orleans Sketches* (ed. Collins), pp. 61-70.

"Home." The New Orleans *Times-Picayune*, Feb. 22, 1925, p. 3. Reprinted in *Mirrors of Chartres Street*, pp. 19-25; in *New Orleans Sketches* (ed. Nishizaki), pp. 32-39; and in *New Orleans Sketches* (ed. Collins), pp. 73-79.

"Jealousy." The New Orleans *Times-Picayune*, Mar. 1, 1925, p. 2. Reprinted in *Faulkner Studies*, III (Winter 1954), 46-50; in

Jealousy and Episode: Two Stories by William Faulkner, Minneapolis: Faulkner Studies, 1955, pp. 1-6; in *New Orleans Sketches* (ed. Nishizaki), pp. 23-31; and in *New Orleans Sketches* (ed. Collins), pp. 83-90.

"Cheest." The New Orleans *Times-Picayune,* Apr. 5, 1925, p. 4. Reprinted in *Mirrors of Chartres Street,* pp. 27-32; in *New Orleans Sketches* (ed. Nishizaki), pp. 93-99; and in *New Orleans Sketches* (ed. Collins), pp. 93-98.

"Out of Nazareth." The New Orleans *Times-Picayune,* Apr. 12, 1925, p. 4. Reprinted in *Mirrors of Chartres Street,* pp. 35-43; in *New Orleans Sketches* (ed. Nishizaki), pp. 69-79; and in *New Orleans Sketches* (ed. Collins), pp. 101-110.

"The Kingdom of God." The New Orleans *Times-Picayune,* Apr. 26, 1925, p. 4. Reprinted in *Mirrors of Chartres Street,* pp. 45-51; in *New Orleans Sketches* (ed. Nishizaki), pp. 53-60; and in *New Orleans Sketches* (ed. Collins), pp. 113-119.

"The Rosary." The New Orleans *Times-Picayune,* May 3, 1925, p. 2. Reprinted in *Mirrors of Chartres Street,* pp. 53-58; in *New Orleans Sketches* (ed. Nishizaki), pp. 12-18; and in *New Orleans Sketches* (ed. Collins), pp. 123-128.

"The Cobbler." The New Orleans *Times-Picayune,* May 10, 1925, p. 7. Reprinted in *Mirrors of Chartres Street,* pp. 61-64; in *New Orleans Sketches* (ed. Nishizaki), pp. 19-22; and in *New Orleans Sketches* (ed. Collins), pp. 131-134.

"Chance." The New Orleans *Times-Picayune,* May 17, 1925, p. 7. Reprinted in *Mirrors of Chartres Street,* pp. 67-73; in *New Orleans Sketches* (ed. Nishizaki), pp. 40-47; and in *New Orleans Sketches* (ed. Collins), pp. 137-143.

"Sunset." The New Orleans *Times-Picayune,* May 25, 1925, p. 7. Reprinted in *Mirrors of Chartres Street,* pp. 75-85; in *New Orleans Sketches* (ed. Nishizaki), pp. 80-92; and in *New Orleans Sketches* (ed. Collins), pp. 147-157.

"The Kid Learns." The New Orleans *Times-Picayune,* May 31, 1925, p. 2. Reprinted in *Mirrors of Chartres Street,* pp. 87-93; in *New Orleans Sketches* (ed. Nishizaki), pp. 61-68; and in *New Orleans Sketches* (ed. Collins), pp. 161-167.

"The Liar." The New Orleans *Times-Picayune,* July 26, 1925, pp. 3 and 6. Reprinted in *New Orleans Sketches* (ed. Collins), pp. 171-184.

"Episode." The New Orleans *Times-Picayune,* Aug. 16, 1925, p. 2. Reprinted in *Eigo Seinen* (Tokyo), Dec. 1, 1954; in *Faulkner Studies,* III (Winter 1954), 51-53; in *Jealousy and Episode,* pp. 7-9; in *New Orleans Sketches* (ed. Nishizaki), pp. 7-11; and in *New Orleans Sketches* (ed. Collins), pp. 187-190.

"Country Mice." The New Orleans *Times-Picayune,* Sept. 20, 1925, p. 7. Reprinted in *New Orleans Sketches* (ed. Collins), pp. 193-207.

"Yo Ho and Two Bottles of Rum." The New Orleans *Times-Picayune,* Sept. 27, 1925, pp. 1-2. Reprinted in *New Orleans Sketches* (ed. Collins), pp. 211-223.

MISCELLANEOUS PIECES

"To the Voters of Oxford." A broadside printed in Oxford, 1950. Reprinted (with very slight changes) in *The New Yorker,* XXVI (Nov. 25, 1950), 29; original text reprinted in Hodding Carter's "Faulkner and His Folk," the *Princeton University Library Chronicle,* XVIII (Spring 1957), 98-99.

"Notice" [to hunters]. The Oxford *Eagle,* Oct. 22, 1959, p. 7. The full text is reprinted in *Time,* LXXIV (Nov. 2, 1959), 29. [This is an exhortation to hunters on his land not to shoot his horses, his cow, or other hunters.]

LETTERS

To the Editor, *The Mississippian,* IX (Apr. 7, 1920), 1. Reprinted in Martha Mayes's "Faulkner Juvenilia," *New Campus Writing No. 2,* ed. Nolan Miller, New York: Bantam Books, 1957, p. 144. [A commentary on his parodist, who had evoked the piece "The Ivory Tower" a few weeks earlier.]

To the Editor, *The Forum,* LXXXIII (Apr. 1930), lvi. [This appears in the issue containing "A Rose for Emily." It is a humorously written "autobiography."]

To Maurice Edgar Coindreau (dated Apr. 14, 1932). Appears (in facsimile) in *The Princeton University Library Chronicle*, XVIII (Spring 1957), Pl. 2. [Concerns translations of Faulkner's short stories and a critical commentary on him by Mr. Coindreau.]

To Maurice Edgar Coindreau (dated Feb. 26, 1937). Appears (in facsimile) in the *Princeton University Library Chronicle*, XVIII (Spring 1957), Pl. 2. [Concerns translations made by Mr. Coindreau of *As I Lay Dying* and *The Sound and the Fury*.]

To the President of the League of American Writers. In *Writers Take Sides: Letters about the War in Spain from 418 American Authors*. New York: The League of American Writers, 1938, p. 23. [A reply to a questionnaire from Donald Ogden Stewart, in which Faulkner records his opposition to Franco.]

To the Editor, the Memphis *Commercial-Appeal*, July 12, 1941, p. 4. [Ironic reflections on flabby army discipline evoked by the once-notorious "Yoo-hoo" incident and General Lear.]

To the Editor, the Oxford *Eagle*, Mar. 13, 1947, p. 5. Reprinted, slightly changed, in the *Eagle*, Dec. 21, 1950, p. 25. [A comment on the newspaper's attempts to save the old Oxford courthouse building.]

To the Editor, the Memphis *Commercial-Appeal*, Mar. 26, 1950, Sec. IV, p. 4. [Remarks on the justice in sentencing a white killer (Leon Turner) of three Negro children in Attala County, Mississippi.]

To the Editor, the Memphis *Commercial-Appeal*, Apr. 9, 1950, Sec. IV, p. 4. [Further comments on the subject of the letter of Mar. 26.]

To the Editor, the Oxford *Eagle, Sept.* 14, 1950, p. 13. Reprinted in the *Eagle*, Dec. 21, 1950, p. 25, and in Hodding Carter's "Faulkner and His Folk," the *Princeton University Library Chronicle*, XVIII (Spring 1957), 100-101. [An ironic statement on the question of legalizing beer in Lafayette County, related to his broadside, "To the Voters of Oxford."]

To the Editor, *Time,* LVI (Nov. 13, 1950), 6. [An attack on the critics of Hemingway.]

To the Secretary of the American Academy of Arts and Letters (dated June 12, 1950). In *Proceedings of the American Academy of Arts and Letters and the National Institute of Arts and Letters,* Second Series, No. 1, 1951, p. 19. [This acknowledges the medal given Faulkner by the Academy.]

To Richard Walser. In *The Enigma of Thomas Wolfe,* ed. Richard Walser, Cambridge: Harvard University Press, 1953, p. vii. [This is an explanation of Faulkner's frequently misquoted remarks that Wolfe was "the greatest American writer of modern times."]

To the Editor, *The New York Times,* Dec. 26, 1954, Sec. IV, p. 6. (dated Dec. 22, 1954). [A comment on the "man versus machine" argument, stemming from the crash of an Italian airliner at Idlewild.]

To the Editor, the Memphis *Commercial-Appeal,* Feb. 20, 1955, Sec. V, p. 3. Reprinted in the *New York Times Book Review,* Mar. 13, 1955, p. 8. [A humorous bit of logic-chopping concerning the relative shiftlessness of Negroes and whites.]

To the Editor, the Memphis *Commercial-Appeal,* Mar. 20, 1955, Sec. V, p. 3. Reprinted in a slightly different form and slightly abbreviated in "On Fear: The South in Labor," *Harper's Magazine,* CCXII (June 1956), 29. The complete letter is reprinted in Hodding Carter's "Faulkner and His Folk," the *Princeton University Library Chronicle,* XVIII (Spring 1957), 102-103. [This concerns the school integration question.]

To the Editor, *The New York Times,* Mar. 25, 1955, p. 22 (dated Mar. 18, 1955). [This is an attack on the politicians who were responsible for expelling the Metropolitan of the Russian Orthodox Church from this country.]

To the Editor, the Memphis *Commercial-Appeal,* Apr. 3, 1955, Sec. V, p. 3. Reprinted in Hodding Carter's "Faulkner and His Folk," the *Princeton University Library Chronicle,* XVIII (Spring 1957), 103-104. [This concerns the school integration question.]

To the Editor, the Memphis *Commercial-Appeal*, Apr. 10, 1955, Sec. V, p. 3. [This concerns the school integration question.]

To the Editor, the Memphis *Commercial-Appeal*, Apr. 17, 1955, Sec. V, p. 3. [This concerns the school integration question.]

To the Editor, *Life*, XL (Mar. 26, 1956), 19. [This is an explanation of his article, "A Letter to the North," *Life*, XL (Mar. 5, 1956), 51-52. It concerns the school integration question.]

To the Editor, *The Reporter*, XIV (Apr. 19, 1956), 7. [This is a disavowal of remarks attributed to him in an interview with Russell Warren Howe in *The Reporter*, XIV (Mar. 22, 1956), 18-20. It concerns the school integration question.]

To the Editor, *Time*, LXVII (Apr. 23, 1956), 12. [This concerns the same as the letter to *The Reporter*. *Time* had quoted excerpts from the interview.]

To the Editor, *Time*, LXVIII (Dec. 10, 1956), 6 and 9. [This concerns the Suez crisis.]

To the Editor, *The New York Times*, Dec. 16, 1956, Sec. IV, p. 8 (dated Dec. 11, 1956). [This concerns the Suez crisis.]

To the Editor, *Time*, LXIX (Feb. 11, 1957), 8. [This concerns the Suez crisis.]

To the Editor, *The New York Times*, Oct. 13, 1957, Sec. IV, p. 10 (dated Oct. 7, 1957). [A statement, stemming from the Little Rock troubles, about the necessity for all free peoples "to federate into a community dedicated to the proposition that a community of individual free men not merely must endure, but can endure."]

To the Editor, *The New York Times*, Aug. 28, 1960, Sec. IV, p. 10 (dated Aug. 24, 1960). [This is a statement criticizing the behavior of Pilot Francis Powers in connection with the "U-2 incident."]

To Sherwood Anderson. Reproduced in facsimile in James B. Meriwether, *The Literary Career of William Faulkner*, Princeton University Library, 1961, Pls. 27, 28, and 29. [This undated letter refers to the Jackson family, which Faulkner and Anderson invented, and to their various exploits. Some of the story appears in *Mosquitoes*, pp. 277-281, and Faulkner mentions, in his article on Anderson in *The Atlantic Monthly,* how he and Anderson used to think up fantastic tales concerning the Jacksons.]

INTERVIEWS

[From time to time newspapers and news magazines have printed fragments of interviews with and comments by Faulkner. None of those are listed here. This listing consists only of those interviews and conferences of some length which have a sense of completeness about them.]

Bouvard, Loic. "Conversation with William Faulkner" (translated from the French by Henry Dan Piper). *Modern Fiction Studies,* V (Winter 1959-1960), 361-364. [From *Bulletin de l'association amicale universitaire France-Amérique,* Jan. 1954, pp. 23-29.]

Breit, Harvey. "A Walk with Faulkner." The *New York Times Book Review,* Jan. 30, 1955, pp. 4 and 12. Reprinted in same author's *The Writer Observed,* Cleveland: The World Publishing Company, 1956, pp. 281-284.

Dominicus, A. M. "An Interview with Faulkner" (translated from the Italian by Elizabeth Nissen). *Faulkner Studies,* III (Summer-Autumn 1954), 33-37. [From *La Fiera Letteria* (Rome), Feb. 14, 1954.]

Grenier, Cynthia. "The Art of Fiction: An Interview with William Faulkner." *Accent,* XVI (Summer 1956), 167-177.

Gwynn, Frederick L., and Blotner, Joseph L., eds. *Faulkner in the University: Class Conferences at the University of Virginia 1957-1958.* Charlottesville: The University of Virginia Press, 1959. [A somewhat different version of the material on pages 125-127 appeared in *The University of Virginia Magazine,* II (Feb. 1957), 7-13 and (Spring 1958), 32-37, under the title "William Faulkner on Dialect." A different version of the material on pages 57-70 appeared in *College English,* XIX (Oct. 1957), 1-6, under the title "Faulkner in the University: A Classroom Conference."]

Howe, Russell Warren. "A Talk with William Faulkner." *The Reporter*, XIV (Mar. 22, 1956), 18-20.

Jelliffe, Robert A, ed. *Faulkner at Nagano*. Tokyo: Kenyusha, Ltd. 1956. [A large segment of the interview material in this book appeared in *Esquire*, L (Dec. 1958), 139, 141, and 142, but in an entirely different sequence and apparently much edited.]

Rasco, Lavon. "An Interview with William Faulkner." *The Western Review*, XV (Summer 1951), 300-304. [This contains the remarks on Wolfe, Hemingway, *et al.*, that Faulkner was forced for years to explain or disavow.]

Stein, Jean. "The Art of Fiction XII: William Faulkner." *The Paris Review No. 12* (Spring 1956), 28-52. Reprinted in *Writers at Work: The Paris Review Interviews*, ed. Malcolm Cowley, New York: The Viking Press, 1958, pp. 119-141.

BOOKS CONTAINING NONFICTION PROSE

Faulkner, William. *Jealousy and Episode*. Minneapolis: Faulkner Studies, 1955. A limited edition of 500 copies. [Two of the sketches from the New Orleans *Times-Picayune*.]

Faulkner, William. *Mirrors of Chartres Street*. Minneapolis: Faulkner Studies, 1953. With an introduction by William Van O'Connor. A limited edition of 1000 copies. [Eleven of the sixteen sketches from the *Times-Picayune*. Those not included are "Country Mice," "Episode," "Jealousy," "The Liar," and "Yo Ho and Two Bottles of Rum."]

Faulkner, William. *New Orleans Sketches*. Edited and with an introduction and notes (in Japanese) by Ichiro Nishizaki. Tokyo: The Hokuseido Press, 1955. [Thirteen of the sketches from the *Times-Picayune*. Those not included are "Country Mice," "The Liar," and "Yo Ho and Two Bottles of Rum."]

Faulkner, William. *New Orleans Sketches*. Edited and with an introduction by Carvel Collins. New Brunswick: Rutgers University Press, 1958. [Contains all sixteen of the sketches from the *Times-Picayune* and "New Orleans" from *The Double Dealer*.]

Faulkner, William. *Salmagundi*. Edited and with an introduction
  by Paul Romaine. Milwaukee: The Casanova Press, 1932. A
  limited edition of 525 copies. [Besides five poems (see bibliography to the poetry) this contains "New Orleans," "On Criticism," and "Verse Old and Nascent: A Pilgrimage," all from
  The Double Dealer.]
Faulkner, William. *William Faulkner: Early Prose and Poetry*.
  Boston; Little, Brown and Co., 1962. Edited and with an introduction and notes by Carvel Collins. [Besides nineteen
  poems (see bibliography to the poetry) this contains "Landing
  in Luck," "The Hill," "American Drama: Eugene O'Neill,"
  "American Drama: Inhibitions," and reviews of books by W.
  A. Percy, Conrad Aiken, Edna St. Vincent Millay, and Joseph
  Hergesheimer, all from *The Mississippian,* and "On Criticism"
  and "Verse Old and Nascent: A Pilgrimage," from *The Double
  Dealer*.]
Gwynn and Blotner, eds. *Faulkner in the University* (see under
  Interviews). [In addition to classroom conferences, this contains
  two of Faulkner's addresses: "A Word to Virginians," pp. 209-
  212, and "A Word to Young Writers," pp. 241-245.]
Jelliffe, Robert A., ed. *Faulkner at Nagano* (see under *Interviews*). [Besides interviews and colloquies, this contains "Message Given at Nagano," pp. 175-177, "Impressions of Japan,"
  pp. 178-184, "To the Youth of Japan," pp. 185-187, and the
  Nobel Prize Address, pp. 204-206.]

Appendix IV

THE FICTION

NOT TAKING into account his early sketches, Faulkner had published up to the time of his death in 1962, seventeen novels and seventy-six short stories. Thirty-two of the stories can be disposed of briefly, for they have become parts of larger units. Seven are in *The Unvanquished,* six in *Knight's Gambit,* nine in *Go Down, Moses,*[1] four have been absorbed into *The Hamlet,* two into *The Town,* one into *Absalom, Absalom!,* one into *Requiem for a Nun,* and one into *The Mansion.* The one remaining has been reprinted in *Big Woods.* Of the other forty-four, thirty-nine have been brought together in the *Collected Stories.*[2] The other five consist of two individually published limited edition stories, "Idyll in the Desert" and "Miss Zilphia Gant," and three uncollected stories, "Once Aboard the Lugger," "Thrift," and "Afternoon of a Cow." Of the seventy-six stories sixty-two were first published in magazines.[3]

The fiction which lies outside the Yoknapatawpha series consists of nineteen stories and five novels. Four of the stories— "Thrift," "The Leg," "The Brooch," and "Honor"—and two of the novels—*The Wild Palms* and *A Fable*—have possibly some remote relationship to the series, however, even though they are not actually a part of the history of the county. Some of the

[1] There are only seven stories in *Go Down, Moses,* but two of them, "The Fire and the Hearth" and "The Bear," are each made up of two stories which were originally published separately.

[2] There are forty-two stories in the *Collected Stories,* but three of them have become parts of novels.

[3] *The American Caravan,* in which "Ad Astra" first appeared, is treated here as a magazine.

Yoknapatawpha stories, on the other hand, stand completely independent of the overall relationship of the others, being about characters who do not appear in any of the other stories and novels.

No chronological sequence of publication accounts for those pieces which are about Yoknapatawpha County and those which are not, for while 1929 was the publication date of the first Yoknapatawpha County fiction, all of the non-Yoknapatawpha short stories appeared after that date, as did *Pylon, The Wild Palms,* and *A Fable.* While some of the stories, such as those about World War I, may have been written before 1929, in all likelihood not all of them were, and the three novels, as both internal and external evidence show, are all post-1929. Nor is there any consistent pattern in the nature of the non-Yoknapatawpha fiction itself. Two stories, "Crevasse" and "Turnabout," are stories of World War I. One story, "Victory," and one novel, *Soldiers' Pay,* are about veterans of that war. One story, "Golden Land," and one novel, *Mosquitoes,* have in common a portrayal of sophisticated life among the wealthy and the artistic, the former in Hollywood, the latter in New Orleans. Three stories, "Fox Hunt," "Black Music," and "Carcassonne," are connected through the interrelationship of characters appearing in them. The others vary widely, from the almost plotless descriptive and atmospheric story of digging for buried treasure in "Once Aboard the Lugger," to the heavily plotted and suspense-filled "Mistral" and "Doctor Martino." These others include the stunt pilot novel, *Pylon*; a story of a love triangle involving a novelist and a poet, "Artist at Home"; a story about the relationships of sailors on board and ashore, "Divorce in Naples"; an ironically twisted love story among tuberculosis patients in the Arizona desert, "Idyll in the Desert"; a story of an old lady's burial insurance money being embezzled by her criminal son, "Pennsylvania Station"; and the scatologically humorous self-parody, "Afternoon of a Cow."

Of the four stories and two novels which may have tangential relationship to the Yoknapatawpha series, "The Brooch" is the most doubtful. All we know is that Howard Boyd and his mother live in a "little lost Mississippi hamlet," which could or could not be located in Yoknapatawpha County. There is no reference to any other known person or place of Yoknapatawpha County in the story. The other five pieces, however, have more tangible relationships. "The Leg," a semi-war story, has nothing to do with Jefferson or Yoknapatawpha County or any of their inhabitants, but the narrator, an American named Davy who has lost a leg in battle, could quite conceivably be the same "I" who was "trying to get used to a mechanical leg," and who tells about John Sartoris' death in "All the Dead Pilots." And in the latter story, part of Sartoris' background in England before he went to France is related to the narrator by a man named Ffollansbye, presumably the same Ffollansbye—since his function in both stories is identical—who related the background of Mac-Wyrglinchbeath in "Thrift." The story "Honor" is about Buck Monaghan, a former World War I aviator and later a car demonstrator. The story, like the others, has nothing to do with Yoknapatawpha County, but in "Ad Astra" Monaghan is one of Bayard Sartoris' companions, and in *Sartoris* Bayard meets him in Chicago. Monaghan also pops up in *A Fable*. There he is identified as an American flyer in the squadron to which Gerald David Levine has been assigned. An even closer tie between the France of *A Fable* and Yoknapatawpha County is revealed through an American private, a Negro from Mississippi, named Philip Manigault Beauchamp. Although he is identified only as from Mississippi, Beauchamp is obviously a well-known Yoknapatawpha County name.[4]

Faulkner himself has revealed the relationship of *The Wild Palms* to the Yoknapatawpha saga. While the title story is set in New Orleans, Chicago, Wisconsin, Utah, San Antonio, and the gulf coast of Mississippi, and has nothing to do with Yoknapatawpha County and its inhabitants, the "counterpoint" story, "Old Man," does have something to do with them. As a story it

---

[4] The name "Manigault" is also connected with Yoknapatawpha County. That was the original of "Mannigoe," the family name of Nancy in *Requiem for a Nun*.

does not, for it is not set in the county nor does it ever mention the place or any of its people. But according to the map which Faulkner drew for *The Portable Faulkner,* the location of the tall convict's birth, childhood, and youth is placed near the Old Frenchman's Place. He was born across the Yoknapatawpha River from Will Varner's domain, however, which would make Okataba County his birthplace.

Some of the Yoknapatawpha stories themselves belong there only by grace of their having been definitely located there, for they have little or no interrelationships with other stories in the saga. "Miss Zilphia Gant" opens in a "settlement . . . less than a village, twenty miles from the railroad in a remote section of a remote county" some seventy-five miles from Memphis. The remote county turns out to be Yoknapatawpha, for although it remains unnamed throughout the story, after Mrs. Gant has disposed of her husband and his partner Mrs. Vinson, she moves with her daughter Zilphia to "Jefferson, the county seat." The "settlement" itself is apparently Frenchman's Bend, for one of the people of Jefferson calls the place "the Bend." No familiar figure of either place appears in the story, and the Miss Eunice Gant, a clerk in the luggage department of Wildermark's, who appears in *The Town,* seems to be no relation of theirs. In "Elly" the central character and her parents live in Jefferson, but as in "Miss Zilphia Gant" there is no reference to anything from other stories in the series. The same is true of "That Will Be Fine," except that Mottstown as well as Jefferson is a part of the setting. And it is possible that the Jefferson livery stable proprietor known as Mr. Harris in *Sanctuary* is the father of the narrator of this story, for his father George owned a livery stable in Jefferson. Whether the economy of so small a town as Jefferson could support more than one livery stable is a moot question.

Several other stories have only loose relationships to the series. "Mountain Victory" and "Lo!" are tied together inasmuch as the Major Saucier Weddel of the former is the son of the Francis Weddel of the latter, but except for their undetermined and tenuous relationship with the Indian background of Northern

Mississippi and Yoknapatawpha County they are not actually a part of the series. The Grenier Weddel of *The Town* may be a descendant, for both his first and last names come from the early history of the county. "Uncle Willy" contains all new characters, but the narrator does mention having seen the sheriff take Darl Bundren to the asylum, and the Christian drugstore appears prominently in *The Town,* where Uncle Willy is instrumental in the capture of Montgomery Ward Snopes. It is in *The Town* that we discover it is Uncle Willy's drugstore in which Skeets McGowan works. "Beyond" brings in the well-known Doctor Peabody, but otherwise contains no reference to other known Jefferson citizens. "Death Drag" does not even mention Jefferson by name. When the pilot of the stunt plane asks the name of the town, all that is reported is: "One of the small boys told him the name of the town." In the map drawn for *The Portable Faulkner,* however, Jefferson was noted as the locale for the story, and one character, Captain Warren, later appears in "Knight's Gambit." The garageman, Mr. Harris, may also be the former livery stable owner of the same name in *Sanctuary.* The story "Hair" has all new characters in it, except that the barber Hawkshaw also appears in "Dry September," and the shop where he works, Maxey's, appears in *Light in August.* The John McLendon of "Dry September" is also in *Light in August,* and is undoubtedly the Jackson McLendon referred to by Chick Mallison in *The Town* and called Captain McLendon in *The Mansion.*

A more complicated problem is posed by the stories "Red Leaves" and "A Justice." There are a number of confused and conflicting accounts of the entire Yoknapatawpha County history, some in dates, some in names, and some in differing versions of the same event. Most of them are resolvable, however, when one grants that the saga is not documented history but legend and lore. These two stories, though, are so anachronistic and so conflicting in their accounts of stories related elsewhere that they disturb the history almost beyond reconciliation.

As a story by itself "Red Leaves" is a masterpiece. It tells of the pursuit and capture of the Negro body servant of a dead

Indian chief so that the servant may be buried with his master according to the custom of the people. Quiet and restrained, it presents a magnificent picture of man that far transcends the particular of the immediate situation. But viewed in relation to the cycle of Yoknapatawpha County history, the story contradicts other accounts of the Chickasaw dynasty. While the story of "Doom" (Ikkemotubbe) is correct in its overall details—his trip to New Orleans, his friendship with de Vitry, the origin of the name "Doom," and his accession to the chieftainship through the sudden and mysterious death of his uncle and cousin (unnamed here)—it disagrees with the more frequently related account by having Issetibbeha the son of Ikkemotubbe.[5] In "Red Leaves" Doom and his son Issetibbeha are already dead, and Moketubbe has become chief. Elsewhere it was the eight-year-old son of Moketubbe (or in another version of Issetibbeha and Moketubbe) whom Ikkemotubbe poisoned, and he remained chief of the Chickasaws until their removal to Oklahoma in the 1830s.

"A Justice" relates the story of Sam Fathers. The dates and circumstances vary from other accounts, and it was Jason Compson I, not Carothers McCaslin, who had bought him and his mother from Ikkemotubbe. According to this story Sam is not the son of Ikkemotubbe but of an Indian named Crawfish-ford, shortened for convenience to Craw-ford, and a Negro slave woman, wife of another Negro. Hence the original name for Sam: Had-Two-Fathers. There are other variants. Ikkemotubbe, for instance, is called a Chocktaw chief, and although the story of his succession to the chieftainship follows pretty well the general account, it is here, and only here, that his English pseudonym David Callicoat is mentioned. Also, it is said that Issetibbeha was still living when Ikkemotubbe returned from New Orleans, and that Ikkemotubbe poisoned both him and his son, instead of just the grandson as the other accounts relate. The chief anachronism, however, is that the story is related by Quentin Compson. According to one definite account, Quentin was born

[5] He is not called Ikkemotubbe in the story, but as "Doom" he is unmistakably the same person as the other "Doom"—who is Ikkemotubbe.

in 1891 (1889 is a better approximation). According to "The Bear," Sam Fathers died in 1883. Quentin's age is not given in "A Justice," but he was old enough to have listened to Sam's story with interest and to have remembered it.

Other evidence suggests that "A Justice" was a separate short story which eluded its author's scrutiny when it came to the integration of the Yoknapatawpha story. By this I mean that it seems almost certain that the final synthesis of Yoknapatawpha County and Jefferson history was not a definite pattern in Faulkner's mind when he began writing it. (The later inclusion of "Old Man" and "Death Drag" would help support this.) If one examines some of the magazine stories in relation to their later appearance in book form he will note that what were originally separate short stories have been revised so that their place in the whole series has become more consistent. "The Old People," for example, in its magazine publication, is a first-person story, which, although the narrator is nameless, is almost certainly also related by Quentin Compson. Its relationship with "A Justice" is obvious. We are told that Sam Fathers' father "sold them both [Sam's parents] and the child too (his own son) to my great-grandfather almost a hundred years ago." We are told also that "he [Sam] had lived on our farm four miles from Jefferson, though all he ever did was what blacksmithing and carpentering was needed." This is almost identical with what Quentin says about Sam in "A Justice." There is continual reference to "my father" by the narrator, Tennie's Jim is called Jimbo, and Uncle Ike McCaslin is referred to as a person other than the narrator. Sam used to come to "my father's" office in town. "Lion," which was later rewritten as part of "The Bear," is another case in point. Here the narrator is called Quentin by name. In the revised version the point of view is shifted to third person and the boy is Ike McCaslin, but here he appears as "Uncle Ike," another character in the story. In the original story Quentin is sixteen; in the revised version Ike McCaslin is sixteen. (One might also point out that Quentin, who killed himself in 1910, refers here to Dempsey and Tunney, who boxed in the 1920s.)

The revised version is much more clearly consistent with the overall history, so it is not too much to assume that "A Justice" was a story that for one reason or another failed to be taken into consideration when its author was revising the whole Yoknapatawpha County history.

The integration of the story can be seen in other places. Those stories which later became a part of *The Hamlet* were originally self-sustaining pieces, but when they were incorporated into the novel they became an unmistakable part of the whole. "Fool About a Horse," which is a story about Ab Snopes told by Ratliff in the novel, was originally a first-person story about "Pap." Most of the characters remain the same except that Cliff Odum in the novel was known as Odum Tull in the story, while in the novel and elsewhere Tull's first name is Vernon. The store where the cream separator was bought is called Cain's store in the novel; in the story it was called Ike McCaslin's store. Snopes does not appear. "The Hound," which became in *The Hamlet* the story of Mink Snopes's murder of Jack Houston, has as the murderer a man called Ernest Cotton. He is not in the novel. "Spotted Horses" is much the same in content, although in its original version it was a first-person story told, presumably, by Ratliff, for the narrator "was trying to sell a machine to Mrs. Bundren." In "Lizards in Jamshyd's Courtyard" Ratliff is called Surrat (as he was in *Sartoris*),[6] Vernon Tull is a bachelor, Will Varner a Methodist lay preacher, and Snopes is said to have bought the Old Frenchman's Place.

Even more interesting is the picture of Lucas Beauchamp as he progressed from the magazine stories to "The Fire and the Hearth." In the later version, as in *Intruder in the Dust,* he is presented as a dignified character, and his language has the dignity befitting him. In the magazine stories, on the other hand, his language is typical dialect, with, for example, such conventional dialect spellings as "gwine" for "going," "wuz" for

---

[6] This was a deliberate and not an absent-minded change, made because there was a real person named V. K. Surrat.

"was," and "ef'n" for "if." The expression "I seed hit work" is changed, in the book, to "I saw it work."

In his "note" to *The Mansion* Faulkner said that "the purpose of this note is simply to notify the reader that the author has found more discrepancies and contradictions than he hopes the reader will," and elsewhere he stated about his characters: "These people I figure belong to me and I have the right to move them about in time when I need them." Even so, with remarkably few exceptions, the final versions of most of the stories and novels are so closely integrated that one can follow characters—even minor characters—with such a familiar feeling of greeting old acquaintances that the reader soon figures that they belong to him too.

BIBLIOGRAPHY:

SHORT STORIES

[This lists chronologically the original publication and final disposition only. Because a number of excerpts from novels were originally printed in magazines and because a number of the stories later became parts of novels, this listing goes according to what the original publication states: those called "stories" are listed here; those called "excerpts" are listed in another category.]

"A Rose for Emily." *The Forum,* LXXXIII (Apr. 1930), 233-238. Revised slightly and reprinted in *These 13* and in *Collected Stories.*

"Honor." *The American Mercury,* XX (July 1930), 268-274. Reprinted in *Doctor Martino and Other Stories* and in *Collected Stories.*

"Thrift." *The Saturday Evening Post,* CCIII (Sept. 6, 1930), 16-17, 78 and 82. Uncollected, but reprinted in *O. Henry Memorial Award Prize Stories of 1931,* ed. Blanche Colton Williams, Garden City: Doubleday, Doran & Co., 1931, pp. 153-169.

"Red Leaves." *The Saturday Evening Post,* CCIII (Oct. 25, 1930), 6-7, 54, 56, 58, 60, 62 and 64. Revised and reprinted in *These 13* and in *Collected Stories.* A section was further revised for inclusion in *Big Woods,* pp. 99-109 (unnumbered).

"Dry September." *Scribner's Magazine,* LXXXIX (Jan. 1931), 49-56. Revised and reprinted in *These 13* and in *Collected Stories.*

"That Evening Sun Go Down." *The American Mercury,* XXII (Mar. 1931), 257-267. Revised and reprinted as "That Evening Sun" in *These 13* and in *Collected Stories.*

"Ad Astra." *The American Caravan,* IV (1931), 164-181. Revised and reprinted in *These 13* and in *Collected Stories.*

"Hair." *The American Mercury,* XXIII (May 1931), 53-61. Revised and reprinted in *These 13* and in *Collected Stories.*

"Spotted Horses." *Scribner's Magazine,* LXXXIX (June 1931), 585-597. Rewritten and expanded for *The Hamlet,* pp. 309-380.

"The Hound." *Harper's Magazine,* CLXIII (Aug. 1931), 266-274. Reprinted in *Doctor Martino and Other Stories;* rewritten for *The Hamlet,* pp. 250-296.

"Fox Hunt." *Harper's Magazine,* CLXIII (Sept. 1931), 392-402. Reprinted in *Doctor Martino and Other Stories* and in *Collected Stories.*

"All the Dead Pilots." In *These 13* (first publication, 1931) and in *Collected Stories.*

"Carcassonne." In *These 13* (first publication, 1931) and in *Collected Stories.*

"Crevasse." In *These 13* (first publication, 1931) and in *Collected Stories.*

"Divorce in Naples." In *These 13* (first publication, 1931) and in *Collected Stories.*

"A Justice." In *These 13* (first publication, 1931) and in *Collected Stories.* A section was revised for inclusion in *Big Woods,* pp. 139-142 (unnumbered).

"Mistral." In *These 13* (first publication, 1931) and in *Collected Stories.*

"Victory." In *These 13* (first publication, 1931) and in *Collected Stories.*

"Doctor Martino." *Harper's Magazine,* CLXIII (Nov. 1931), 733-743. Reprinted in *Doctor Martino and Other Stories* and in *Collected Stories.*

Idyll in the Desert. New York: Random House, 1931. Separate and only publication, 400 copies printed Dec. 7, 1931.

"Death-Drag." *Scribner's Magazine,* XCI (Jan. 1932), 34-42. Slightly revised and reprinted as "Death Drag" in *Doctor Martino and Other Stories* and in *Collected Stories.*

"Centaur in Brass." *The American Mercury,* XXV (Feb. 1932), 200-210. Reprinted in *Collected Stories;* rewritten for *The Town,* pp. 3-29.

"Once Aboard the Lugger." *Contempo,* I (Feb. 1, 1932), 1 and 4. Uncollected.

"Lizards in Jamshyd's Courtyard." *The Saturday Evening Post,* CCIV (Feb. 27, 1932), 12-13, 52 and 57. Rewritten for *The Hamlet,* pp. 383-421.

"Turn About." *The Saturday Evening Post,* CCIV (Mar. 5, 1932), 6-7, 75-76, 81 and 83. Revised and reprinted in *Doctor Martino and Other Stories* and, as "Turnabout," in *Collected Stories.*

"Smoke." *Harper's Magazine,* CLXIV (Apr. 1932), 562-578. Slightly revised and reprinted in *Doctor Martino and Other Stories* and in *Knight's Gambit.*

Miss Zilphia Gant. Dallas: The Book Club of Texas, 1932. Separate and only publication, 300 copies. With a Preface by Henry Smith.

"A Mountain Victory." *The Saturday Evening Post,* CCV (Dec. 3, 1932), 6-7, 39, 42 and 44-46. Revised and reprinted, as "Mountain Victory," in *Doctor Martino and Other Stories* and in *Collected Stories.*

"There Was a Queen." *Scribner's Magazine,* XCIII (Jan. 1933), 10-16. Reprinted in *Doctor Martino and Other Stories* and in *Collected Stories.*

"Artist at Home." *Story,* III (Aug. 1933), 27-41. Reprinted in *Collected Stories.*

"Beyond." *Harper's Magazine,* CLXVII (Sept. 1933), 394-403. Reprinted in *Doctor Martino and Other Stories* and in *Collected Stories.*

"Elly." *Story,* IV (Feb. 1934), 3-15. Reprinted in *Doctor Martino and Other Stories* and in *Collected Stories.*

"Pennsylvania Station." *The American Mercury,* XXXI (Feb. 1934), 166-174. Reprinted *Collected Stories.*

"Wash." *Harper's Magazine,* CLXVIII (Feb. 1934), 258-266. Reprinted in *Doctor Martino and Other Stories* and in *Collected Stories;* rewritten for *Absalom, Absalom!,* pp. 278-292. [This is the only one of the short stories rewritten for inclusion in a novel which has retained its separate identity *after* its appearance in the novel.]

"A Bear Hunt." *The Saturday Evening Post,* CCVI (Feb. 10, 1934), 8-9, 74 and 76. Reprinted in *Collected Stories;* revised and reprinted in *Big Woods.*

"Black Music." In *Doctor Martino and Other Stories* (first publication, 1934) and in *Collected Stories.*

"Leg." In *Doctor Martino and Other Stories* (first publication, 1934) and, as "The Leg," in *Collected Stories.*

"Mule in the Yard." *Scribner's Magazine,* XCVI (Aug. 1934), 65-70. Reprinted in *Collected Stories;* rewritten for *The Town,* pp. 231-261.

"Ambuscade." *The Saturday Evening Post,* CCVII (Sept. 29, 1934), 12-13 and 80-81. Revised and reprinted in *The Unvanquished.*

"Retreat." *The Saturday Evening Post,* CCVII (Oct. 13, 1934), 16-17, 82, 84-85, 87 and 89. Revised and reprinted in *The Unvanquished.*

"Lo!" *Story,* V (Nov. 1934), 5-21. Reprinted in *Collected Stories.*

"Raid." *The Saturday Evening Post,* CCVII (Nov. 3, 1934), 18-19, 72-73, 75 and 77-78. Revised and reprinted in *The Unvanquished.*

"Skirmish at Satoris." *Scribner's Magazine,* XCVII (Apr. 1935), 193-200. Revised and reprinted in *The Unvanquished.*

"Golden Land." *The American Mercury*, XXXV (May 1935), 1-14. Reprinted in *Collected Stories*.

"That Will Be Fine." *The American Mercury*, XXXV (July 1935), 264-276. Reprinted in *Collected Stories*.

"Uncle Willy." *The American Mercury*, XXXVI (Oct. 1935), 158-168. Reprinted in *Collected Stories*.

"Lion." *Harper's Magazine*, CLXXI (Dec. 1935), 67-77. Rewritten as part of "The Bear" in *Go Down, Moses*.

"The Brooch." *Scribner's Magazine*, XCIX (Jan. 1936), 7-12. Reprinted in *Collected Stories*.

"Fool About a Horse." *Scribner's Magazine*, C (Aug. 1936), 80-86. Rewritten for *The Hamlet*, pp. 31-53.

"The Unvanquished." *The Saturday Evening Post*, CCIX (Nov. 14, 1936), 12-13, 121-122, 124, 126, 128 and 130. Revised and reprinted, as "Riposte in Tertio," in *The Unvanquished*.

"Vendée." *The Saturday Evening Post*, CCIX (Dec. 5, 1936), 16-17, 86-87, 90 and 92-94. Revised and reprinted in *The Unvanquished*.

"Monk." *Scribner's Magazine*, CL (May 1937), 16-24. Reprinted in *Knight's Gambit*.

"An Odor of Verbena." In *The Unvanquished* (first publication, 1938).

"Barn Burning." *Harper's Magazine*, CLXXIX (June 1939), 86-96. Reprinted in *Collected Stories*. [The central episode of this story is retold by Ratliff in *The Hamlet*, pp. 15-21, but the story itself—that of Colonel Sartoris Snopes—is not.]

"Hand Upon the Waters." *The Saturday Evening Post*, CCXII (Nov. 4, 1939), 14-15, 75-76 and 78-79. Reprinted in *Knight's Gambit*.

"A Point of Law." *Collier's Magazine*, CV (June 22, 1940), 20-21, 30 and 32. Rewritten as part of "The Fire and the Hearth" in *Go Down, Moses*.

"The Old People." *Harper's Magazine*, CLXXXI (Sept. 1940), 418-425. Rewritten for inclusion in *Go Down, Moses*; reprinted in *Big Woods*.

"Pantaloon in Black." *Harper's Magazine,* CLXXXI (Oct. 1940), 503-513. Revised and reprinted in *Go Down, Moses.*

"Gold Is Not Always." *The Atlantic Monthly,* CLXVI (Nov. 1940), 563-570. Rewritten as part of "The Fire and the Hearth" in *Go Down, Moses.*

"Tomorrow." *The Saturday Evening Post,* CCXIII (Nov. 23, 1940), 22-23, 32, 35 and 37-39. Reprinted in *Knight's Gambit.*

"Go Down, Moses." *Collier's Magazine,* CVII (Jan. 25, 1941), 19-20 and 45-46. Revised and reprinted in *Go Down, Moses.*

"The Tall Men." *The Saturday Evening Post,* CCXIII (May 31, 1941), 14-15, 95-96 and 98-99. Reprinted in *Collected Stories.*

"Two Soldiers." *The Saturday Evening Post,* CCXIV (Mar. 28, 1942), 9-11, 35-36, 38 and 40. Reprinted in *Collected Stories.*

"The Bear." *The Saturday Evening Post,* CCXIV (May 9, 1942), 30-31, 74 and 76-77. Rewritten as part of "The Bear" in *Go Down, Moses;* that version reprinted, without part 4, in *Big Woods.*

"Delta Autumn." *Story,* XX (May-June 1942), 46-55. Revised and reprinted in *Go Down, Moses.* A section was further revised for inclusion in *Big Woods,* pp. 199-212 (unnumbered).

"Was." In *Go Down, Moses* (first publication, 1942).

"Shingles for the Lord." *The Saturday Evening Post,* CCXV (Feb. 13, 1943), 14-15, 68 and 70-71. Reprinted in *Collected Stories.*

"My Grandmother Millard and General Bedford Forrest and the Battle of Harrykin Creek." *Story,* XXII (Mar.-Apr. 1943), 68-86. Reprinted in *Collected Stories.*

"Shall Not Perish." *Story,* XXIII (July-Aug. 1943), 40-47. Reprinted in *Collected Stories.*

"An Error in Chemistry." *Ellery Queen's Mystery Magazine,* VII (June 1946), 5-19. Reprinted in *Knight's Gambit.*

"Afternoon of a Cow." *Furioso,* II (Summer 1947), 5-17. Uncollected but reprinted in *Parodies: An Anthology from Chaucer to Beerbohm—and After,* ed. Dwight Macdonald, New York: Random House, 1960, pp. 462-473, where it is called a "conscious self-parody." [Unlike the rest of the stories, this was first published in a French translation by Maurice Edgar Coindreau in *Fontaine*, 27-28 (June-July 1943), 66-81, and under a pseudonym, Ernest V. Trueblood.]

"A Courtship." *The Sewanee Review*, LVI (Autumn 1948), 634-653. Reprinted in *Collected Stories*.

"Knight's Gambit." In *Knight's Gambit* (first publication, 1949). [This story runs for over one hundred pages, so it should perhaps be called a novelette. It is shorter than "The Bear," however, and in order to avoid creating a new and extremely small category for them, it is treated as a short story here.]

"A Name for the City." *Harper's Magazine*, CCI (Oct. 1950), 200-214. Rewritten for *Requiem for a Nun*, pp. 3-48.

"Race at Morning." *The Saturday Evening Post, CCXXVII* (Mar. 5, 1955), 26, 103-104, and 106. Revised and reprinted in *Big Woods*.

"By the People." *Mademoiselle*, XLI (Oct. 1955), 86-89 and 130-139. Rewritten for *The Mansion*, pp. 294-321.

EXCERPTS FROM NOVELS

"Absalom, Absalom!" *The American Mercury*, XXXVIII (Aug. 1936), 466-474. From *Absalom, Absalom!*, pp. 7-30.

"The Jail." *The Partisan Review*, XVIII (Sept.-Oct. 1951), 496-515. From *Requiem for a Nun*, pp. 213-262.

"Notes on a Horsethief." *Vogue*, CXXIV (July 1954), 46-51 and 101-107. From *A Fable*, pp. 151-204. [There was a shortened version of this, with minor changes, in *Perspectives USA* No. 9 (Autumn 1954), 24-59; both differ somewhat from the first published version, published separately by the Levee Press of Greenville, Mississippi, in 1950, in a limited edition of 975 copies.]

"The Waifs." *The Saturday Evening Post*, CCXXIX (May 4, 1957), 27, 116, 118 and 120. From *The Town*, pp. 359-371.

"Mink Snopes." *Esquire*, LII (Dec. 1959), 226-230 and 247-264. From *The Mansion*, pp. 3-51.

"Hell Creek Crossing." *The Saturday Evening Post*, CCXXXV

(Mar. 31, 1962), 22-25. From *The Reivers*, pp. 75-91, with an
introductory summary paragraph.
"The Education of Lucius Priest." *Esquire*, LVII (May 1962), 109-
116. From *The Reivers*, pp. 95-115, 132-133, 139-143, and 152-
161, edited to form continuity.

Note: "Spotted Horses," which is all but the last two pages of
Chapter I of Book IV of *The Hamlet* (pp. 309-380), and "Old
Man," which consists of Chapters 2, 4, 6, 8, and 10 of *The Wild
Palms,* are also properly "excerpts" from novels, as in *The Long
Summer* (Book III of *The Hamlet*). They have been extracted
and reprinted, as have segments of some of the other novels, the
last usually to be found in college textbook anthologies of American literature. No attempt has been made to catalog these various and sometimes truncated reprintings. Both *The Faulkner
Reader* and *The Portable Faulkner* contain excerpts from novels
also.

THE NOVELS

Soldiers' Pay. New York: Boni and Liveright, 1926.
Mosquitoes. New York: Boni and Liveright, 1927.
Sartoris. New York: Harcourt, Brace & Co., 1929.
The Sound and the Fury. New York: Jonathan Cape and Harrison
   Smith, 1929.
As I Lay Dying. New York: Jonathan Cape and Harrison Smith,
   1930.
Sanctuary. New York: Jonathan Cape and Harrison Smith, 1931.
Light in August. New York: Harrison Smith and Robert Haas,
   1932.
Pylon. New York: Harrison Smith and Robert Haas, 1935.
Absalom, Absalom! New York: Random House, 1936.
The Wild Palms. New York: Random House, 1939.
The Hamlet. New York: Random House, 1940.
Intruder in the Dust. New York: Random House, 1948.
Requiem for a Nun. New York: Random House, 1951.

A Fable. New York: Random House, 1954.
The Town. New York: Random House, 1957.
The Mansion. New York: Random House, 1959.
The Reivers. New York: Random House, 1962.

COLLECTIONS

These 13. New York: Jonathan Cape and Harrison Smith, 1931.
[All thirteen of the stories in this volume were reprinted in
Collected Stories. See Glossary for contents.]

Doctor Martino and Other Stories. New York: Harrison Smith
and Robert Haas, 1934. [Twelve of the fourteen stories in this
volume were reprinted in *Collected Stories;* one was reprinted
in *Knight's Gambit;* and one was rewritten for *The Hamlet.*
See Glossary for contents.]

The Unvanquished. New York: Random House, 1938. [A cycle
of seven related stories, all but one reprinted (in revised form)
from magazines. Although some critics have argued that *The
Unvanquished* is a novel, Faulkner himself said of the stories:
"I realized that they would be too episodic to be what I considered a novel, so I thought of them as a series of stories. . . ."
See Glossary for contents.]

Go Down, Moses and Other Stories. New York: Random House,
1942. [A cycle of seven related stories, all but one reprinted
(in revised form) from magazines. Editions after the first are
called *Go Down, Moses.* See Glossary for contents.]

The Portable Faulkner, ed. Malcolm Cowley. New York: The
Viking Press, 1946. [Contains twelve stories, five from *These 13,*
two from *Doctor Martino and Other Stories* (all seven of these
to be reprinted in *Collected Stories*), three from *Go Down,
Moses,* and two from *The Unvanquished;* and excerpts from
six novels. Contains also a newly drawn map of Yoknapatawpha
County and the first publication of the Appendix on the
Compsons, both done by Faulkner. See Glossary for contents.]

Knight's Gambit. New York: Random House, 1949. [A cycle of six related stories, all but one of them reprinted from magazines. See Glossary for contents.]

Collected Stories of William Faulkner. New York: Random House, 1950. [Contains forty-two stories, all of them reprinted from *These 13* and *Doctor Martino and Other Stories* and from previously uncollected magazine publication. (See Glossary for contents.]

The Faulkner Reader. New York: Random House, 1954. [Contains eight stories from *Collected Stories,* one from *The Unvanquished,* one from *Go Down, Moses,* four excerpts from novels, one complete novel, and the Nobel Prize Address. There is a Foreword by the author. See Glossary for contents.]

Big Woods. New York: Random House, 1955. [Contains four stories, a prelude, three interludes, and a postlude, all taken (but mostly revised) from previous publications. See Glossary for contents.]

Three Famous Short Novels. New York: Random House, 1958. [Contains "Spotted Horses" from *The Hamlet,* "Old Man" from *The Wild Palms,* and "The Bear" from *Go Down, Moses.*]

Selected Short Stories of William Faulkner. New York: The Modern Library, 1962. [Contains thirteen stories, twelve from the *Collected Stories,* and one ("Race at Morning") from *Big Woods.* See Glossary for contents.]

Appendix V

HISTORIES OF THE PRINCIPAL FAMILIES OF YOKNAPATAWPHA COUNTY

THE CHICKASAWS

THE LAND that later became Yoknapatawpha County and surrounding area was originally Chickasaw country. Information about the Chickasaws is scarce in the Faulkner account, and not all of it consistent. We hear first of a David Colbert, mentioned only once, as the "chief Man of all the Chickasaws in our section" around 1800. He never appears in any of the stories, but in one we are told that his wife was distantly related to Herman Basket's aunt. (David Colbert could not be a variant of David Callicoat, the name assumed by Ikkemotubbe when he returned from New Orleans, for David Colbert was the "chief Man" at the time Ikkemotubbe was still a youth.)

Our first knowledge of the chieftainship places it with Issetibbeha. He had a son Moketubbe, a brother Sometimes-Wakeup, and a sister Mohataha, the mother of Ikkemotubbe. In 1800, when he was a young man, Ikkemotubbe ran away to New Orleans. He stayed away seven years, during which time Issetibbeha died and Moketubbe succeeded to the chieftainship. When Ikkemotubbe returned in 1807 he brought with him a French companion, a Chevalier Soeur-Blonde de Vitry. It was de Vitry who started calling Ikkemotubbe *Du Homme,* later anglicized to "Doom" and translated to "The Man." Ikkemotubbe also brought with him a quadroon slave girl, the mother of Sam Fathers—Ikkemotubbe himself being the father. Ikkemotubbe presumably poisoned the eight-year-old son of Moketubbe, after which Moketubbe abdicated and Ikkemotubbe became chief. He remained chief through the 1830s when the Indians moved west, across the river into what is now Oklahoma, leaving the land east to the white man.

There are other stories connected with the Indians, some of them contradictory to the one above which seems to be the most accurate. One story calls Issetibbeha the son of Ikkemotubbe. Another notes that when Ikkemotubbe returned from New Orleans, calling himself David Callicoat, he was known as a Chocktaw chief. It is also reported that Ikkemotubbe poisoned both his uncle and his cousin. Elsewhere we read that Issetibbeha made a treaty with Jackson about what land belonged to the Indians. And in still another place we hear that in the 1830s the "chief in the Chickasaw Nation" was a half-Frenchman, half-Indian called François Vidal or Francis Weddel, and that it was he who went to Washington to see President Jackson about his people. He too, elsewhere, is called a Chocktaw.

SOURCES:

The reference to David Colbert appears in "A Courtship." The best brief account of Ikkemotubbe's activities to make himself chief appears in "The Old People" (*Go Down, Moses*). The story, or parts of it, appears also in *Requiem for a Nun,* "A Courtship," and "A Justice." This latter story, however, calls Ikkemotubbe a Chocktaw chief, refers to his anglicized name of David Callicoat, relates that Issetibbeha was still living when Ikkemotubbe returned from New Orleans and that Ikemotubbe poisoned both Issetibbeha and his son, contains the only reference to Issetibbeha's brother, and gives a different version of Sam Fathers' paternity. "A Courtship" reports that it was Issetibbeha who met Jackson concerning which land was Chickasaw and which land was the white man's. The inverted story that Issetibbeha was Doom's son (Doom is not called Ikkemotubbe here) appears in "Red Leaves." The name of Ikkemotubbe's mother appears only in *Requiem for a Nun* and *The Mansion,*

although in the latter she is not identified as his mother. Ikkemotubbe appears also in the Appendix to *The Sound and the
Fury,* and is mentioned in *The Town* along with Issetibbeha,
where it is confirmed that Ikkemotubbe was Issetibbeha's nephew.
The story of Francis Weddel's journey to Washington to
see President Jackson is related in "Lo!" A story of his son, Saucier
Weddel, a major in the Civil War (in which Francis Weddel
is called half-French, half-Choctaw) appears in "Mountain
Victory." There was a Grenier Weddel in Jefferson around 1910,
but his descent, if he is of the same family, is not known. He
appears in *The Town.* Issetibbeha, Moketubbe, and Doom
(Ikkemotubbe) are referred to in passing in *The Reivers.*

HABERSHAM

Doctor Samuel Habersham was the first important white man
in Yoknapatawpha County, having come from Carolina with
his eight-year-old son and Alexander Holston and Louis Grenier
around 1800 to become the government agent at the Chickasaw
agency there. He was a friend of Issetibbeha. He is supposed to
have died sometime before 1833 when Jefferson was founded,
although the exact date is not known. His son, according to the
same account, at the age of twenty-five married a granddaughter
of the old Chickasaw chief Issetibbeha and moved in the 1830s
to Oklahoma with the Chickasaws. (Elsewhere in the same account, however, it is stated that he married a daughter of
Ikkemotubbe.)

We find, nevertheless, that during the Civil War there was a
banker in Jefferson named Habersham, whose wife Martha was
a social leader of the time. It was she who virtually forced
Colonel Sartoris and Drusilla Hawk to marry, and her husband
the banker signed the Colonel's peace bond after the latter had
killed the two Burden carpetbaggers.

Almost a century later, in the 1940s, we encounter a seventy-
year-old spinster named Eunice Habersham, possessor of the
oldest name in the county, and presumably the last one by that
name. But there is also a social worker in Jefferson in 1942

known as Mrs. Habersham, a lady who tried to find out the name of the nine-year-old Grier boy when he arrived in Jefferson on his way to Memphis to find his brother Pete. She is perhaps the same person as the Miss Emily Habersham who is instrumental in returning Byron Snopes's half-breed children to Texas.

SOURCES:

Information about Doctor Habersham and his son is to be found in *Requiem for a Nun*. That he was one of the original founders of the county is repeated in *The Town*. "Skirmish at Sartoris" and "An Odor of Verbena" (*The Unvanquished*) provide the information about the banker and his wife Martha. Eunice Habersham appears in *Intruder in the Dust* and is mentioned in *The Town*. The social worker is to be found in "Two Soldiers," while Miss Emily Habersham appears in *The Town*.

HOLSTON

With Doctor Habersham came Alexander Holston, who took care of Habersham's son and acted as a kind of valet and bodyguard to the doctor himself. He established the Holston House in Jefferson, and died in 1839, a "childless bachelor," according to one report, although elsewhere we hear of a Mrs. Holston running the Holston House during the Civil War, and still elsewhere we hear that during the same period there was a Doctor Holston in Jefferson. According to the most recent account, as late as the 1940s the Holston House was still being run by two sisters, the "last descendants" of Alexander.

SOURCES:

The story of Holston's early days in Yoknapatawpha County is told in *Requiem for a Nun* and referred to in *The Town* and *The Mansion*. "Skirmish at Sartoris" (*The Unvanquished*) offers the information about Mrs. Holston, while "My Grandmother Millard" refers to Doctor Holston. There is reference to Alexander Holston in *Intruder in the Dust* and "Hand Upon the Waters" (*Knight's Gambit*). The account of the Holston House still being run by the family appears in *The Mansion*. It is mentioned in *The Reivers*.

GRENIER

Louis Grenier, a Huguenot second son, came with Habersham and Holston to Mississippi. He bought land in the southeastern part of the county—and in the next county as well—and established the first plantation in the county, raising the first cotton and possessing the first slaves. He died in 1837. The family descent is not known, except that in 1905 there was a Dan Grinnup in Jefferson, a descendant shiftless and given to alcohol, and around 1940 or so in the region of the old plantation there was a thirty-five-year-old feeble-minded man named Lonnie Grinnup, who was murdered by a man named Boyd Ballenbaugh for his insurance. Lonnie Grinnup, though he did not know it, was really named Louis Grenier, and he was the last surviving descendant of the first Louis Grenier. The plantation went into decay after the first Grenier's death, and by the 1890s was known merely as the "Old Frenchman's Place," the larger part of it belonging to Will Varner. Varner gave it to Flem Snopes when Flem married his daughter Eula, and later Flem sold it to Homer Bookwright, Henry Armstid, and V. K. Ratliff. By 1930 Lee Goodwin was living there with his common-law wife Ruby Lamar, making bootleg whiskey. The small settlement became known as Frenchman's Bend. There is also a neighboring Grenier County.

SOURCES:

Louis Grenier appears in *Requiem for a Nun* and is referred to in *Intruder in the Dust*, *The Town*, "Hand Upon the Waters" (*Knight's Gambit*), and *The Reivers*. This last also tells about Dan Grinnup and mentions (without naming him) a relative whose description fits Lonnie, whose story is told in "Hand Upon the Waters." Lonnie is referred to in *Intruder in the Dust*. Grenier County is mentioned in *The Hamlet*, where the sale of the old plantation to Bookwright, Armstid, and Ratliff is related. Lee Goodwin's activities there are told in *Sanctuary*. A Grenier Weddel lived in Jefferson around 1910, but his relationship with either the Grenier or the Weddel family is not known. He appears in *The Town*. There is apparently a time discrepancy between Dan and Lonnie Grinnup.

BENBOW

The first Benbow we encounter is a Judge Benbow of Civil War times, who was the executor of Goodhue Coldfield's estate. He had a son named Percy. Little is known of them. There was, however, right after the war an ex-slave who used to drive the Benbow carriage and who called himself Cassius Q. Benbow. He ran off with the Yankee troops and returned after the war to become acting marshall in Jefferson. He was frightened off when Colonel Sartoris killed the two carpetbaggers.

Next we hear of a Francis Benbow, and of his son Will, whose wife's name was Julia. Will and Julia were the parents of Horace and Narcissa Benbow. Horace was born around 1886 or 1887 and Narcissa around 1895. Mrs. Benbow died around 1902. Horace went to Sewanee (University of the South) and later to Oxford (England) and became a lawyer. He had been an enlisted man in World War I. Some time in the early 1920s he married Belle Mitchell, the divorced wife of Harry Mitchell, and moved to Kinston in another county to practice law. Narcissa in 1919 married Bayard Sartoris III and on June 21, 1920, their son Benbow Sartoris was born.

SOURCES:

Judge Benbow is referred to in *Absalom, Absalom!*, "An Odor of Verbena" (*The Unvanquished*), and *The Hamlet*. His son is referred to in *Absalom, Absalom!* Cassius Q. Benbow is mentioned in "Skirmish at Sartoris" (*The Unvanquished*). Francis, Will, and Julia Benbow are mentioned in *Sartoris*. Horace and Narcissa appear in that book, and in *Sanctuary*. Narcissa appears again in "There Was a Queen." She is referred to in *The Town*.

STEVENS

We are told that Stevens is one of the oldest names in Jefferson history, and the name is mentioned as being in the county in the 1830s. One account, in fact, says that it was Stevens, Holston, and Grenier, and not Habersham, Holston, and Grenier who first came to what was to become Jefferson. The first Stevens we meet is a Judge Stevens, who was eighty years old around 1900 and mayor of Jefferson at that time. Next is a Lemuel Stevens, who married Margaret Dandridge, and whose children were Gavin and Margaret, twins. Although a farmer from the French-man's Bend region once called him "Captain" Stevens, he was generally known as Judge Stevens. When his wife died is not known, but the Judge died in 1919 and she had preceded him in death.

Gavin and Margaret were born sometime around 1890. According to one account Gavin studied at Harvard and at Heidelberg, and later returned to the University of Mississippi for a law degree. But in another account he receives his law degree before going to Heidelberg. When not engaged in law practice he was at work translating the Old Testament into classic Greek. He became County Attorney for Yoknapatawpha County and later District Attorney. Early in 1942, he married a Mrs. Harriss, a wealthy widow who had been a childhood sweetheart.

His sister Margaret married a man named Charles Mallison, and they had a son, Charles, Jr., who was born in 1914, although one account makes the time around 1922 or 1924. He went to Harvard and later to the University of Mississippi to study law. He joined the army in 1942, became a bombardier, was shot down in Germany, and spent ten months in a prison camp. His grandfather—whether he was Judge Stevens or on the Mallison side of the family is not clear—was a cousin of Major de Spain.

There was another Stevens, Gowan, who was a second cousin of Charles (their grandfathers had been brothers). His father worked for the State Department in Washington, and when Gowan was a child his father was sent to China or somewhere in Asia, so Gowan lived with the Judge Stevens family in Jefferson. He was thirteen years older than his cousin Charles. In 1931 Gowan married Temple Drake, the daughter of Judge Drake of Jackson, and they had two children, a son called Bucky, born in 1934, and an infant girl, born in 1938, who was killed at the age of six months by her Negro nurse Nancy Mannigoe.

SOURCES:

Requiem for a Nun mentions Stevens as an early name in Jefferson and "Hand Upon the Waters" (*Knight's Gambit*) lists Stevens as one of the founders of Yoknapatawpha County. The first Judge Stevens is referred to in "A Rose for Emily." Information about "Captain" Stevens appears in "Tomorrow" (*Knight's Gambit*), and about Judge Stevens in *The Town, The Mansion,* and *The Reivers.* Reference to Maggie (Margaret) Dandridge being Charles's grandmother is to be found in *Intruder in the Dust.* In "Tomorrow" (*Knight's Gambit*) young Charles reports that his uncle went to law school after returning from Heidelberg; in *The Town* he reports the opposite story. Gavin Stevens appears in *Knight's Gambit* (all of the stories), *Intruder in the Dust, Requiem for a Nun, Light in August,* "Go Down, Moses," "The Tall Men," "Hair," *The Town,* and *The Mansion.* Parts of the last two he relates. Mrs. Mallison appears in *Knight's Gambit, Intruder in the Dust, The Town,* and *The Mansion.* She is mentioned in *Requiem for a Nun.* Her husband appears in *The Town* and *The Mansion.* Charles Mallison, Jr. appears in "Knight's Gambit" and *Intruder in the Dust.* He appears in, and narrates part of, *The Town* and *The Mansion.* He narrates all of the stories "Monk," "Tomorrow," and "An Error in Chemistry" (*Knight's Gambit*). Gowan Stevens appears in *Sanctuary* and *Requiem for a Nun,* and is referred to in *The Town.*

SARTORIS

The history of the Sartoris family begins in 1823 with the birth of John Sartoris somewhere in the Carolinas. He had one brother, Bayard, known only through hearsay as a reckless youth who at the age of twenty-three was shot in the back and killed by a Union army cook when he tried to "capture" some anchovies from the officers' mess. No date is given for either Bayard's birth or death, but the former would have to have been either 1838 or 1839, and the latter before August 1862, because he was killed "prior to the second battle of Manassas." He had never been in Mississippi. A sister, Virginia, was born sometime around 1843, although the exact date is not known. She married a man named Du Pre right at the beginning of the war, and he was killed shortly after at Fort Moultrie. In 1869 she moved to Mississippi to live with her brother's family, and became known to everyone as Aunt Jenny.

John Sartoris is supposed to have arrived in Jefferson in 1839 "with slaves and gear and money." By reckoning, he was only sixteen at the time, and if the record of his birth is correct he must have been rather precocious, for he immediately became a member of the committee to help raise money to finish the courthouse. He married a girl from a family named Millard. She died before the war, and during the war her mother Rosa Millard came to stay with the family while Sartoris, then a colonel, was away fighting. Mrs. Millard was killed near the end of the war by a group of raiders led by a man named Grumby. According to the earliest account (*Sartoris*) John Sartoris and his wife had three children, a son Bayard II, and two daughters, one two years older and one three years younger than he, the two girls having been sent to Memphis to stay with relatives during the war. According to a later account, however ("Ambuscade" in *The Unvanquished*), Mrs. Sartoris died when Bayard was born and no sisters are ever mentiond elsewhere. At the end of the war Colonel Sartoris, as he was generally called, married a distant cousin of his first wife, a girl from Alabama named Drusilla Hawk, who was quite a number of years his junior (she was only eight years older than her stepson). Her fiancé, Gavin Breckbridge, had been killed at Shiloh, and dressed in soldier's clothing she had gone with the Colonel into Virginia to fight alongside him, a situation so disturbing to her mother's sense of decency and decorum that when they returned home she forced them into marriage. Colonel Sartoris shot and killed two carpetbaggers from Missouri, a grandfather and grandson both named Calvin Burden, and so intimidated the Negroes during the Reconstruction that Jefferson and Yoknapatawpha County remained in control of Southern whites. He also, with a partner named Ben J. Redmond (and at the beginning with General Compson as third partner), built a railroad through Jefferson.

The only child of Colonel Sartoris and his first wife (he had no children by Drusilla) who carried on the family history is Bayard II. He was born around 1852 at the Sartoris plantation some four miles north of Jefferson in the house his father had built there. The accounts of his birth date conflict. The earliest account makes him twenty years old in 1869, which would put the date of birth at 1849. A later account makes him twenty-four in the year 1876. During the war the boy Bayard and his Negro companion Ringo (Marengo) became involved in a number of exciting adventures with Grandmother Millard (whom both boys called Granny) and the Union Army, and it was they who ran down and killed the man Grumby who had shot her, nailing him to the wall of a barn and cutting off his right hand to bring back and put over her grave. These adventures, as well as the story of the Colonel's shooting the carpetbaggers and of his own death ten years later, are afterwards related by Bayard himself (in *The Unvanquished* and "My Grandmother Millard"). Bayard's report varies somewhat with another account, for in one record ("There Was a Queen") it is stated that the old plantation house was over a hundred years old, while Bayard relates that the house was burned by the Yankees and that his father built a larger one on the same site after the war.

When things began to settle down Bayard went to Oxford, to the state university, to study law. He was called back home when his father was shot and killed on September 4, 1876, by his erstwhile partner Redmond, who was also his rival for the candidacy to the state legislature. Expected to defend the family honor, Bayard hunted out Redmond, but permitted him to shoot at him and escape, because, as he said, there had already been enough killings in the Sartoris family. That same evening Drusilla left for Montgomery, to the home of her brother Dennison, who was married and studying law there.

Little is known of Bayard's wife and son. The wife is not mentioned, but the assumption is that she died early. There was one son, John II, who married a woman named Lucy Cranston. He had been wounded in the Spanish-American War, and died in 1901 of yellow fever. When his wife died is not recorded. They had twin sons, Bayard III and John III, born March 16, 1893. When they finished high school the boys were sent to the University of Virginia, but caused so much trouble there that it was thought advisable to separate them, so John was sent to Princeton. When war broke out in Europe Bayard went to Memphis to learn flying and later taught there in a flying school. It was there that he met and married Caroline White. Before America's entry into the war the boys joined the Royal Air Corps and were sent to France. John was killed there on July 5, 1918. Before Bayard returned home his wife had died in childbirth, the son dying also. This was on October 27, 1918.

Meanwhile Grandfather Bayard had established a bank in Jefferson known as the Merchants and Farmers Bank. In 1894 he became mayor of Jefferson. His Aunt Jenny continued to live with him. When young Bayard returned home, maladjusted and bitterly upset over his brother's death, he bought a car and proceeded to race it around the countryside. He was involved in several smashups. After one in which he broke his ribs, he was bedridden for some time. During this time he was read to by a friend of the family, Narcissa Benbow, sister of the lawyer Horace Benbow. This led to a kind of romance, which in turn led to their marriage. Bayard continued his reckless driving, even after he had promised Narcissa to stop, and finally only his grandfather would ride with him. It was on one of these maddened rides, in December 1919, that old Bayard Sartoris died of a heart attack, and the grandson fled to the country to stay with some people named MacCallum. From there he fled to Mexico, South America, back to California, Chicago, and finally, on June 11, 1920, he was killed in a crash near Dayton, Ohio, where he was testing an airplane.

On the same day his son was born. Aunt Jenny insisted that he be named John after his uncle, but his mother named him Benbow. He was raised by his mother at the old Sartoris home, where, around the age of ninety, Aunt Jenny died. The boy Benbow (called Bory by his mother) is the last of the Sartorises, and the last we hear of him is in 1942, when, as an officer in the United States Army, he is in England on some secret mission.

The Sartoris Negroes

The history of the Sartoris Negroes begins with Joby, Colonel Sartoris' body servant whom he brought with him from Carolina. Joby and his wife Louvinia took care of the Sartoris household during the war. They had two sons, Simon and Lucius (Loosh). Simon was away at war with the Colonel, while Loosh and his wife Philadelphia stayed at home. Simon had a son Marengo (Ringo), who was the constant companion of the young Bayard Sartoris, both being the same age. Joby and Simon, and all the female slaves, were entirely devoted to the family, but after getting ideas from the Yankees Loosh tried freedom for a while. He returned home, however, when he found that freedom alone did not provide him food and shelter.

Like the history of their white masters, the history of the slaves (and later hired help) of the Sartoris family is not clear during the period between the war and the beginning of the twentieth century. In 1919, when the chronicle is picked up, we find an elderly Simon Strother, grandson of old Joby, acting as Bayard II's driver and household servant. He had a wife named Euphronia, who is now dead. The early account gives, as children of Simon, Elnora the cook, and Caspey, recently returned from World War I. There is also a sixteen-year-old Isom, grandson of Simon and nephew of Caspey.

A more recent account ("There Was a Queen") calls Simon

"Elnora's mother's husband," and Caspey Elnora's husband. It is also stated that Elnora is a half-sister of Bayard Sartoris II, implying that old Colonel Sartoris was her father. Since the Colonel died in 1876 and his contemporaries among the Negroes were at least three generations older than Elnora, the chronology becomes confusing here.

Sometime near the end of June 1920 Simon was found dead with a fractured skull in the cabin of a mulatto girl, Meloney Harris, to whom he had presumably given the sixty-seven dollars and forty cents held in trust by him as treasurer of the Negro Baptist Church society so she could open a beauty parlor. She had formerly been a maid at the Harry Mitchell home in Jefferson. Later we hear that Caspey is in the penitentiary for stealing.

SOURCES:

The fullest account of the Sartoris family is to be found in *Sartoris,* which, while set in 1919 and 1920, sketches in much background material. The story of the Civil War, with emphasis on Grandmother Millard and the Colonel, is to be found in Bayard's account in *The Unvanquished* and "My Grandmother Millard," which is essentially an isolated story belonging to *The Unvanquished.* The death of John Sartoris III is related in "All the Dead Pilots," and a glimpse of his brother afterwards but before he returns home from Europe is to be seen in "Ad Astra." The story of Aunt Jenny's death and of Narcissa's solution to the problem of some anonymous letters sent her by Byron Snopes is related in "There Was a Queen." More about the widowed Narcissa is to be found in *Sanctuary,* while Benbow Sartoris' activities in World War II are briefly mentioned in the title story in *Knight's Gambit.* There are of course many references to this well known family to be found elsewhere in the history. Reference to Bayard II as mayor of Jefferson appears in "A Rose for Emily." A mention of his death is to be found in *Requiem for a Nun,* and Colonel Sartoris' shooting of the Burdens is told of in *Light in August.* A great deal of the Sartoris history is briefly recapitulated in *The Town* and *The Mansion.* The Colonel and Bayard II are mentioned in *The Reivers.*

COMPSON

The history of the Compson family begins in 1699 in Glasgow, Scotland, with the birth of Quentin MacLachan Compson. His father was a printer. The boy was orphaned, and raised by his mother's family in Culloden Moor in the Perth Highlands. When he reached manhood, Quentin Compson took part in the Jacobite uprising, and then fled to America to the Carolinas. Here, after the American Revolution started, he fled once more—in 1779, at the age of eighty—to Kentucky, taking his infant grandson, Jason Lycurgus Compson, with him. Quentin MacLachan Compson died in Harrodsburg, Kentucky, at about eighty-four years of age, in 1783, although the exact age and date cannot be documented.

His son, Charles Stuart Compson, became an officer in the British Army and fought the American rebels in Georgia. He was wounded and left for dead in a Georgia swamp, but finally, four years later, managed to reach Kentucky, where his father and son were. There he tried schoolteaching, but gave that up and turned to gambling. He associated himself with the plot to join the Mississippi Valley to Spain, and when that failed he fled the country with his son—probably south to New Orleans, although this can be only conjecture.

The history is dropped there, to be picked up in 1811, when the son, Jason Lycurgus, then probably in his early thirties, appeared in Mississippi at the Chickasaw agency in Okataba County, and within a year had become a partner in the agency there. In 1813 he traded a racing horse to the Indian chief Ikkemotubbe for a square mile of land in Yoknapatawpha County, in what was later to become almost the center of Jefferson. Here the Compson plantation was built. (A later account says that it was Mohataha who "granted" the land, not to Jason Lycurgus but to Quentin Compson, and the date is put at 1821.)

Whom Jason Lycurgus Compson married and who his children were is not made known in the record. Different accounts conflict. One descendant—who must have been a son—was a second Quentin MacLachan Compson, who later became governor of Mississippi. According to one account (the Appendix to *The Sound and the Fury*) he was the father of Jason Lycurgus Compson II, who was a young man in 1833 and had married a non-Jefferson girl sometime before 1838. This record calls Jason II the "son of a brilliant and gallant statesman," and calls Quentin IV the "greatgreatgranddaughter" of the governor. But another account (*Requiem for a Nun*) calls Jason II "General Compson, the first Jason's son," and does not mention the governor. A still later account (*The Town*) makes the general and the governor the same person. He "had not only been a Confederate brigadier, but for two days he had been Governor of Mississippi too." There is also a confusion between the two Jasons. In one account Jason II was an important figure in the development of Jefferson, and the only person in the county to become a friend of the stranger Thomas Sutpen, who arrived in Jefferson in 1833. Elsewhere it is recorded that Jason I was the one who helped to found Jefferson and who befriended Sutpen. At all events, Jason II was the one who became a brigadier general when the war broke out, and it was he who put the first mortgage on the Compson place.

There was another Compson, one with no recorded first name, who must have been a son of the governor and a brother of the general (or the brother of the general-governor), although his relationship with the family has not been established. We hear about him from Bayard Sartoris II. According to Bayard, this Mr. Compson "had been locked up for crazy a long time ago because in the slack part of the afternoons he would gather up eight or ten little niggers from the quarters and line them up across the creek from him with sweet potatoes on their heads and he would shoot the potatoes off with a rifle. . . ." His place in the chronicle is not clear, but his existence—if he is one of *the* Compsons—does help to establish the fact of insanity in the family.

The general's son was named Jason Richmond Compson, and despite the different middle name he was known as Jason III. He was a lawyer who married a girl named Caroline Bascomb. They had four children: Quentin II, born (probably) in 1889,

Candace (Caddy), born in 1891, Jason IV, born in 1893, and Maury, born in 1895. The youngest was named for Mrs. Compson's brother, Maury L. Bascomb, but the name was later changed to Benjamin when it was discovered that the child was an idiot. It was Quentin who renamed him, and Quentin and Caddy called him Benjy.

When all the children were still under ten (probably around 1898) their grandmother, whom they called "Damuddy," died. It is not clear whether she was Mr. or Mrs. Compson's mother. In 1900 old General Compson, who spent most of his later years hunting with Major de Spain in the Tallahatchie bottom country in northwestern Yoknapatawpha County, died there.

The children of Jason Compson III grew up in a household in which the father drank increasingly, the mother had frequent spells of imaginary illnesses, and the uncle moved shiftlessly in and out of the family existence. When it came time for the eldest son to go to college, Mr. Compson decided to send him to Harvard, and he sold a portion of the Compson domain, supposedly Benjy's portion, to a golf club to help pay the expenses. About the same time the daughter Caddy became engaged to a banker from Indiana named Sydney Herbert Head, but only after she had become pregnant by a fellow called Dalton Ames. She married Herbert, as she called her fiancé, on April 25, 1910. On June 2 of the same year, Quentin committed suicide in Cambridge by drowning. He did this out of a confused sense of guilt concerning the family honor which Caddy's behavior supposedly besmirched. The following year Caddy's daughter was born, and she was named Quentin after the dead brother. At the same time Herbert Head divorced Caddy, and Mrs. Compson took the baby, refusing to let its mother even see it. For years, however, Caddy sent money for the child's care, which her brother Jason appropriated for his own use.

In 1912 Mr. Compson died. In 1913 the idiot Benjy molested some girls so the family had him castrated. With the death of Mr. Compson Jason took over as head of the household. He had been disappointed earlier because he had been promised a position in Herbert Head's bank, but when Caddy's marriage with her husband fell through there was no possibility for that. So Jason got a job in a farmers' supply store in Jefferson, and, according to one report, saved enough to send himself to school in Memphis where he learned to class and grade cotton, and then set up his own business as a buyer and seller of cotton. Jason continued to embezzle the money his sister sent periodically for the support of her child, and refused to allow the young Quentin any contact with her mother. Finally, on the night of April 7, 1928, when she was seventeen, Quentin took the money Jason had hidden away—it was almost seven thousand dollars—and ran away with a carnival pitchman.

According to one account Mrs. Compson died in 1933 and Jason had Benjy committed to the state aslyum in Jackson. He then sold the Compson house to a man who had moved in from the country, who turned the old mansion into a boarding house. Jason moved to a small place above his store, living alone but consorting with a prostitute he had picked up in Memphis. But according to a later account Jason had Benjy committed before his mother had died, and then had to have him released and brought back home to quiet his mother's weeping and complaining. Two years after he was brought home Benjy set fire to the house, burning himself to death and completely destroying the house.

Caddy meanwhile had remarried in 1920, this time to a motion picture executive. They were divorced in 1925. In 1940 she was in Paris, and it was rumored that she had become the mistress of a German general of the occupation.

In the account containing the burning of the Compson home by Benjy, Jason is reported to have used the insurance money to build a house for his mother and himself downtown. In 1929 he had bought back the land his father had sold in 1910 to the golf club. Instead of opening his own cotton grading business, as the earlier report had mentioned, he had, while still in high school, started working in Ike McCaslin's hardware store and, *à la* Flem Snopes, was soon the chief man there. He had not removed the mortgage from the old place, however, and had had to borrow more money from the bank to finish his new house. During World War II he conceived a plan for selling the old Compson domain at a huge profit by starting a rumor that the federal government was considering the land as an airfield. The terrain was completely unfit for an airfield, but he presumably gambled on local ignorance in such matters to make the rumor seem plausible. At any rate, it seemed to the local citizenry that Flem Snopes had met his match and had taken the bait, for by January 1943 it was known that he owned the Compson lands. The airfield was of course not built there and the land stood idle throughout the war's duration. But at war's end and with a looming housing shortage in prospect, Flem turned the land into a housing project and reaped far more money than he would have otherwise. The subdivision was named Eula Acres.

The history of the Compson family breaks off here. By the middle 1940s, so far as we know, there were Jason, Caddy, and young Quentin of Compson blood still remaining. But Caddy was too old to have more children, Jason was a middle-aged bachelor, and the young Quentin was lost. She was "doomed to be unwed," we are told. The Compson lands had already been metamorphosed into a subdivision and renamed. Thus the Compson family and Compson name, so important in Yoknapatawpha County history disappeared with the present generation.

The Compson Negroes

Only the colored help of the family of Jason Compson III is known. The help consisted of Roskus (Rocius) and Dilsey, and their children, Versh (Virgil), T. P., and Frony (Euphronia), and Frony's son Luster. T. P. and Frony were about the same age as the Compson children. At the time of Mr. Compson's death T. P. was eighteen, which would make him about Benjy's age. Versh was older, and he took care of young Benjy. Although the exact date cannot be verified, it must have been in 1910, when Caddy was married and Quentin killed himself, that Frony was married. Luster and young Quentin are about the same age, which would make late 1910 or early 1911 his birth date. It was Luster who took care of the grown Benjy.[1]

Roskus apparently died in the 1920s. Sometime earlier, about the time of Mr. Compson's death, Versh had gone away to Memphis. T. P., who took care of Benjy during the teens, also left for Memphis, probably about the time of Roskus' death. Dilsey, Frony, and Luster were still in Jefferson in 1928, and Dilsey and Luster were still working for the Compsons.

When Mrs. Compson died, Jason, who had always feared Dilsey, got rid of her. Frony had married a Pullman porter meanwhile (probably a second marriage, but that is not made clear), and had moved to St. Louis. But Dilsey refused to move that far from Jefferson, so Frony moved back to Memphis to make a home for her. By 1943 Dilsey was still alive, and still living with Frony in Memphis.

Another Negro associated with the Compsons was Nancy Mannigoe, who did their washing in the 1890s, and used to cook for them when Dilsey was not well. She was married to a man named Jesus. Nancy was a dope addict who used to consort with a white man named Stovall, a cashier in the bank and a deacon in the Baptist church, and she was made pregnant by him. Jesus was a violent and jealous man, and Nancy was in terror over the possibility of his killing her, especially when she had to walk home at night from the Compson place, and she used every pretext she knew either to remain overnight at the Compson's or to get the Compson children to go home with her. Many years later she became a nursemaid to the two children of Gowan Stevens and his wife Temple Drake, and was hanged for having killed their six-months-old child.

---

[1] Although in *Absalom, Absalom!* Shreve recalls to Quentin that Quentin and Mr. Compson used to go hunting accompanied by Luster, Luster could not yet have been born at the time Quentin committed suicide. In *The Sound and the Fury* Quentin refers to a time Versh used to go hunting with him—which would be more accurate chronologically. The family name of Roskus and Dilsey is not mentioned by any of the Compsons, but on the way to church Easter morning Dilsey is addressed as "Sis'" Gibson.

SOURCES:

The story of the Jason Richmond Compson family is to be found chiefly in *The Sound and the Fury* and in the "Appendix" attached to it, which sketches in both ancestry and the final disposition of most of the people involved. More about Quentin, his father, and the old General may be gleaned from *Absalom, Absalom!*, in which the story of Thomas Sutpen is revealed primarily through their eyes. "Skirmish at Sartoris" (*The Unvanquished*) gives the account of the "crazy" Compson, while his wife is referred to a number of times throughout that book. The Nancy story, as well as a good insight into the Compsons themselves, is to be found in "That Evening Sun" (related by Quentin), while the conclusion of her story is related in *Requiem for a Nun*. More about Jason Compson I appears in the same book. Something about the General as an old man can be found in "The Old People" and "The Bear" (*Go Down, Moses*). One anachronistic story, related, like "That Evening Sun," by Quentin, is "A Justice," about Sam Fathers. (One or two other anachronistic stories originally related by Quentin were later rewritten.) The authority for the identification of Nancy Mannigoe with the Nancy of "That Evening Sun" comes from Faulkner himself (*Faulkner in the University*, p. 79). There is some contradictory problem concerning her age. In the novel it is said that she is "about thirty—that is, she could be almost anything between twenty and forty." Even forty would be an impossibility, for if the time of "That Evening Sun" is 1898 and the time of *Requiem for a Nun* is 1938, she would have to have been closer to sixty in the latter account. But it was in conection with Nancy that Faulkner made his remark that he sometimes moved his characters about in time when he needed to. The Compsons are mentioned frequently in *The Town* and *The Mansion*. It is in the former that the general and the governor are identified as the same person. And it is in the latter where the story that Mohataha granted the land to Quentin Compson in 1821 appears, as well as the story of Jason Compson's dealings with Flem Snopes. The General is mentioned in *The Reivers*.

McCASLIN-EDMONDS

The history of the McCaslin and Edmonds families begins in 1772 with the birth of Lucius Quintus Carothers McCaslin in the Carolinas. Early in the nineteenth century he came to Mississippi and settled in the northeastern corner of Yoknapatawpha County on land bought from the Chickasaws, some seventeen miles from what was later to become Jefferson. He married, but the record ignores his wife. Twin sons, Amodeus and Theophilus, were born to them around 1800, before the arrival of the family in Mississippi. No date is recorded for their birth, but we are told that Isaac McCaslin's father, who was Theophilus, was "near seventy" when Isaac was born in 1867. (Bayard Sartoris II had said that they were past seventy in the early years of the war, but his account is perhaps not so trustworthy as Isaac's.) When the twins grew old they were known to everyone as Uncle Buck (Theophilus) and Uncle Buddy (Amodeus). A daughter was also born to L. Q. C. McCaslin and his wife. She is given no first name in the record, but it was probably Carolina, since the colored couple Terrel and Tennie had named one son Amodeus and a daughter "Callina," and had wanted to name another son Theophilus. The first of the McCaslins, the father, died on June 27, 1837.

The McCaslin twins embarked on a project to free their slaves some ten years before the war, turning the plantation house over to them, and the two men themselves lived in a two-room log house along with a dozen dogs or so. According to Bayard Sartoris, they used to lock the slaves in the big house at night, and worked out an involved system whereby the Negroes would buy their freedom by working on the plantation—a system Colonel Sartoris called fifty years ahead of its time. When the war broke out the twins, although no longer young, wanted to enlist, and after some argument it was decided that one should go and the other stay home. To settle the question, they played three hands of draw poker. Uncle Buck lost so he stayed home. Uncle Buddy became a sergeant with the army in Virginia.

Uncle Buddy had won another poker game earlier, this time from Hubert Beauchamp, an acquaintance living in another county twenty-two miles away. The issue was whether the McCaslins were to buy a slave belonging to Beauchamp or he was to buy one belonging to them, since their slave was always running away to be with the Beauchamp slave. The result was that not only did the McCaslins win Tennie, the Beauchamp slave girl, but also Hubert Beauchamp's sister, Miss Sophonsiba (whom her brother called Sibbey). The whole thing had been a trick of Beauchamp to get his sister off his hands and married to Uncle Buck McCaslin. Uncle Buck and his wife had one son, Isaac Beauchamp McCaslin, who was born in 1867. Uncle Buddy never married. Uncle Buck and Uncle Buddy both died in the same year at the age of seventy. The exact date is not known, but it was probably 1870, since both were living in 1869 and had been dead "almost five years" by 1874. The death of Uncle Buck's wife is not recorded, although she had died before her son was ten years old.

The son of Theophilus and Sophonsiba, Isaac, was raised by his cousin McCaslin Edmonds and taught to hunt by the part-Indian, part-Negro, part-white Sam Fathers. Inheriting his uncle's and father's feelings toward the land, he relinquished it, at the age of twenty-one, to his cousin and moved to Jefferson, where he took up carpentering and (according to a later report) opened a hardware store. He married the daughter of his partner sometime between 1888 and 1895, and moved into a small house in Jefferson which her father had built for them. Isaac's wife was never happy over his having given up his inheritance for a mere fifty dollars a month which McCaslin Edmonds, and later his son and grandson, gave him, but she could never make him reconsider his decision. After her death (around 1920) Isaac continued to live in the house, but he kept only one small room, allowing his wife's sister and her children to live in the rest. Isaac, who became known as Uncle Ike to nearly everyone, had no children, and when he died in 1947 at the age of eighty the McCaslin name was extinguished. Chick Mallison, who may have been confused by a decade or two, once (in *Intruder in the Dust*) noted that Uncle Ike was "still alive at ninety," but at that time he could not yet have reached eighty.

Through old Lucius Quintus Carothers McCaslin's daughter, who married an Edmonds, another branch of the family carried on. Little is known of the daughter and her husband, nor of their son, but their grandson, McCaslin Edmonds, who was born in 1850, was the one who raised Isaac, and who received the McCaslin lands which Isaac had repudiated. He was known generally as Cass Edmonds. He was married and had one son, Zachary Taylor Edmonds, known as Zack, who was born around 1875. His son, Carothers Edmonds, called Roth, was born in March 1898, at which time Zack's wife died, according to one account, although in 1905 there was a Mrs. Zack Edmonds, perhaps a second wife, living with Zack on the McCaslin lands. Zack died sometime around 1921. The boy Roth was raised by Mollie, the wife of Lucas Beauchamp. At last report, Carothers Edmonds was still living and running the family plantation, but since he was a bachelor in the 1940s, the likelihood of his marrying and perpetuating that branch of the family legitimately was small. He did become a father, but not within the bounds of lawful wedlock.

The all-white blood of old L. Q. C. McCaslin was destined to be carried along in the Priest family. A great-granddaughter named Sarah, probably a sister of McCaslin Edmonds, was born in 1854 and in 1869 married a distant cousin named Lucius Quintus Carothers Priest. There were young descendants from them still in Jefferson as late as 1961.

The McCaslin-Edmonds Negroes (Beauchamp)

From Carolina old Lucius Quintus Carothers McCaslin had brought the slave Rocius (Roskus), his wife Phoebe (Fibby), and their son Thucydides, who was born in 1779. On the death of McCaslin in 1837 Roskus and Fibby were freed but refused to leave. Thucydides was given ten acres of land by McCaslin's will, which he refused, as he did an offer of two hundred dollars cash from the two McCaslin sons. In December 1841, however,

he took the two hundred, which he had earned in the interven-
ing years, and set up a blacksmith shop in Jefferson. Roskus
died on January 12, 1841, and Fibby died on August 1, 1849.

Geneological complications begin with Eunice, a slave bought
by McCaslin in New Orleans in 1807, and married to Thucydides
in 1809. The following year a daughter Thomasina was born
to Eunice. She was not the daughter of Thucydides, however,
but of McCaslin himself. Then when the girl, who was called
Tomey, was twenty-three, she died giving birth to a son Terrel,
in June 1833. Six months before, on Christmas day 1832, her
mother Eunice had committed suicide by drowning herself. The
reason for the mother's suicide was that McCaslin was the father
of his own daughter's child. When McCaslin died four years
later he left "Tomey's Turl," as Terrel was called, a thousand
dollars in his will, to be given the boy on his twenty-first birthday. The mildly submitting cuckold Thucydides died in Jefferson on February 17, 1854, without, one gathers, ever having
produced any children of his own.

The Negro son-grandson of McCaslin fell in love with a slave
girl at Warwick, the home of Hubert Beauchamp, and was constantly running away to the Beauchamp plantation twenty-two
miles away. So Uncle Buddy McCaslin and Hubert Beauchamp
played a game of poker to see who would buy the one or the
other slave so they could be married. Uncle Buddy won Tennie,
and she and Terrel were married in 1859. They were not permitted the name McCaslin, so they took the name Beauchamp.
The same year a son, Amodeus McCaslin Beauchamp, was born
to them, but died in infancy. A daughter named Carolina
McCaslin Beauchamp was born in 1862, and another nameless
child of unidentified sex was born in 1863, both of which also died.
Then on December 29, 1864, another son was born. His parents
wanted to name him Theophilus McCaslin, but because the
other two bearing the names of the McCaslin family had died,
they were persuaded to choose a non-family name, so the child
was called James Thucydides, and became known as Tennie's
Jim. A daughter, Sophonsiba, was born in 1869, and became
known as Fonsiba. Another son, born on March 17, 1874, was

named for his white grandfather (and great-grandfather as well), but instead of calling himself Lucius Quintus Carothers McCaslin Beauchamp when he grew up, he changed the first name to Lucas, and became known simply as Lucas Beauchamp, or occasionally as Luke.

The original legacy of one thousand dollars left by Carothers McCaslin was increased by his two sons to one thousand dollars apiece for each of the surviving three children of Turl and Tennie, to be paid them when each reached his majority. Jim, who disappeared on the night of his twenty-first birthday, December 29, 1885, was never heard from again directly. The report was that he married, settled in Indianapolis, and died there around 1938. We know that he had one granddaughter and one grandson. Shortly after his disappearance Isaac McCaslin traced him as far as Jackson, Tennessee, and there lost track of him, so Isaac returned with the money intended for Jim. The following year, when the girl Fonsiba was seventeen, she married a northern Negro who had a land grant farm near a hamlet called Midnight, Arkansas, and in December 1886, just five months after she had left the McCaslin lands, Isaac went to find her living in destitution on a barren farm. He arranged with the local banker to have her share of the money doled out to her in monthly payments of three dollars, so that the whole amount would last over a period of twenty-eight years and perhaps keep her from starving for that long a time. Isaac did not have to travel to find Lucas. He had remained on the land, and on the morning of March 17, 1895, he appeared at Isaac's home in Jefferson for his share of the money, taking not only his own thousand dollars, but the thousand intended for Jim as well.

The history of Jim and Fonsiba is cut off after they leave, but that of Lucas continues. In 1896 he married a girl named Mollie from a Jefferson family—called Worsham in one chronicle, Habersham in another. Lucas and Mollie had three children, only two of which are known. The eldest was Henry, who was born in 1898 and grew up with Roth Edmonds. He disappeared from the chronicle early. There was an unnamed daughter who married and died in childbirth, leaving a son Samuel Worsham Beauchamp, whom Mollie raised. Known as Butch Beauchamp, at nineteen he left the country for Jefferson, where he entered into a life of gambling and fighting. He got into trouble by robbing Rounceville's store in Jefferson, and was put in jail. He escaped, fled north, and finally, at the age of twenty-six, was electrocuted at the penitentiary in Joliet, Illinois, for killing a Chicago policeman. Another daughter of Lucas and Mollie, named Nathalie and called Nat, married a young man named George Wilkins and moved to Detroit with him. Mollie Beauchamp died in what can be approximated as either 1939 or some time in the 1940s. At the last report Lucas was still living.

Among the remaining Beauchamps there was a youth called Bobo Beauchamp, reported to be a grandson of James, who left the McCaslin lands probably in 1904, and went to Memphis, where he got a job in the stables of the wealthy Mr. van Tosch, and then got into trouble through gambling debts. This was in 1905.

The history of the Beauchamps ends with a baby born to a granddaughter of James Beauchamp and to Roth Edmonds, thus making the intermixing of McCaslin and Negro blood even more inextricably fused.

Other McCaslin-Edmonds Negroes

Several other slaves (or hired help), not related to old Roskus or to the Beauchamps, occupy a place in the McCaslin history. One was Percival Brownlee, a twenty-six-year-old Negro whom Theophilus McCaslin bought from General Forrest on March 3, 1856, to use as a bookkeeper. Discovering that Brownlee could not keep books, nor plow, nor take care of the cattle, he tried to get rid of him by freeing him, but Brownlee refused to leave. In October of the same year McCaslin renamed him Spintrius. He later disappeared, and in 1862 reappeared on the plantation, conducting revival meetings among the Negroes, only to disappear again when the Union Army came through. In 1866 he reappeared once more, this time in Jefferson with an army paymaster, but he ran away again when Uncle Buck McCaslin happened to encounter him crossing the Square. He was last heard of twenty years later in New Orleans, the prosperous owner of a house of prostitution there.

In the year 1859 the McCaslin twins had a slave called Jonas, who took care of their horses. In 1905 a forty-five-year-old Negro named Ned William McCaslin, who claimed to be descended from old McCaslin himself, worked as coachman for Lucius Quintus Carothers Priest. He died in 1934. In the 1940s an elderly Negro called Isham accompanied Roth Edmonds on hunting trips. Many other colored folk, some never mentioned by name, mostly hired help or renters on the Edmonds land, appear briefly in the chronicle, none of them significant to the unfolding of family history with one exception. That exception was Sam Fathers, the son of the Chickasaw chief Ikkemotubbe and a quadroon slave girl, who Ikkemotubbe himself sold to old Carothers McCaslin in 1809, when Sam was two years old, along with his mother and foster father. Sam Fathers grew up to know woodcraft and hunting as no one else, and it was he who taught Isaac McCaslin the lore of the woods. Sam died following the hunt in which Boon Hogganbeck killed the bear Old Ben in the year 1883.

SOURCES:

The source book for most of the McCaslin-Edmonds-Beauchamp history is the collection *Go Down, Moses*. Further history of Lucas Beauchamp is to be found in *Intruder in the Dust*. Uncle Buck McCaslin's part in helping to capture the killer of Rosa Millard is told in "Vendée" (*The Unvanquished*), and references to the family are to be found scattered throughout the Yoknapatawpha County records. Some of them are contradictory. Lucius Priest the second (in *The Reivers*) says that the first McCaslin came from Carolina in 1813, although he must have been in Yoknapatawpha County before 1809. Priest also calls McCaslin

Edmonds Zack's uncle. And Chick Mallison, whose awareness of local history seems to be even more hazy, in *The Town* called Roth Edmonds the son of McCaslin Edmonds instead of the grandson, as the record states. He also said that Ike McCaslin was Roth's uncle. There is reference to the McCaslins and Edmondses in *The Town, The Mansion,* and *The Reivers. The Mansion* tells about Ike McCaslin's hardware store. *The Reivers* introduces us to Zack Edmonds' wife Louisa, and tells us about Sarah Edmonds, old McCaslin's great-granddaughter, who married Boss Priest. *The Town* contains a character called Tomey's Turl Beauchamp, but since he was only thirty years old around 1909-1910, he could not be the same person as the one who was born in 1833, old Carothers McCaslin's own son. A Negro private in World War I from Mississippi named Philip Manigault Beauchamp, who appears in *A Fable,* may or may not be of this family.

PRIEST

The Priest family, related to the McCaslin-Edmonds family, are relative newcomers insofar as we have a record of them. The family begins with Lucius Quintus Carothers Priest, who was born in Carolina sometime around 1847. The Priests were distant relatives of the McCaslins, the name Lucius Quintus Carothers being carried along in both branches of the family. Young Priest's mother died in 1864 and in 1865 he came to Mississippi in search of his family's relatives. Here he met Sarah Edmonds, old L. Q. C. McCaslin's great-granddaughter, who was born in 1854, and married her in 1869. They had a son Maury, who married a girl named Alison Lessep, and they had four sons: young Lucius Quintus Carothers, born in 1894, two younger boys, Maury and Lessep, whose exact birth dates are not known, and Alexander, born in 1905.

The elder Priest, known generally as "Boss Priest," was a lawyer who became president of the Bank of Jefferson sometime before 1900. The son Maury ran a livery stable in Jefferson. That is all the information we have on the family to date, except that the younger Lucius was still alive in 1961 and had a young grandson with the same name.

There was another Priest in Jefferson around 1910, named Maurice Priest. His relationship to the Priest family, if any, is unknown.

SOURCES:

All the information about the Priest family and their relationship to the McCaslin-Edmonds family is to be found in *The Reivers*. Maurice Priest appears in *The Town*.

SUTPEN

The history of the Sutpen family is more circumscribed than are the histories of the other important Yoknapatawpha County families, for it exists almost solely within the lifespan of Thomas Sutpen himself—the man who sought to establish for himself a family name and station among the planter aristocracy of Jefferson and failed.

Unlike the others, who had come from Carolina, Sutpen came from Virginia. He was born in the mountains of what later became West Virginia in 1807 of Scottish and English forebears, into a family of poor whites. Sutpen had two older brothers who left home when he was a child and were not heard of after, several older sisters, and one sister nine or ten years younger than himself. His mother died when he was about ten, and his father then took him and his sisters to the Tidewater section of Virginia. This was in 1817. On the journey one of the older sisters, who was unmarried, gave birth to a child, and the trip was further enlivened by the father's frequent bouts with drunkenness.

During the three years that the young Thomas Sutpen remained in the Tidewater region he learned many things that he had never before realized: he learned about wealth and position and individual importance, and decided that he too would achieve such goals. He had found out in the three months he had attended school that there was a place called the West Indies where poor men went and became rich, so in 1820, at the age of fourteen, he ran away to Haiti. (Quentin Compson, in telling the story to Shreve McCannon, said that 1823 was the year, saying also that Sutpen was "a boy of fourteen or fifteen who had never seen the ocean before.") Sutpen ended up working for a sugar planter of French descent, and in 1827 married his employer's daughter, Eulalia Bon. They had a son, Charles, in 1829 (this acording to the record; the tombstone reads: "Died . . . May 3, 1865. Aged 33 years and 5 months). Charles later took his mother's maiden name. When Sutpen discovered that his wife had Negro blood he divorced her. This was in 1831. Eulalia later moved to New Orleans with her son. The date of her death is not recorded.

In 1833 Sutpen arrived in Jefferson. He stayed at the Holston House long enough to buy one hundred acres of virgin timber land twelve miles northwest of Jefferson from Ikkemotubbe. With the help of an imported French architect and some Haitian Negroes, Sutpen built a huge house on the land, which he named Sutpen's Hundred.

Among the slaves he had brought with him from Haiti were two females, and in 1834 one of them gave birth to a daughter who was named Clytemnestra and called Clytie. Sutpen was the father. He needed to establish a family, however, so when the house was finished he set about to find for himself a woman of respectable background so he could beget a son to carry on the family name. The woman Sutpen chose to mother his family was Ellen Coldfield, the daughter of a small Jefferson merchant named Goodhue Coldfield, who had come in 1828 from Tennessee with his mother, his sister, his wife, and his daughter Ellen. The daughter had been born in Tennessee on October 9, 1817 (the geneology calls it 1818). Much later, in 1845, a daughter Rosa was born to Goodhue Coldfield and his wife, the wife dying in childbirth. His mother had died meantime, the exact date not being recorded.

Sutpen and Ellen Coldfield were married in 1838. A year later a son Henry was born, and two years after that, on October 3, 1841, a daughter Judith was born.

When Henry Sutpen finished school he enrolled at the state university in Oxford. There, in 1859, he met Charles Bon, an older student from New Orleans, and they became friends. At Christmas time he brought Charles home and soon Charles and Judith became engaged, but by the following Christmas, with the possibility of marriage imminent, Sutpen forbade it, and Henry, because of his strong attachment for Charles, repudiated his birthright, and went away with Charles. Henry did not know at the time that Charles was his and Judith's half-brother. Charles meanwhile had been consorting with an octoroon mistress in New Orleans, and in 1859 a son Charles Etienne de Saint Velery Bon was born to them.

When the war broke out Charles and Henry joined the army with a university group and became a part of General Compson's regiment. Sutpen helped Colonel Sartoris to raise a regiment in Yoknapatawpha County and became second in command. They went off to Virginia, and the following year, during an election, Sartoris was deposed and Sutpen became colonel. While he was away Mrs. Sutpen died, on January 23, 1863.

Meanwhile the sister of Goodhue Coldfield had eloped with a horse-trader, and Rosa kept house for her father. When, during the war, the aunt's husband was captured and put in a prison camp in Rock Island, Illinois, Mr. Coldfield refused to allow her to return home, and he even kept Rosa from watching the soldiers march in the street. Finally, after some soldiers had raided his small store, he nailed himself up in the attic of his home, and Rosa fed him by hauling up a pail of food daily on a rope and pulley arrangement outside the attic window. He died in his self-imprisonment in 1864.

Near the close of the war Charles and Henry returned to Sutpen's Hundred, and just as they arrived there, on May 3, 1865, Henry, who had been told of Charles's parentage by his father, shot Charles to keep him from marrying Judith, and then ran away (one account—"Wash"—says that Henry was killed in the war.) When she heard the news of Charles's death and Henry's disappearance, Rosa Coldfield moved out to the plantation to be with Judith.

At the war's end Sutpen returned to find the plantation in

ruins from lack of care. Still obsessed with the idea of a son to carry on the family name, he proposed to Rosa Coldfield. They became engaged, whereupon he made her an offer that they try to produce a son, and if successful he would marry her. Insulted by such a proposition, Miss Rosa left Sutpen's Hundred and returned to Jefferson. This was in 1866, only a year after she had moved out to the country to be with Judith.

Sutpen, in order to support himself and his family, since the plantation was not able to support them, opened a little crossroads store, catering to what Quentin Compson and Shreve McCannon later called "freed niggers" and "white trash," and got Wash Jones to clerk for him.

Jones, whose background was unknown, was a squatter who had moved into an abandoned fishing camp on Sutpen's place in 1850 with his daughter Melicent. Three years later she gave birth to a daughter Milly, who was raised on the Sutpen plantation. The father was unknown. What happened to Milicent is not recorded, but it was rumored that she went to Memphis and died in a brothel there. Jones himself after his fashion took care of Sutpen's Hundred while the owner was away at war.

When Sutpen discovered that Rosa Coldfield would not participate in his experiment to produce a male heir, he begin, in 1867, to try his tactics on the fourteen-year-old Milly, succeeding to the extent that she became pregnant, and on August 12, 1869, gave birth to an unnamed girl. When he discovered that the child was female, Sutpen spurned the girl, and as he left the cabin Jones killed him with an old rusty scythe. Later in the day, when the sheriff came after him, Jones killed Milly and the baby with a butcher knife and then died resisting arrest. (Another account—"Wash"—states that he also set fire to the cabin.)

A year later the son of Charles Bon and his New Orleans mistress appeared at Sutpen's Hundred, and the year after that Judith sent Clytie to New Orleans to bring him back to the plantation to live. The boy, Charles Etienne de Saint Velery Bon, his white and colored blood in constant conflict, in 1879 returned to New Orleans and there married a full-blooded

Negress. They returned in 1881 to Sutpen's Hundred to remain. In 1882, a son, later known by the name of Jim Bond, was born. Charles died in 1884, at which time Judith Sutpen also died, on February 12, both of them from smallpox, according to the record. According to Mr. Compson's account, however, the County Medical Officer had told General Compson that it was yellow fever, while at another time Mr. Compson, forgetfully, had told Quentin that Judith "died peacefully of no particular ailment." What happened to the wife of Bon is not recorded.

The land had meanwhile been sold to Major de Spain, who turned it into a hunting ground, but Clytie and Jim Bond, a rather slow-witted "saddle colored" man, stayed on in the now dilapidated house. Then in 1906 or thereabout, Henry Sutpen, an old man of sixty-seven, returned to the plantation to die. Rosa Coldfield, suspecting that there was someone at the old place besides the two colored people, took Quentin Compson out with her on a September afternoon in 1909 and discovered Henry. After thinking it over for about three months, she returned in December to bring him back to Jefferson, but before she could do anything, Clytie (perhaps in fear that Henry would be turned over to the police for Charles Bon's murder) set fire to the old house, and she and Henry were destroyed in the blaze. The Negro Jim Bond, the last remaining descendant of Thomas Sutpen, disappeared and was never heard of again. Rosa Coldfield died on January 8, 1910.

SOURCES:

The complete account of the Sutpen family is contained in *Absalom, Absalom!* with its accompanying Chronology and Geneology, although the narrative and the record do not agree on all counts, perhaps because a great deal of the narrative is a secondhand relay by Quentin Compson from material he got from his father's memory. Another account of Wash Jones's killing of Sutpen and his granddaughter may be found in "Wash," although some of the details vary from the longer account. (It is here the statement is made that Henry Sutpen was killed during the war.) Bayard Sartoris in "An Odor of

Verbena" (*The Unvanquished*) recapitulates briefly a good part of the Sutpen story. In "The Bear" (*Go Down, Moses*) is found the information that Major de Spain got the land from Sutpen. Reference to the arrival of Sutpen in Jefferson and the information that it was his French architect who designed the Yoknapatawpha County courthouse are to be found in *Requiem for a Nun*. Sutpen is mentioned as an old Yoknapatawpha County family name in *The Town*. Thomas Sutpen's "vast kingly dream" is referred to in *The Reivers*.

McCALLUM

The McCallum family has a special place in Yoknapatawpha County history because it is one of the few rural lower class white families that is treated with profound admiration and respect. No long account has been devoted to the McCallums, but they appear on a number of occasions in a number of different places in the history. Only one generation, that of those born between 1865 and 1895, is shown fully, but a brief glimpse of the father and of the third generation is afforded the reader.

The first one we meet is Anse McCallum (he is called Virginius MacCallum in *Sartoris*). He was born around 1845. His mother's maiden name was Carter. When the Civil War broke out he walked all the way to Virginia to join the Confederate forces. He returned home in 1866, married, and settled in east central Yoknapatawpha County in the region of Beat Four, just south of the McCaslin lands. He produced five sons, Jackson, Henry, Raphael Semmes and Stuart (twins), and Lee. After the death of his first wife he remarried and had one more son, Buddy. Anse McCallum is known to have once gone to Texas to bring back some horses. Following his second wife's death, he lived with his sons on the farm until his own death around 1925 or 1926.

We first see the family in 1920, when Bayard Sartoris goes out to their farm after the sudden death of his grandfather. The twin Sartorises, Bayard and John, used to hunt with the McCallums when they were younger, before the war.

Jackson, the eldest McCallum, was born in 1868. He was a

quiet man, shy and impractical. Henry was born in 1870. He had a "squat tubby figure . . ., mild brown eyes, and . . . capable, unhurried hands." He was the family cook and maker of the best whiskey in the surrounding country—a fact to which Ratliff once testified when he offered some to Ab Snopes. Unlike the other brothers, Henry did not care for hunting. The twins Raphael Semmes and Stuart were born in 1876. Raphael, called Rafe, was the most loquacious of the brothers, and the one who liked horses. Bayard Sartoris injured himself trying to mount one of Rafe's horses, and Max Harriss bought another of his horses in an attempt to get Captain Gualdres killed. Stuart was shy, a stay-at-home, and the farmer of the family. So retiring was he that Samson (at whose place the Bundrens stayed overnight on their way to take Addie's body to Jefferson) could never remember his name but only that he was Rafe's brother. Lee, the least talkative of all, was the youngest son of Anse's first wife. Buddy, the only son of his second wife, was born in 1895. He had been in World War I and had been decorated by both the French and American governments. He had brought back with him a Luger, which he later traded to the Gowries for some hounds. It was that gun which Crawford Gowrie used to kill his brother Vinson and Jake Montgomery and later himself.

Buddy McCallum was the only one of the brothers who married. He had twin sons, Lucius and Anse. His wife died (the date is not recorded), and when the boys were old enough they went to an agricultural college for a year. When the draft law went into effect in 1940 the boys, out of ignorance of the law, failed to register, and when a federal agent came to arrest them their father sent them to Memphis to enlist. That same day he (Buddy) had his foot amputated after an accident on the farm. There is a time shift here, for in 1925 Matt Levitt, a northerner who worked in a garage in Jefferson and courted Linda Snopes, got into a fight with Anse McCallum, Buddy's son, and at that time Buddy already had an artificial leg. Also, the young Anse McCallum would not likely have been old enough to get into a fight with a twenty-one-year-old man in 1925.

Between the decadent old aristocracy (like the Compsons and the Sartorises) and the greedy materialistic upstarts (like the Snopeses), the McCallums represent a healthy middle way. They are plain and unassuming, but highly conscious of their own integrity and self-sufficiency.

SOURCES:

Most of the background of the McCallum family is to be found in *Sartoris* (where Anse is called Virginius and the family named spelled MacCallum). The story of Buddy's two sons and the draft board is to be found in "The Tall Men." (Henry is the only one of the sons not mentioned in this story.) In *The Hamlet* there is an unidentified man referred to as "Old Man Hundred-and-one McCallum," and McCallum is mentioned there as being a name local to the Frenchman's Bend region. Also in *The Hamlet* Ratliff refers to the McCallum whiskey. Stuart—referred to only as Rafe's twin brother—appears in *As I Lay Dying,* where the name is again spelled MacCallum. Reference to Buddy's trading his Luger to the Gowries appears in *Intruder in the Dust.* Reference to Rafe's selling a horse to Max Harriss is to be found in "Knight's Gambit" and in *The Mansion.* The account of the fight between young Anse McCallum and Matt Levitt is in *The Town.* There is another time shift with Rafe: in *Sartoris* he is forty-four in 1920; in "The Tall Men" he is forty-five in 1940.

SNOPES

The history of the Snopes family begins during the Civil War, with Ab (Abner) Snopes then a full-grown man. He was supposedly a handyman around the Sartoris plantation while the Colonel was away at war. While virtually nothing is known about his forebears, we do find out that his youngest sister married a man named Grimm, and that they had a son named Eustace Grimm, a young tenant farmer who lived in the next county. Presumably, also, I. O. Snopes and perhaps Mink Snopes were Ab's brothers, although the terms "cousin" and "uncle" are used interchangeably in reference to the Snopes clan. We see Ab Snopes primarily as a horse trader, and it was he who worked with Granny Millard in her horse-and-mule-stealing activities. He would take those animals rounded up to Memphis to sell back to the Union Army. He is pictured as a shifty, untrustworthy character, and young Bayard Sartoris and his companion Ringo even thought at one time that he might be Grumby, the man who killed Granny. He was reported to have a crippled foot, the result of having been shot by Colonel Sartoris when he tried to steal the Colonel's horse.

Ab later married a girl from Jefferson, a girl he called Vynie, and rented some land from Anse Holland in Beat Four, twenty-eight miles northeast of Jefferson. They had no children. It was while Ab was living there that he was bested in a horse-trading deal by the fabulous Pat Stamper, and became soured on life according to V. K. Ratliff, the sewing machine salesman. This must have been around 1876 or 1877, for according to Ratliff, Ab Snopes had hidden out in the woods until Colonel Sartoris had finished building his railroad.

We next meet him some twenty-five years later, when he came to rent from Will Varner at Frenchman's Bend. Before that he had had two encounters with those he had rented from—one with a Mr. Harris and one with Major de Spain. In both instances he had got revenge for alleged injury by burning their barns. Before he appeared at Varner's, Snopes had spent the winter on the McCaslin lands just north of Beat Four. His wife had died meantime and he had remarried, a woman he called Lennie, and had four children—Flem, Colonel Sartoris (called Sarty), and twin girls, one of them known by the name of Net. The family also included his wife's widowed sister, known only as Lizzie.

By the time Ab Snopes and his family arrived in Frenchman's Bend the younger boy, Colonel Sartoris, was no longer with them. He had run away from home the night his father had burned Major de Spain's barn. Ratliff had recalled that there had been a younger son, but did not known what had become of him. Ab settled on the Varner land, and Joby, Will Varner's son, gave Flem a job in the store—primarily to protect the land, so Ab would not burn Varner's barn. Flem soon took over, and it was not long before he had a cousin Eck (Eckrum) Snopes running the Varner blacksmith shop.

Flem, because he was impotent, could have no children of his own. But when Eula Varner became pregnant from a young man named Hoake McCarron the family married her to Flem, sent them on a honeymoon to Texas, where the baby daughter was born, and gave them the Old Frenchman's Place for a wedding present. (Ratliff suggested that there was something more than merely "giving" the place to Flem, that Flem had used his own devious methods to get hold of it, but the general belief was that it was a wedding present.) By this time Flem was a pretty big local operator, and he was involved—one is not sure exactly to what extent—in Buck Hipps's auction of the spotted horses at Frenchman's Bend. Finally Flem achieved his biggest *coup* by salting the garden of the Old Frenchman's Place with silver dollars, and then selling it to Henry Armstid, Odum Bookwright, and V. K. Ratliff. For his part of the payment Ratliff gave a mortgage on his half of a sidestreet eating place in Jefferson, which he owned in partnership with his cousin Grover Cleveland Winbush. Flem thereupon moved his family to Jefferson and became a restaurant operator, with Eula acting as waitress. Flem soon took over his partner's half of the restaurant, and shortly after that he was out of the restaurant altogether, having become superintendent of the city's power plant. The local rumor (which proved to be true) was that he got the position by allowing the incoming mayor, Manfred de Spain, to sleep with his wife.

When Bayard Sartoris II, who had founded the Merchants and Farmers Bank in Jefferson, died in 1919, de Spain moved into the presidency of the bank and Flem followed him as vice-president. But meanwhile other Snopeses took up the slack whenever there was a vacancy. When Flem left the restaurant Eck and his family moved in from Frenchman's Bend to run it. Because Eck was honest and "innocent," Gavin Stevens always claimed that he was not a Snopes at all, that his mother had been unfaithful to her Snopes husband when she received the seed which produced Eck. But aside from his honesty and industry Eck was like a Snopes in other respects. Some six months after his arrival in Frenchman's Bend Eck had married one of the daughters of the family where he boarded, and ten months after that had a child. At about the same time appeared another boy, about six years old, the son of Eck by a former marriage. He was not named until much later, at which time he became known as Wallstreet Panic Snopes. The younger son was named Admiral Dewey Snopes. Presumably, according to a later account, Eck graduated from Varner's blacksmith shop to Varner's sawmill, for shortly before he moved to Jefferson he had broken his neck in an accident at the mill resulting from a wager that he and another man could pick up one of the large cypress logs and set it on the mill. He did not last long in the restaurant, for his honesty and naïveté were not good for business and Flem fired him. Through the influence of the Masons he got a job as night watchman for an oil company's storage tank near the depot. In 1917 Eck was killed in an explosion of the tank when he carried a lighted lantern into it in search of a lost little boy.

Meanwhile Flem had got the Commercial Hotel, a sidestreet boarding house, away from its owners, the Rouncewells, renamed it the Snopes Hotel, and put Mrs. Eck to work running it. And another Snopes, I. O., had taken Eck's place in the restaurant. I. O., apparently following in Eck's steps, had inherited the Varner blacksmith shop even though he knew nothing about blacksmithing (Eck had done all the work). One day when Eck was away I. O., while shoeing Zack (Jack?) Houston's horse, pounded a nail into the quick and Houston picked him up and dumped him into the cooling tub. I. O. then became the local schoolteacher and married a local girl, a relative of Mrs. Vernon Tull. Within a year they had a son, Clarence, and shortly after that (as soon as biologically possible) they had twins, which they named Vardaman and Bilbo. But it seems that I. O. had already been married and was the father of a five-year-old son amed Montgomery Ward. (An early account attributes another son, St. Elmo, to I. O. Snopes, and a late account attributes a younger brother, Doris, to Clarence.) When I. O. succeeded Eck in the Jefferson restaurant, his first wife followed him to the town and moved into the Snopes-owned hotel, while his second remained in Frenchman's Bend with her three children.

Only one more of the older generation Snopeses moved to Jefferson and he did not remain long. That was Wesley Snopes, the father of Byron and Virgil. He used to sing at revival meetings until someone caught him in an empty cotton house with a fourteen-year-old girl and he was tarred and feathered and driven out.

Several of the Snopeses remained in the Frenchman's Bend region, or if they did not history does not record their activities elsewhere. One was Launcelot Snopes, known as Lump, who in 1908 or thereabout took over Flem's place in the Varner store when Flem's activities got too diversified for store clerking. About the same time there was a twenty-one-year-old idiot, Isaac (Ike) Snopes, known only as a cousin of Flem, Mink, and Eck, who lived in the Littlejohn Hotel and helped Mrs. Littlejohn with the work. He fell in love with a cow belonging to Jack Houston and Houston gave the cow to him. Ike kept the cow in a barn back of the hotel and made love to it there. People used to come and watch, so they got rid of the cow, and to pacify the boy Eck bought him a toy cow. There were other Snopeses, farmers in the neighborhood, one of them living there and farming as late as 1940.

One of the local farmer Snopeses who achieved a great deal of notoriety was Mink Snopes. He was a cousin of Flem's, apparently, and lived on a small, poorly producing farm not far from Jack Houston. A cow belonging to Mink ran away to Houston's pasture and Houston impounded it and then forced Mink to work out the cost before he would return the cow. This occurred in 1908 when Flem was on his honeymoon in Texas. Mink worked up a grudge against Houston and shot him to death. Mink was arrested, tried, and convicted, and sent to Parchman for life. During his imprisonment in the Jefferson jail and during the trial he kept expecting Flem to come and get him out, which Flem did not do. So he transferred his grudge to Flem, and spent his time in prison plotting revenge. His lawyer had told him that with good behavior he could probably get out in twenty or twenty-five years, and Mink settled down patiently to wait.

Meanwhile other things were happening to other Snopeses. In 1910 Ab Snopes and his old maid daughter and the twin sons of I. O. Snopes, Vardaman and Bilbo, moved to a small garden farm about a mile or so outside Jefferson. Ab settled there and began raising watermelons, and spent his time watching over them with a shotgun in the hope of catching the town boys stealing them. How long Ab lived there is not known, but as late as 1924 he was reported to have shot the Roebuck boy in the back, after which he had to use stones to rout the boys, for the sheriff forbade the use of a gun.

The elder of the two sons of Wesley Snopes, Byron, was sent to Memphis to a business school by Colonel Sartoris (Bayard II, that is) and when he got out he was given a job in the bank. Byron used to write anonymous love letters to Narcissa Benbow, and sometimes would climb a tree outside her bedroom window to watch her. When Narcissa married young Bayard Sartoris, Byron stole the letters back. Near the end of World War I he was drafted, but within three weeks or so was released for reasons of health. It seems that every night before retiring Byron would tape a plug of tobacco to his left armpit, thus causing his heartbeat to increase. Sometime in 1919 he embezzled some money from the bank and fled to Mexico. Nothing was heard of him for ten years, when Flem received "by express" four of his halfbreed children which he had bred by a Mexican Indian woman. After several weeks of quiet terror, first in Jefferson and later in Frenchman's Bend, they were returned the same way to Byron.

The non-Snopes son of the non-Snopes Eck, Wallstreet Panic, followed his non-Snopes way independently. When he was twelve years old he entered kindergarten and by the time he was nineteen he had finished high school. Meanwhile he had taken a job in a local grocery and started a paper route, which he got his brother and some other local boys to run. When his father was killed and his mother received a thousand dollars insurance money, Wallstreet bought half interest in the grocery and it was not long before he owned all of it. He married, and then began expanding his business. He bought the store next door and turned it into a warehouse. Later he bought an abandoned livery stable for a warehouse, and turned the two stores into a super-market—the first in Jefferson. He bought an empty lot back of his store and turned it into a parking lot. Soon he decided to go into the wholesale grocery business, and by the 1940's he was living with his family in Memphis and was head of a large whole-sale grocery chain supplying extensive sections of Tennessee, Mississippi, and Arkansas.

Flem Snopes in the meantime pursued his upward way with determination. When he became vice-president of the bank, he added to his reverence for money a desire for respectability, and he used the same methods to obtain both. His daughter—or step-daughter—Linda was growing up, and Flem used her and her mother as props of respectability in a house furnished by a Memphis furniture store according to Flem's ideas of what re-spectability should be. But he had another reason for keeping them a part of his property. Will Varner, almost as shrewd in his ways as Flem, had willed his money to Eula and her de-scendants, and Flem knew he had no means of getting hold of it unless he had them. And part of his way of maintaining re-spectability was to rid Jefferson of any Snopes who might bring disgrace on the name.

One of the first things he had to do after becoming vice-presi-dent was to take care of Montgomery Ward Snopes, I. O.'s eldest son. Montgomery Ward had gone to France with Gavin Stevens with the YMCA (the early report has it with Horace Benbow). While there he turned the canteen he was operating into a brothel, and when he was kicked out he went to Paris and opened another one. He returned to Jefferson after the war wearing a beard and a cape in the French manner, rented a store from Jason Compson, and opened a photography shop which he called "Atelier Monty." After the first year he seemed to be doing no picture-taking business, but his nighttime business with young men from all over Yoknapatawpha County and from neighboring counties was enormous. All kinds of rumors spread, but when the place was raided nothing but photography equipment was found. Montgomery Ward said it was a kind of club. What it turned out to be was a profitable business in reproducing French postcards which he had brought back with him. Such activity was a federal offense, so Flem, with ideas of his own to put into operation, had moonshine whiskey substituted for developing fluid in the containers in Montgomery Ward's shop, thus making a state offense which took precedence over the federal offense. Montgomery Ward was convicted and sent to Parchman for two years. What Flem wanted was to get Montgomery Ward to Parchman where he could get Mink Snopes to try to escape, thus adding to his term, for with good behavior Mink was eligible to be released within five years. The ruse worked, and Mink was given another twenty years.

With that out of the way Flem could turn his attention to another troublesome Snopes, I. O. (Wallstreet Panic was doing well, so Flem did not worry about him; Flem had tried to cause a little trouble in the hope of profiting from the business, but it did not work.) I. O. Snopes had turned a business of buying mules in Memphis for sale to local farmers into a really prosperous venture by having the mules tied to a blind curve on the railroad and having them struck and killed by a freight train. The railroad paid more per mule than the farmers did. This worked well until Lonzo Hait, the man who did the work for I. O., was himself killed along with the mules he was tying to the tracks. Mrs. Hait claimed the mules had belonged to her husband and the railroad paid her eight thousand and five hundred dollars for her husband and the mules. After some trouble with Mrs. Hait over the money he thought should belong to him in payment for the mules, Flem stepped in and paid I. O. nine hundred dollars to "move back to Frenchman's Bend and never own a business in Jefferson again." In order to make the point stronger, he sold the Snopes Hotel where I. O. had been living.

Flem was all set now to go after what he really wanted—de Spain's position as president of the bank. He had kept Linda from going away to college after she finished high school for fear she would meet someone and get married and then he would be farther away than ever from the Varner money. By devious means he got her to make a will in his favor which he promptly took to Frenchman's Bend to show Mrs. Varner. This led Will to storm into Jefferson and the whole business of Eula's relations with de Spain was brought to a climax. In order to save Linda from disgrace, Eula killed herself, after which de Spain left town. Flem succeeded to the presidency of the bank and in addition moved into the de Spain mansion, which he had remodeled with two-story columns in the old Southern tradition.

Meanwhile, back in Frenchman's Bend, another Snopes was growing up and starting to make a name for himself. That was Clarence Snopes, I. O.'s second son. He had been in a gang of young toughs until he began to get on Will Varner's nerves, so Will made him constable. As Clarence continued to make a nuisance of himself, Varner had him moved from constable to district supervisor to state representative to state senator. He remained state senator for about fifteen years (safely outside of Frenchman's Bend) until in 1945 he (or Will Varner) decided to run for United States representative. This was too much for Ratliff, the sewing machine salesman, so he devised a trick, combined with a bit of blackmail, to have Clarence removed. The trick was to rub the back of Clarence's trouser leg with the reeds neighborhood dogs used to urinate against, whereupon they transferred their attentions to his legs. It was suggested to Will Varner that if Clarence withdrew his candidacy the story would not be made public. Varner, in his usual fashion, withdrew Clarence without notifying him first.

Another Snopes whose activities need to be mentioned is Virgil, the younger brother of Byron Snopes. With Fonzo Winbush, the nephew of Grover Cleveland Winbush, he went to

Memphis in the early 1920's to enter barber college. Warned to stay at a boarding house where the managing lady was motherly, they saw Miss Reba Rivers—who looked motherly to them—and took a room at her house of prostitution, not knowing its real nature, and went to other, cheaper places for their own pleasures. It was not long before they encountered Clarence Snopes at one of the houses, in one of his regular tours of duty, and Clarence soon discovered a phenomenon which as a good Snopes he at once turned to monetary gain. It seems that Virgil was so constituted sexually that he could satisfy two girls in succession. Such a feat of endurance was unbelievable to most men, and Clarence had no difficulty in getting them to bet on the outcome. He almost always won the bet, and on one occasion he really reaped rich rewards when Virgil was able to handle three girls in a row.

The activities of Clarence and Virgil did not impinge upon Flem's domain, so after having taken care of Mink for another twenty years, got rid of Montgomery Ward and I. O., and succeeding to the presidency of the bank, he was doing well for himself. His daughter Linda had left for New York right after her mother's suicide, and there she met and married a sculptor named Barton Kohl, who was a Communist, and when the Spanish Civil War broke out they went to Spain. Kohl was killed and Linda made deaf (in separate accidents), and she returned to Jefferson and kept house for her father.

In the meantime two more Snopeses showed up in Jefferson, but both were apparently imported by Flem himself to take care of some projects of his. The first was Watkins Products (Wat) Snopes, a carpenter who remodeled the de Spain house for Flem. This, apparently, was in 1927 or 1928. He returned again in 1943 to remodel the Compson carriage house into a two-story house for another Snopes, Orestes (Res), a bachelor put there by Flem to act as a nuisance to old man Meadowfill in the hope that Meadowfill would sell his land to Snopes to be included in the development of the subdivision he was building on the old Compson lands.

But in 1946 another Snopes, whom Flem did not invite, returned to Jefferson. That was Mink Snopes, who, after thirty-eight years in prison, had come to fulfill a mission he had set for himself back in 1908. That was to kill Flem, which he did, after which he returned to his old home in Frenchman's Bend and rested in what had once been its basement, for the old house had collapsed from lack of upkeep. There Gavin Stevens and Ratliff found him, gave him some money turned over to him by Linda, and then Mink set out on his way, his work completed.

So, by the late 1940s there were no more Snopeses left in Jefferson nor was the community any longer represented legislatively by a Snopes. Snopesism, if not destroyed, was at least for the time inactivated.

SOURCES:

The activities of Ab Snopes during the Civil War are to be found in *The Unvanquished*. His activities thereafter, and most of the information about the Snopeses around the turn of the century in Frenchman's Bend, are contained in *The Hamlet*. The period from 1908 to 1929, centering in Jefferson, is recorded in *The Town*. And from 1929 to 1946 the history is to be found in *The Mansion*. All three accounts do not agree, nor do they agree in every case with accounts of the Snopeses to be found elsewhere. There is also a certain amount of overlapping, of retelling the same story, sometimes with variations, among the three. *Sartoris* tells something about Flem's banking activities and about those of Byron Snopes. The early peregrinations of Montgomery Ward Snopes are related there also. News of Clarence and Virgil is to be found in *Sanctuary*. The boy Colonel Sartoris Snopes appears in "Barn Burning." I. O. Snopes appears briefly among the men at the telegraph office in *The Sound and the Fury*. In *As I Lay Dying* Jewel Bundren rides a Snopes horse, and reference is made to another Snopes whose uncle is Flem. Another Snopes is shown briefly in "Shingles for the Lord." ("Centaur in Brass" and "Mule in the Yard" are not considered here, for their substance has been incorporated into *The Town*.) Flem is mentioned in passing in *The Reivers* as having been "murdered ten or twelve years ago. . . ."

ISSETIBBEHA'S

Hunting & fishing camp where Wash Jones killed Sutpen. Later owned by Major De Spain

TALLAHATCHIE RIVER

GO DOWN,
McCaslin
Edmonds • MOSES
WAS

WASH
THE BEAR
A JUSTICE
RED LEAVES

Sutpen's •
Hundred

John Sartoris' Railroad

CHICKASAW
ABSALOM,
ABSALOM!

Where by 1820 his people had learned to call it "The Plantation" just like the white men did

PATENT

Sartoris •

RAID
AN ODOR OF VERBENA
A ROSE FOR
EMILY
Grierson
Burden •

THE UNVANQUISHED

SANCTUARY
Where Lee Goodwin was jailed tried & lynched

THE SOUND
AND THE
FURY

PERCY GRIMM

LIGHT IN
AUGUST

Airport

THAT
EVENING
SUN

DEATH
DRAG

Compson's Mile

for which Jason I swapped Ikkemotubbe a race horse & the last fragment of which Jason IV sold in order to become free

JEFFERSON
and
YOKNAPATAWPHA
COUNTY
Mississippi
1945

SPOTTED
HORSES

THE
HAMLET
Varner's Crossroads

Old Frenchman Place where Popeye murdered Tawmmy •

YOKNAPATAWPHA RIVER

OLD MAN
Here was born the convict & grew a man & sinned & was transported for the rest of his life to pay for it

Surveyed & mapped for this volume by
WILLIAM FAULKNER

This map was drawn by William Faulkner for *The Portable Faulkner*, edited by Malcolm Cowley and published by The Viking Press. Permission to reproduce it here has kindly been granted by the publishers.

THE GEOGRAPHY
OF YOKNAPATAWPHA COUNTY

YOKNAPATAWPHA COUNTY consists of 2,400 square miles. It had, as of a 1936 census, a population of 15,611, of which 6,298 were whites and 9,313 were Negroes. It is bounded on the north by the Tallahatchie River and on the south by the Yoknapatawpha River. Jefferson is in almost the exact geographic center. The whole eastern part of the county is pine hill country except for a small section in the southeast, which is rich river-bottom land. There is also a small section of pine hill country in the southwest corner of the county.

To the northwest (and extending beyond the later county boundaries) was a heavily wooded land early granted by the government to Issetibbeha, chief of the Chickasaws, as the Chickasaw Domain. His nephew and successor, Ikkemotubbe, in the 1830s sold one hundred acres of it some twelve miles from Jefferson to Thomas Sutpen, who built a plantation there. After Sutpen was killed in 1869 the land was bought by Major de Spain, who turned it into a hunting ground. The hunting lands near the river were known locally as Big Bottom. After 1883, when Old Ben, the bear, was finally captured and killed and Sam Fathers died, de Spain sold the lumber rights to a local sawmill, and most of the timber was cut down. The sawmill was at a nearby settlement called Hoke's, and the bridge which crossed the river a few miles below the hunting camp was known as Coon Bridge. Somewhere in this neighborhood, but not in Yoknapatawpha County itself, were two camps, one known as

Hog Bayou and the other as Hollyknowe. Twenty-eight miles from the Hollyknowe camp was a settlement called Van Dorn.

In the northeast part of the county, seventeen miles from Jefferson are the McCaslin lands, first settled by Lucius Quintus Carothers McCaslin, who arrived there between 1800 and 1807. The land up through the 1940s remained in the hands of Mc-Caslin descendants, the last owner being Carothers (Roth) Edmonds. Just south, and perhaps a little east of the McCaslin property is a section known as Beat Four, so called because of the number of its survey co-ordinates. It is a small rural settlement where live such people as the Gowries, the Workitts, the Ingrums, and the McCallums. There is a store there, known as Fraser's, four miles from the McCaslin plantation. Also in Beat Four is a rural church known as Caledonia Chapel. On the road between Jefferson and Beat Four is a bridge called Nine Mile Branch Bridge, and in the Beat Four region itself is another bridge called the Three Mile Bridge.

In the southeast corner of the county is the land settled by Louis Grenier in the early days of the nineteenth century. After his death in 1837 the place changed hands several times, until some time in the 1880s or so when it came into the possession of Will Varner. It is known simply as the Old Frenchman's Place. A small settlement which grew up there later is called Frenchman's Bend. It is twenty-two miles from Jefferson. Besides Varner's store and blacksmith shop, there is Littlejohn's Hotel and Quick's sawmill in Frenchman's Bend. Other local names, mostly farmers, are Tull, Armstid, Bookwright, Ratliff, and Turpin. The Snopeses, who were not originally from Frenchman's Bend, all descended on the settlement around 1900 and got their start there. Because of the importance of Will Varner to the neighborhood, the place is sometimes called Varner's Corners or Varner's Mill. Somewhere near Frenchman's Bend are two small settlements known as Burtsboro Old Town and Inverness, and another known as Remish, named for the parlor organs sold by Ratliff and manufactured by the Remish Musical Company of South Bend, Indiana.

Just four miles north and slightly to the west of Jefferson is the Sartoris plantation, settled by John Sartoris around 1839. It remained in Sartoris hands, the last ones living there being the widow and son of Bayard Sartoris III. A small creek running through the Sartoris lands is called Hurricane Creek, known locally as Harrykin Creek. This probably runs into a swamp four miles from Jefferson known as Hurricane Bottoms.

Within Jefferson itself (actually in the southeast corner) was the Compson land, a square mile Jason Lycurgus Compson got from Ikkemotubbe in 1813. Piece by piece, parts of the land were mortgaged or sold, and finally Jason Compson IV, the last remaining Compson in Jefferson, sold the place. After World War II it was turned into a housing development and named Eula Acres.

Jefferson is the county seat of Yoknapatawpha County. Like many southern towns it is built around the courthouse square. Its two Negro sections are called Freedmantown and Nigger Hollow. One road runs straight north and south through Jefferson, another east and west. There is another road running to the northwest past the Sutpen place, another to the northeast past Beat Four and the MsCaslin lands. Somewhere on this road is another settlement called Mount Vernon. One more main road runs to the southeast, past Frenchman's Bend. The railroad built by Colonel Sartoris in the early 1870s parallels the north and south highway to the west. Jefferson is seventy-five miles southeast of Memphis and forty miles from Oxford. Near Jefferson is a small place known as Peddlers Field Old Town. Some of the local places of business in Jefferson are the Holston House, a hotel; the Savoy Hotel, a sidestreet rooming house; the Commercial Hotel (often called Rouncewell's because it was owned by a family of that name), another sidestreet hotel which around 1910 was renamed the Snopes Hotel and then in the 1920s renamed the Jefferson Hotel; Christian's Drugstore; Rogers' Cafe; Dixie Cafe; Maxey's Barber Shop; Wildermark's, the big department store; the Watts Hardware Store; the McCaslin Hardware Store; and the Blue Goose, a cafe, and Lilley's, a store, both patronized by Negroes. From time to time there were other well-known places in Jefferson, such as Montgomery Ward Snopes's photography shop and Wallstreet Panic Snopes's supermarket.

Jefferson has two banks, the Bank of Jefferson, which was founded in the 1830s, and the Merchants and Farmers Bank, which was founded around 1900 by Bayard Sartoris II. It has an academy, usually known as the Female Academy. The local weekly is called the Yoknapatawpha *Clarion*.

Not far from Jefferson is an elevation known as Seminary Hill. There are other place names not readily identifiable as to location. One is called New Market. Another is called Wyott's Crossing, which is probably north of Jefferson on the Tallahatchie River. Whether it is the same place as one called Old Woyttsport is not known, but one would guess that it is. There is a Samson's Bridge, apparently somewhere across the Yoknapatawpha River between Mottstown and Jefferson. The old Backus farm, somewhere right outside Jefferson, was renamed Rose Hill when it was turned into a showplace by the bootlegger Harriss from New Orleans. And finally there is a place called Hickahala Bottom, a lowland where Ab Snopes hid the horses and mules he stole from the Federal troops during the Civil War.

The southwest quarter of Yoknapatawpha County is completely unknown. There are no settlements, no plantations, and none of the inhabitants of the county are known to have dwelt there. Besides the fact that there is a small pine hill section there, nothing else is known about it. There is not even a road running through it.

The county directly south of Yoknapatawpha, across the Yoknapatawpha River, is Okataba County. Its county seat is Mottstown. According to the map, the Bundrens lived in Okataba County, just across the river from the Old Frenchman's Place. Three miles from the Bundren farm is a settlement called New Hope. Near there, also in Okataba County, was the birthplace of the tall convict. Other neighboring counties are Grenier County, possibly to the east, Mott County (although Mottstown is in Okataba County), Crossman County, probably to the north, which has two towns called Glasgow and Hollymount, Cumberland County, and Minton County.

THE DOCUMENTS
OF YOKNAPATAWPHA COUNTY

THE DOCUMENTS of Yoknapatawpha County history present several problems. First of all, there are some direct contradictions in names and dates. Second, differing versions of the same story may be given, so that there may be several possibilities concerning the actuality of events. Third, often no names are given at all, or else only first names. And fourth, time is frequently mentioned only in generalities—that is, in such terms as "ten or fifteen years ago" and the like. Reference to the same thing in several places may sometimes more closely define time, place, and character. When there are contradictions, the majority accounts, if any, may be taken as the most accurate. And when there are just two conflicting versions the more credible is assumed to be the more correct. Those short stories which eventually became absorbed in novels are not considered here. Among them are such pieces as "Centaur in Brass" and "Mule in the Yard" (both in the *Collected Stories*) and "By the People," a separately published piece which appeared after the *Collected Stories*. The only exception is "Wash," which alone of all the stories continued its independent existence after its material became a part of *Absalom, Absalom!* It is considered a separate document here. Because the documents cover the history of a group of people whose lives are closely interrelated, few of the documents remain isolated from the others. Hence the breakdown here by families does not by any means imply that information about them cannot be found elsewhere. A case in point is Gavin Stevens and

Charles Mallison, Jr. Only one book (*Knight's Gambit*) really "belongs" to them. Yet *Intruder in the Dust* (Beauchamp) and *The Town* and *The Mansion* (Snopes) are almost as much theirs as they are of the people who receive the central focus.

Most of the documents cover action taking place in the twentieth century. There are some documents of the Civil War period, and parts of others on pre-Civil War days, enough of both to sketch in important aspects of the history. But except for "The Old People" and "The Bear"—which take place in a kind of isolation—"An Odor of Verbena," part of *Absalom, Absalom!*, and perhaps a couple of incidents involving Ab Snopes, there is almost nothing directly concerning the period 1870-1900. And even those stories which are set in that period are chiefly about matters relating more to earlier or later events than to events directly concerned with that period of history. There are a number of lapses in the family histories: The activities of the Compson family (except for a reference to the General's hunting experiences) between the time of the Civil War and the 1890s are not told us. Bayard Sartoris II is seen during the Civil War period and around 1919, but his marriage and the birth of his son are merely alluded to. Ab Snopes's activities between the Civil War period and the 1890s are only hastily sketched in. We know far more about the Civil War generation and the generation born in the 1890s than we do of the generation between the two. Just as the whole southwestern section of Yoknapatawpha County has never been explored, so is a great deal of Yoknapatawpha County history of the Reconstruction period and immediately after destined never to be recorded. But even had its author remained alive, it would not likely have been recorded, for the reason that, according to Faulkner, the period lacks drama: "From '70 on to 1912-14, nothing happened to Americans to speak of."

Released during the lifetime of Faulkner there were, relating to Yoknapatawpha County history, a total of forty-two separate documents, consisting of twelve novels, three collections, and twenty-seven individual short stories. Following is a brief examination of the documents, relating them to time and place and to their connection with families. The date in parenthesis after each document is the date of its first publication.

DOCUMENTS RELATING TO THE INDIANS

"A Courtship" (1948). About the rivalry of Ikkemotubbe and David Hogganbeck for the hand of Herman Basket's sister. The time is around 1798 or 1799, for it was shortly before Ikkemotubbe left for New Orleans. To establish the time of Ikkemotubbe's New Orleans sojourn one must go elsewhere. From "The Old People" we learn that Ikkemotubbe had been away seven years. Two years later he sold Sam Fathers and his mother and foster father to Carothers McCaslin, and that event occurred "seventy years ago." The time of "The Old People" is 1879. Thus Sam and his parents were sold in 1809, Ikkemotubbe returned in 1807, and he left for New Orleans in 1800. The story is a first-person narrative, related in retrospect by a person whose father was one of the lesser suitors for the young lady's hand.

"Red Leaves" (1930). About the flight and capture of Issetibbeha's Negro body servant when Issetibbeha died. The time is somewhere between 1800 and 1807. We read in *Requiem for a Nun* that Issetibbeha was a friend of Doctor Habersham, who arrived in the neighborhood around 1800. Therefore Issetibbeha was chief when Ikkemotubbe left for New Orleans. According to the best accounts Issetibbeha was dead when Ikkemotubbe returned in 1807. (This disregards an obvious contradiction with the other documents that Issetibbeha was Doom's son, Doom being Ikkemotubbe.) The story is a third-person objective narrative.

"A Justice" (1931). About the parentage of Sam Fathers. The time is a period just preceding his birth, so judging from information derived from "The Old People" it would be around 1808. An anachronistic story, since it is a first-person framework story related by Quentin Compson with the inner story related by Sam.

"Lo!" (1934). About the trip of Francis Weddel to see President Jackson concerning the Indians in Mississippi. Since Jackson's term of office was 1829-1837, the time of the story would have to be within that eight-year period. This coincides with the time period of the other Indian stories, for it concerns, in part, the removal of the Indians to Oklahoma, which occurred in the mid-1830s. Related to "Mountain Victory," the story about Francis Weddel's son. Although in "Lo!" Weddel is called half-French, half-Chickasaw, in "Mountain Victory" Major Weddel says that his father was half-French, half-Chocktaw. To accept the latter as the more probable would clarify the situation, for these two stories could then refer to a different part of Mississippi than Yoknapatawpha County, which most accounts name as the land of the Chickasaws. This would agree, too, with the fact that nothing of Yoknapatawpha County is referred to in either of the stories. A third-person objective narrative.

"Mountain Victory" (1932). About the trip to his home in Mississippi after the war of Major Saucier Weddel and his death at the hands of east Tennessee partisans. The time is 1865, right after the end of the fighting. Related to "Lo!" The story is a third-person objective narrative. Except for its relationship to "Lo!" and a reference to "The Man" (Du homme, Doom, Ikkemotubbe), this is actually not a Yoknapatawpha County story.

DOCUMENTS RELATING TO THE SARTORIS FAMILY

The Unvanquished (1938). A chronicle of the Sartoris family during the Civil War.

"Ambuscade" (1934). About how the young Bayard Sartoris and his companion Ringo tried to help the progress of the war by shooting a Yankee horse, and how Granny Millard hid them. The time is summer 1863, for it is right after the fall of Vicksburg. A first-person narrative related by Bayard Sartoris.

"Retreat" (1934). About the attempt and failure of Granny Millard to take the boys and the family silver to Memphis, and of Loosh's defection to the Yankees. The time is about a year after "Ambuscade," for Bayard recalls "last summer" when he and Ringo saw their first Yankee soldier. The narrative device here (and throughout the seven stories) is the same as in "Ambuscade."

"Raid" (1934). About a trip to Hawkhurst in Alabama, and Granny Millard's talking a Yankee colonel into returning the mules and silver taken from Sartoris. The time, according to a dated letter, is August 1863, yet the action occurs after the action of "Retreat."

"Riposte in Tertio" (1936, as "The Unvanquished"). About the mule-stealing activities of Granny Millard, with the help of Ab Snopes, and of her death at the hands of Grumby's raiders. The time is probably 1864, because there is a reference to the order "Colonel Dick had given us in Alabama last year," which was dated August 14, 1863, although Bayard says that he was fifteen (he was twelve in "Ambuscade").

"Vendée" (1936). About the revenge of Bayard and Ringo, with the help of Uncle Buck McCaslin, for the murder of Granny. The action follows immediately after that of "Riposte in Tertio."

"Skirmish at Sartoris" (1935). How Colonel Sartoris routed the carpetbaggers and saved Jefferson for the Southern whites. The time is spring 1865, right after the close of the war.

"An Odor of Verbena" (1938). About the death of Colonel Sartoris and the flight of his killer. The time is (or should be) 1876, for according to the Colonel's tombstone (in *Sartoris*) he was killed September 4, 1876. But here Bayard says it is October, and that he (Bayard) is twenty-four years old. As he was twelve in 1863, according to that reckoning the time should be 1875.

"My Grandmother Millard" (1943). How Granny Millard, with the help of General Forrest, overcame the obstacles to the marriage of two Sartoris cousins. The time is between April 4, 1862 (the fall of New Orleans) and July 4, 1863 (the fall of Vicksburg). The story is a first-person narrative related by Bayard Sartoris, and is therefore a fugitive piece belonging to the *The Unvanquished* series.

"All the Dead Pilots" (1931). About the death of John Sartoris III in a plane crash when he was shot down over enemy lines. According to a letter quoted here, he was killed on July 4, 1918. According to *Sartoris* he was killed on July 5. Also, Aunt Jenny Du Pre is called Mrs. Virginia Sartoris here. The story is a first-person narrative related by a mail censor.

"Ad Astra" (1931). About American and British flyers in Amiens in the autumn of 1918, right at the close of the war. Bayard Sartoris III is one of the men. The story is a first-person narrative related by one of the men.

Sartoris (1929). The major record of the Sartoris family, covering the period 1919-1920, but sketching in a lot of background material. The novel deals directly with the return of Bayard Sartoris III from World War I, his marriage to Narcissa Benbow, the death of his grandfather (Bayard of *The Unvanquished*), the birth of his son, and his own death. The dating of major events is within the novel itself. The story is a third-person objective narrative.

"There Was a Queen" (1933). About Narcissa Benbow Sartoris' solution to the problem of the anonymous letters sent her by Byron Snopes, and about the death of Aunt Jenny Du Pre. The time is 1930, derived from the statement that Benbow Sartoris, who was born in 1920 (as stated in *Sartoris*) is ten years old. The time here would therefore be shortly after the time of *Sanctuary*, also 1930, for Aunt Jenny was still alive at that time. The story is a third-person objective narrative.

DOCUMENTS RELATING TO THE COMPSON FAMILY

The Sound and the Fury (1929). While literally covering only four days—June 2, 1910, and April 6, 7, and 8, 1928—the novel actually relates the history of the Compson family from about 1898 to 1928. This is the family of Jason Richmond Compson and Caroline Bascomb and their four children, Quentin, Candace, Jason, and Benjamin, and Candace's illegitimate daughter Quentin. The "Appendix as a Foreword," first written for *The Portable Faulkner* and later reprinted in the Modern Library edition of the novel, briefly sketches the family history from 1699 to 1945. Dating all the events poses problems, but the major events can be approximated with a certain amount of accuracy. We know that Benjy is thirty-three in 1928. We know the difference in age among the four children. From those we can get the year of birth of each, and then when something happens—for example, when Quentin is nine, Caddy seven, and Jason five, such as the death of Damuddy—we know the year is 1898. (The chronology to *Absalom, Absalom!*" lists Quentin's birthdate as 1891, but according to the reckoning here, the date would be 1889.) We know that Quentin killed himself in June 1910, so at Mr. Compson's funeral when Mrs. Compson says, "Having the two of them like this, in less than two years," we can assume he died in 1912. Some dates are given specifically in the Appendix. To help unscramble the time in the Benjy section (where most of the events are recorded but recorded chronologically unselectively) one has to note which of the three caretakers of Benjy—Versh, T. P., or Luster—is with him. The story is revealed by the stream-of-consciousness method and by objective presentation. We get first a complete perspective of the whole story, completely unselective, through the eyes of the idiot Benjy. Then we get a highly selective and slanted point of view from the thought processes first of Quentin and then of Jason. Finally there is a third-person objective view, not of the whole thirty-year history, but of the consequences as they appeared on Easter Sunday, April 8, 1928.

"That Evening Sun" (1931). About Nancy, the Compson family washerwoman, and her fear of the jealousy of her husband Jesus. The time is 1898, derived from the statement that Quentin is nine, Caddy seven, and Jason five at the time (see *The Sound and the Fury* for dates). While this story is perhaps more closely related to the Gowan Stevens-Temple Drake history than it is to the Compson history (Nancy is a key figure in *Requiem for a Nun*), it is important here for the insight it gives into the characters of the Compsons. A first-person narrative, related by Quentin Compson, although he is relating events which took place "fifteen years ago," which would make the time of the telling 1913, or three years after his death.

DOCUMENTS RELATING TO THE McCASLIN-EDMONDS-BEAUCHAMP FAMILY

Go Down, Moses (1942).

"Was" (1942). About the runaway slave, Tomey's Turl, and his sweetheart Tennie, and Uncle Buddy McCaslin's winning of Tennie from Hubert Beauchamp. The time is 1859, as derived from an entry in the ledger kept by Uncle Buck and Uncle Buddy McCaslin, excerpts of which are to be found in the fourth part of "The Bear." The story is revealed by a double-focus method. It begins in the present with Uncle Ike McCaslin, and then goes back to his cousin McCaslin Edmonds, who was nine years old at the time, and presents the story by third-person method but from the point of view of the nine-year-old Edmonds boy.

"The Fire and the Hearth" (1942). Expanded from "Gold Is Not Always" and "A Point of Law" (both 1940). About Lucas Beauchamp, the discovery of his still, and his hunting for buried treasure. The time is 1941. According to the McCaslin ledger he was born in 1874. At the time of the present story he is sixty-seven. A third-person objective narrative.

"Pantaloon in Black" (1940). About Rider, a sawmill worker who became crazed with grief when his six-months' bride died. Related to the McCaslin-Edmonds-Beauchamp history only through the circumstance that Rider lived on land rented from Roth Edmonds. The time is 1941. When Rider was married he lit a fire on the hearth just as Lucas Beauchamp had done "forty-five years ago." The forty-five years ago, we know from "The Fire and the Hearth," was 1896. A reference in another place suggests a different dating, however. In *Requiem for a Nun,* whose own time is 1938, Temple recounts a story identical in all its major points with this one, saying that it occurred "before my time in Jefferson," which, if it were the same person and event, would make the action of the story prior to 1932. A third-person objective narrative.

"The Old People" (1942). Rewritten from a 1940 version. About Ike McCaslin as a boy and his initiation into the rites of hunting by Sam Fathers. The time of the major action is 1879. In "The Bear" the date for Isaac McCaslin's birth is given as 1867. At the time of his initiation he is twelve. (It is here we are told that Ike would live to be eighty, which would make the year of his death 1947, or *after* the time of this story's publication.) "The Old People" also gives us, in a brief recapitulation of Sam Fathers's heritage, our most precise dating of historical material about the Indians. A third-person narrative from the point of view of the young Ike McCaslin.

"The Bear" (1942). Expanded from "Lion" (1935) and "The Bear" (1942). The major action is about the killing of the bear Old Ben, and the death of Sam Fathers, but throughout, and in part four especially, a tremendous amount of background (and later) information is given. The time of the major action is 1883, for the boy Ike was sixteen at the time. The story is revealed by third-person narrative, but from shifting points of view corresponding to the different ages of Ike McCaslin.

"Delta Autumn" (1942). About a hunting trip taken by Ike Mc-Caslin when he is an old man. Here we encounter the grand-daughter of Tennie's Jim (James Beauchamp), who has been living as mistress to Roth Edmonds and who has a child by him. The time is roughly 1940. This may be established by a reference to Roosevelt and Willkie, and by the statement that this country is not at war but the possibility is that it soon may be. A third-person objective narrative, but partly from Ike McCaslin's point of view.

"Go Down, Moses" (1941). About the execution of Samuel Worsham Beauchamp for murder, and the attempts of his grandmother, Mollie Beauchamp, to get his body returned home. The story offers no evidence for precise dating, but its nature suggests contemporaneity with its date of composition. The presence of Mollie Beauchamp would date it before *Intruder in the Dust*. A third-person objective narrative, partly from the point of view of Gavin Stevens.

Intruder in the Dust (1948). The story of how Lucas Beauchamp was arrested for the murder of Vinson Gowrie, and how Chick Mallison, with the help of Aleck Sander, Eunice Habersham, and his uncle Gavin Stevens, brought the real culprit to justice. The time is difficult to establish because of conflicting evidence. At the time of the action Lucas' wife Mollie had been dead for over a year. She was alive in 1941, the time of "The Fire and the Hearth." Therefore the time here should be 1943 at the earliest. A reference to "the German after 1933 . . . or the present Russian" suggests that the time is post-World War II. These two pieces of evidence are consistent. But other evidence suggests either 1930 or 1940. At the time of the action Chick is sixteen. According to one document (*Knight's Gambit*, p. 196) Chick was born circa 1924, thus making him sixteen in 1940. But according to other documents (*The Town*, p. 103, *The Mansion*, pp. 179, 208, *et passim*) he was born in 1914, making him sixteen in 1930. Faulkner himself (*Faulkner in the University*, p. 141) puts the time "about 1935 or '40." A third-person narrative from the point of view of Chick Mallison.

A DOCUMENT RELATING TO THE PRIEST FAMILY

The Reivers (1962). About how Boon Hogganbeck, Ned William McCaslin, and the eleven-year-old Lucius Priest one day in May 1905 "borrowed" the boy's grandfather's car and went to Memphis, where they stayed at Miss Reba's and got directly involved in a horse race. Also about Boon's marriage and the birth of his son. The specific date of the action is given in the novel. More a story of Boon Hogganbeck than of the Priests, *The Reivers* nevertheless gives us a lot of information about some of them in passing. A first-person narrative, told by the now elderly Lucius in 1961 (that date is also given) to his young grandson of the same name; Lucius begins the whole story with the two words: "Grandfather said."

DOCUMENTS RELATING TO THE SUTPEN FAMILY

Absalom, Absalom! (1936). The story of the Sutpen family, covering a period from 1807 to 1910, with emphasis upon 1833 to 1869. The chronology and geneology listed at the end of the book establish the dates of important events, even though they disagree in a few places with the dates within the novel. A third-person narrative, revealed, for the most part, through Rosa Coldfield, Mr. Compson (Quentin's father), and Quentin. Since a great deal of the material is the attempt on the part of Quentin Compson to recreate the story on hearsay for his roommate at Harvard, Shreve McCannon, conflicting reports offer no real obstacles.

"Wash" (1934). About Wash Jones's killing of Thomas Sutpen for spurning Wash's granddaughter Milly, his killing of Milly and her bastard child, and his (probable) death in trying to resist arrest. The time is 1869, established by the chronology appended to *Absalom, Absalom!,* the story being retold there. A third-person narrative.

DOCUMENTS RELATING TO THE GOWAN
STEVENS-TEMPLE DRAKE FAMILY

Sanctuary (1931). The story of the rape of Temple Drake by Popeye and of the lynching of Lee Goodwin by the people of Jefferson because of his alleged guilt. The time is 1930. This we know from the ages of both Horace Benbow and Benbow Sartoris. In *Sartoris* Horace is thirty-three; in *Sactuary* he is forty-three. In *Sartoris* Benbow was born in 1920; in *Sanctuary* he is ten years old. A third-person objective narrative.

Requiem for a Nun (1951). A three-act play with a prose prelude to each act. The play tells the story of Temple Drake Stevens' realization of her own guilt in the death of her six-months-old baby. The first and third prose sections tell the background history of Jefferson. (The second prose section, about the state capital Jackson, is non-Yoknapatawpha County material.) The dramatic sections cover the period 1938. This we know because the activities of Temple and Gowan at the time of *Sanctuary* happened "eight years ago." The time of the first and third prose sections covers roughly the period from 1800 to 1840, with some projection into later times. A sufficient number of dates is given in these sections to make the references clear. For instance, we know from *Absalom, Absalom!* that Thomas Sutpen arived in Yoknapatawpha County in 1833. Here we read that "a man named Sutpen . . . had come into the settlement that same spring" that Jefferson was named. We also read that Doctor Habersham was dead, and that "in the sixth year old Alec Holston died" and "two years before, Louis Grenier had died," thus making the dates of their deaths 1839 and 1837, respectively. There is a possible discrepancy here with *The Town*. In *Requiem for a Nun* Gavin is often addressed by both Gowan and Temple as "Uncle Gavin," and Mrs. Mallison is referred to as "Aunt Maggie." Yet in *The Town* we learn that not only is Gowan a first cousin once removed of Gavin and Margaret, but he makes a special point to correct people when they call Gavin and Margaret his uncle and aunt. The dramatic sections reveal the story in conventional dramatic technique. The prose sections are third-person objective narrative. Related to "That Evening Sun" through the character of Nancy Mannigoe.

DOCUMENTS RELATING TO THE SNOPES FAMILY

"Barn Burning" (1939). About Ab Snopes and his conflicts with Mr. Harris and Major de Spain. The time is roughly the late 1890s, or shortly before Ab's arrival in Frenchman's Bend. A third-person narrative related from the point of view of the boy Colonel Sartoris Snopes.

The Hamlet (1940). The story of the arrival of the Snopes family in Frenchman's Bend. The time covered is from 1902 to 1908. We are told that Eula Varner is thirteen at the time the Snopeses arrive in Frenchman's Bend. In *The Town* we are told that Eula was born in 1889. In *The Mansion* we are told that Mink Snopes killed Jack Houston in 1908, when Flem was on his honeymoon in Texas. Since shortly after that Flem moved to Jefferson, we can set the terminal date around that time. (There is a seasonal discrepancy between *The Hamlet*, where Mink's trouble with Houston occurs in September, and *The Mansion*, where it occurs in the spring.) The story is revealed by third-person objective narrative, although some of the episodes (especially past ones bearing on the present story) are related by Ratliff.

The Town (1957). The story of the arrival of Flem Snopes in Jefferson up to his becoming president of the Sartoris bank. The time covered is from 1908 to 1929. The narrative picks up immediately following that of *The Hamlet* and ends two years after the suicide of Flem's wife Eula. She killed herself in 1927. The story is all first-person narrative, related by Chick Mallison, Gavin Stevens, and V. K. Ratliff. Of the twenty-four chapters, Chick relates ten, Gavin eight, and Ratliff six. Since Chick is for the most part not directly involved in the action as the other two are, his sections act as a kind of Greek chorus, sketching in more objective information.

The Mansion (1959). This continues the story of Flem Snopes up to his murder in 1946. While ostensibly it begins in 1929, picking up from *The Town*, large sections recapitulate earlier action, going back to 1908, when Mink Snopes murdered Jack Houston. Many specific dates are given in the novel itself, and besides Flem's and Mink's activities, various sections are given over to information about other Snopeses. Of the eighteen chapters, ten (chiefly those devoted to Mink Snopes) are third-person narratives. Three are first-person narratives by Chick Mallison, three by Ratliff, one by Gavin Stevens, and one by Montgomery Ward Snopes.

DOCUMENTS RELATING TO THE FARMERS IN THE FRENCHMAN'S BEND REGION

"The Tall Men" (1941). About the twin sons of Buddy McCallum and their encounter with the draft law of 1940. The time is between October 16, 1940, when the draft law went into effect, and December 7, 1941, when America entered the war. A third-person objective narrative.

"Two Soldiers" (1942). About the enlistment of Pete Grier and about his nine-year-old brother's attempt to go along with him. The time is early 1942, shortly after Pearl Harbor, and shortly before the time of "Shall Not Perish." Like that story and like "Shingles for the Lord," this a first-person narrative related by the nine-year-old Grier boy.

"Shingles for the Lord" (1943). About how Res Grier accidently set the church, which he was helping to reroof, on fire. the time is around 1940, or shortly after the time of the WPA. A first-person narrative related by the Grier boy.

"Shall Not Perish" (1943). About the death of Pete Grier in World War II when a troop transport was torpedoed. The time is 1942, derived from the statement: "Pete and I would walk the two miles down to Old Man Killegrew's house last December, to listen to the radio tell about Pearl Harbor and Manila." Like "Shingles for the Lord" and "Two Soldiers," a first-person narrative related by the Grier boy.

DOCUMENTS RELATING TO VARIOUS RESIDENTS OF JEFFERSON

"A Rose for Emily" (1930). About how Miss Emily Grierson kept her lover, Homer Barron, faithful to her for over thirty years. The time is around 1928-1930, although in retrospect it goes back to the 1890s. The date 1894—when Colonel (Bayard) Sartoris was mayor—is given, and elsewhere it is stated that "Colonel Sartoris had been dead almost ten years." He died in December 1919 according to *Sartoris*. A greater length of time is suggested, however, by the statement that, even after "almost ten years" had passed, "Each December we sent her a tax notice." A first-person "author-observant" narrative.

"Dry September" (1931). About the lynching of Will Mayes for an alleged attack on Miss Minnie Cooper. The time is not definite, but it is probably around 1930, for the McLendon who appears in *Light in August* and the barber who appears in "Hair" are also in this story. A third-person objective narrative.

"Hair" (1931). About Henry Stribling (Hawkshaw), the barber, his paying off the mortgage on his dead sweetheart's home, and his marriage to Susan Reed. The time is 1930, but covers a period going back to 1905 (specific dates are given in the story). The barber appears also in "Dry September." A first-person narative related by a travelling salesman for a work shirts and overalls company.

"Death Drag" (1932). About the appearance of some stunt flyers in Jefferson. A reference to Coolidge implies a time between 1923 and 1928. A first-person "author observant" narrative.

Light in August (1932). A story of the odyssey of Lena Grove in search of the father of her unborn child, of the love of Byron Bunch for her, of the strange case of the Reverend Gail Hightower, and of the short unhappy life of Joe Christmas. The major action covers the years 1929 to 1932. There are a number of ways one can arrive at the dates. Joanna Burden's father had run away from home when he was fourteen and stayed away sixteen years. The date he returned is given as 1866, which would mean he was born in 1836. He married his second wife when he was fifty (1886) and Joanna was born two years later (1888). She was forty-one when Joe Christmas arrived in Jefferson, which would make the year of his arrival 1929. Elsewhere we learn that Hightower was eight years old in 1890, making his birth year 1882. He was fifty when he died, which would be 1932. Joe murdered Miss Burden earlier the same year and he himself was killed the same year. Since Joe was thirty-three when he arrived in Jefferson he would be thirty-six when he was killed. There is a time discrepancy between here and "Skirmish at Sartoris" (*The Unvanquished*). Joanna says that she "was not born until fourteen years after Calvin [her half-brother] was killed" by Colonel Sartoris. That would make the year 1874. But according to young Bayard Sartoris' account, his father killed the two Burdens in 1865. Although approximately only three years are covered in the action of the novel, by means of flashback technique the whole of Joe Christmas' life is related, as is the story of Joanna Burden's grandfather and father and Hightower's early married life. The story of Lena's and Byron's trek into Tennessee at the close of the novel is revealed to the reader through the conversation of a furniture dealer and his wife as they lie in bed. The overall story, however, is a third-person objective narrative.

Miss Zilphia Gant (1932). About the protective custody of Zilphia by her mother after her father had run off with another woman (and they had been killed by Mrs. Gant), and Zilphia's symbolical motherhood after her own husband had been driven away by her mother. The time covers a period of about forty-two years, for Miss Zilphia is an infant when the story opens and is forty-two when it closes. There is nothing in the story to date it, and it has no reference to any of the other stories and novels. Specifically a first-person "author observant" narrative, for Chapter II opens: "They told me in the town . . . ," but for all practical purposes this is a third-person objective narrative.

"Beyond" (1933). About the death of Judge Allison, his going to heaven, and his experiences there. The time is around 1930. This can be derived from the statement that the room in which the Judge died had been "familiar for sixty-five years," and that his son was born in 1903 when the Judge was thirty-seven. A third-person narrative related from the point of view of the Judge.

"Elly" (1934). About the eighteen-year-old Elly who caused the death of her grandmother and Paul de Montigny, the man she wanted to marry, in a car accident because her grandmother resented the affair and Paul refused to marry her. There is no evidence to date the story precisely, but it is about modern Jefferson. Unrelated to any of the other Yoknapatawpha County stories. A third-person objective narrative.

"That Will Be Fine" (1935). About the amorous exploits of the narrator's Uncle Rodney and the consequences thereof. The time is Christmas, probably sometime during the first decade of the twentieth century, for the father of the narrator owns a livery stable and cars are not mentioned in the story. No last name of the family is given, although it is possible that it might be Harris, for in *Sanctuary* appears a Mr. Harris who owned a livery stable in earlier days in Jefferson, and in "Death Drag" a Mr. Harris rented a car to the flyers. Most of the action takes place not in Jefferson but in Mottstown. A first-person narrative related by the seven-year-old Georgie, a nephew of Uncle Rodney.

"Uncle Willy" (1935). About Hoke ("Uncle Willy") Christian, a drugstore owner in Jefferson, and his attempts to free himself from the conventions which bound him. The time is probably around 1931, for there is a reference to Darl Bundren's being taken to the asylum, which occurred "one day last summer" (see dating for *As I Lay Dying*). Although most of the characters in this story do not appear elsewhere, we discover later that Skeets McGowan worked in Uncle Willy's drugstore and that Uncle Willy in 1923 was involved in uncovering the nocturnal activities of Montgomery Ward Snopes (*The Town*).

We also hear that by 1938 (*The Mansion*, p. 201) Uncle Willy was dead. A first-person narrative related by an unnamed fourteen-year-old boy.

A DOCUMENT RELATING TO THE BUNDREN FAMILY

As I Lay Dying (1930). The story of the Bundren family and their attempt to get the body of Addie Bundren from their home near Frenchman's Bend to Jefferson for burial during a period of flooded rivers. Assuming that the novel is not science fiction (that is, that it does not record events taking place *after* its date of publication), we can set the time as 1930. Dewey Dell at the time of the action is seventeen and Jewel is the next older, making him, let us say, eighteen. We are told that when Jewel was fifteen it was twenty-five years before that that Flem Snopes had brought the spotted horses from Texas. Subtracting twenty-eight years from the latest possible date, which would be 1930, we get 1902, the year that Flem Snopes arrived in Frenchman's Bend. While this is certainly off by a few years, it is close enough for general, if not precise, historical accuracy. 1930 is probably the best dating, even though many of the same characters appear in both *As I Lay Dying* and *The Hamlet*, thus suggesting that the time period of the two novels is closer together than other evidence indicates, Tull, Armstid, Varner, and even Houston (who, if the same one, was killed in 1908) all appear. And Will Varner who was sixty at the time of the opening of *The Hamlet*, would be close to ninety by 1930. That need not bother us, however, for according to *The Mansion* he was still alive and very much active in 1945. The presence of cars as a commonplace on the highways in *As I Lay Dying* helps to make 1930 an acceptable date. The story is revealed wholly through the interior monologues of fifteen different people, including, besides the seven members of the Bundren family, Vernon and Cora Tull, Henry Armstid, Doctor Peabody, Reverend Whitfield, a farmer named Samson, a Mottstown druggist named Moseley, and the Jefferson drugstore clerk Skeet MacGowan.

A DOCUMENT RELATING TO GAVIN STEVENS

Knight's Gambit (1949). A record of Gavin Stevens as lawyer-detective.

"Smoke" (1932). About the murder of Anselm Holland and Judge Dukinfield and Gavin Stevens' trapping of the murderer. We are told that Judge Dukinfield had been chancellor for seventeen years and that Gavin "had been county attorney for almost as long as Judge Dukinfield had been chancellor." According to "Tomorrow," Gavin would be about twenty-nine when he became county attorney. Since from other evidence ("Knight's Gambit" and *The Town*) he was born around 1890, it would be 1919 when that happened. The date of first publication of the story being 1932, that would make thirteen years, which could reasonably be "almost as long as" seventeen years, and thus the time of the action can be put contemporary with the date of publication. A first-person "author observant" narrative related by a member of the jury.

"Monk" (1937). About Stonewall Jackson Odlethrop ("Monk"), his execution for a murder he was not really responsible for, and Gavin Stevens' discovery of the real murderer. This story offers no internal evidence for dating. In fact, specific dates are given only as "19—." A first-person narrative related, presumably, by Chick Mallison, since the lawyer is called "Uncle Gavin."

"Hand Upon the Waters" (1939). About how Lonnie Grinnup, the last remaining descendant of Louis Grenier, was murdered, and how Gavin Stevens was almost killed trying to get evidence on the murderer. Like "Monk," this story offers no internal evidence for dating. (Dan Grinnup in 1905, according to *The Reivers*, had an unnamed cousin who closely resembled Lonnie, and Lonnie was still alive at the time of *Intruder in the Dust* [about 1940], but both dates are too extreme for that period of Gavin Stevens' life.) There is an apparent discrepancy here with other documents relating to early Yoknapatawpha County history. Elsewhere we are told that Habersham, Holston, and Grenier were the three "founders" of the county. But here it is Stevens, Holston, and Grenier. A third-person objective narrative.

"Tomorrow" (1940). About the arrest of a man named Bookwright for the murder of Buck Thorpe, a mistrial, and final acquittal, and one of the few cases "lost" by Gavin Stevens. The time of the story is "more than twenty years ago" when Stevens was twenty-eight, which would make the year 1918. But this particular story is full of discrepancies with other accounts, some of them completely irreconcilable. In *The Town* we are told that Gavin went to law school after he got his M.A. from Harvard and before he went to Heidelberg. The time there would be around 1912, for he left in 1913 for Heidelberg, stayed on in Europe (except for a brief sojourn home) throughout the war, and did not get home until 1918. Here (as in *Intruder in the Dust*) we are told that he had gone to law school after Harvard and Heidelberg, and that at the age of twenty-eight he was "only a year out of the state-university law school." Since both this and *The Town* account are related by Charles Mallison, Jr., we do not even have the choice of one account's being more reliable than the other. Also, at the time of the action Chick was twelve years old. And since he is recounting it over twenty years later, he would be in his early or middle thirties. From no other source can any of this be substantiated. According to "Knight's Gambit," Chick was eighteen in 1942. This would make the time of the story 1936 (not 1918), and the relating of it sometime in the late 1950s. But according to *The Town* and *The Mansion*, Chick was born in 1914. By that reckoning the time of the story would be 1926 (again, not 1918), and the relating of it sometime in the late 1940s. And in no other source can we find a sixteen-year age difference between Gavin and Chick. A first-person narrative related by Chick Mallison.

"An Error in Chemistry" (1946). About Joel Flint's murder

of his wife and father-in-law, and Gavin Stevens' seeing through his impersonation of his father-in-law. Except for the fact that Gavin here has "prematurely white hair," there is no evidence to date the story. A first-person narrative, related, apparently, by Chick Mallison.

"Knight's Gambit" (1949). About how Max Harriss tried to kill Captain Sebastian Gualdres by substituting a wild, spirited horse for the captain's regular mount, and how Gavin Stevens (with the help of his nephew) prevented the murder. Also about the marriage of Gavin to the widowed mother of Max. The time here can be set precisely. It opens on Thursday evening, December 4, 1941, and runs through Sunday, December 7, and then covers a day in the spring of 1942. Much background material is covered by recapitulation, however. We are told here that Gavin went back to Heidelberg in 1919 to work on a Ph.D. degree and stayed away from Jefferson for five years. He was, however, according to *The Town* and *The Mansion*, at home at least part of that time, for he was in Jefferson in 1923, which was the year of the Montgomery Ward Snopes affair. A third-person narrative presented from the point of view of Chick Mallison.

TWO DOCUMENTS RELATING TO THE HUNTING LANDS

"A Bear Hunt" (1955). Revised from a 1934 version. About how V. K. Ratliff cured Lucius Hogganbeck's hiccups and how Old Man Ash Wylie got revenge for a twenty-year-old grievance. From practically any approach this story offers contradictory evidence for dating. It is about the de Spain hunting lands "twenty miles from town," the setting for "The Old People" and "The Bear." But it is a much later time, about the time of *The Town*, for the younger de Spain has the hunting lands. Yet we hear at the close of "The Bear" that Major de Spain sold the timber rights of the place after Sam Fathers' death in 1883 and never went back there to hunt. (The later hunting grounds were some two hundred miles from Jefferson, over in the Delta region, the setting for "Delta Autumn" and "Race at Morning.") Since the younger de Spain is called a banker, the time here (from the evidence of *The Town*) would have to be after 1920. But the narrator is a grandson of old General Compson, and he (the narrator) is likely to be Quentin, who died in 1910, unless, of course, he is Jason, and that is not likely. But confusion does not end there. Here the banker de Spain has a wife and married daughters, while in *The Town* he is a bachelor. Also, at the time the incident at the hunting grounds took place, Ratliff "hadn't never even seen Jefferson in them days," which would put the time back before that of *The Hamlet,* and hence brings the time back closer to that of "The Bear." Matters are not helped any when we learn (in *The Reivers*) that Lucius was born in 1906. The story is revealed by a framework method. It is begun by the first-person narrator (the grandson of General Compson) who introduces the characters and sets the scene. The story is then taken over by Ratliff, who relates the major episode. (This is the revised version, which appeared in *Big Woods*, not the original, which is in the *Collected Stories.*)

"Race at Morning" (1955). About an unnamed twelve-year-old boy on a hunting trip with a Mister Ernest, who took him into his home after the boy's mother had run off with a "roadhouse feller" and his father had disappeared. It is apparently the boy's last hunting trip for some time because Mister Ernest is sending him to school. The time is roughly around 1940, or the time of "Delta Autumn." Ike McCaslin is an old man, Roth Edmonds, Walter Ewell, and Will Legate are all members of the hunting party, and it is many years after the old hunting lands in Yoknapatawpha County have been abandoned to the sawmill. Except for the presence of Ike McCaslin, Roth Edmonds, Will Legate, and Walter Ewell, and a reference to "Yoknapatawpha, where they lived," this is not a Yoknapatawpha County story. Mister Ernest and the boy do not live in Yoknapatawpha County. A first-person narrative related by the twelve-year-old boy.